THE MYSTERY
OF BIRTH AND DEATH
Redefining the Self

RAMTHA

THE MYSTERY OF BIRTH AND DEATH
Redefining the Self

JZK
PUBLISHING,
A DIVISION OF JZK, INC.

The Mystery
of Birth and Death
Redefining the Self

ISBN # 1-57873-038-4

Other Titles by JZK Publishing,
a division of JZK, Inc.:

A Beginner's Guide to Creating Reality, REVISED AND EXPANDED ED.
Ramtha
The Children's View of Destiny and Purpose
The Mystery of Love
The Plane of Bliss

JZK Publishing,
a division of JZK, Inc.
P.O. Box 1210
Yelm, Washington 98597 USA
360.458.5201
800.347.0439
www.ramtha.com / info@ramtha.com

Weary with toil, I haste me to my bed,
  The dear repose for limbs with travel tir'd;
But then begins a journey in my head,
To work my mind, when body's work's expir'd:
For then my thoughts (from far where I abide)
Intend a zealous pilgrimage to thee,
And keep my drooping eyelids open wide,
Looking on darkness which the blind do see:
Save that my soul's imaginary sight
Presents thy shadow to my sightless view,
Which, like a jewel hung in ghastly night,
Makes black night beauteous, and her old face new.
        Lo, thus, by day my limbs, by night my mind
        For thee, and for myself, no quiet find.

— *William Shakespeare*
Sonnet XXVII

TABLE OF CONTENTS

PUBLISHER'S NOTE   xi

NOTE ON TRANSLATIONS   xxi

1. INTRODUCTION: BEGINNING THE PATH
   TO ENLIGHTENMENT   1

2. THE WHEEL OF REINCARNATION   5

   OUR CHOICES BEFORE WE WERE BORN   6
   LIVING IN THE PAST   10
   THE SHADOW ASPECT OF THE SELF   12
   THE ART OF DETACHMENT AND UNCONDITIONAL LOVE   17
   IT IS POSSIBLE TO OWN IT ALL IN ONE LIFETIME   22
   RAMTHA'S LEARNING TO DETACH FROM HIS PHYSICAL BODY   24
   THE EGYPTIAN BOOK OF THE DEAD   27
   THE IMPORTANCE OF CHANGE FOR THE SOUL'S JOURNEY   29

3. THE LAST BATTLE AGAINST TYRANNY AND SLAVERY   33

   THE CONQUEST OF OUR PERSONAL LIMITATIONS   34
   VISION OF THE COLLAPSE OF HUMAN CONSCIOUSNESS   37
   STRATEGY TO PRESERVE THE TRUTH OF OUR DIVINE INHERITANCE   40
   USING EMOTIONAL ENERGY AS A TOOL FOR CHANGE   44

4. REDEFINING THE SELF AS THE SPIRITUAL SELF   51

   ABOLITION OF THE SELF THROUGH BLAME AND VICTIMIZATION   52
   THE DARK NIGHT OF THE SOUL   56
   JUDGMENT DAY AND THE LIFE REVIEW   59
   MAPPING OUR NEW LIFE ON THE PLANE OF BLISS   63
   THE VALUE OF EXPERIENCING A NEW INCARNATION   69
   THE ANIMAL NATURE OF HUMANITY   73
   REDEFINING THE SELF BY CHOOSING OUR SPIRITUAL NATURE   78
   SUMMARY: THE SPIRITUAL WALK OF THE MASTER   82
   RESOLUTION   93
   INSTRUCTIONS ON THE PRACTICAL APPLICATION
   OF THESE TEACHINGS   104

5. DEATH AND THE REVELATION OF OUR
   ULTERIOR MOTIVE   109

   REVELATION OF OUR ULTERIOR MOTIVE   110
   FREEDOM FROM THE DECEIT OF THE PAST   122
   BEING AN HONORABLE AND IMPECCABLE PERSON   128
   COULD IT BE THAT YOU ARE ALREADY DEAD?   130
   THE VOID, POINT ZERO, THE MIRROR CONSCIOUSNESS, AND
   OUR HUMAN INCARNATION   136
   NEAR-DEATH EXPERIENCES AND THE EGYPTIAN RITES OF PASSAGE 147
   TO A MASTER THERE IS NO BIRTH AND DEATH, ONLY CREATION 153
   OUR HEART WEIGHED AGAINST A FEATHER   164
   COMMON THOUGHT IS WHAT CREATES OUR DAILY LIFE   169
   YOU ARE GODS, THE CREATORS OF REALITY   173
   BEING CONSISTENT IN THE DISCIPLINES OF THE GREAT WORK   177
   TRIUMPH OVER DEATH AND THE ALCHEMY OF TRANSMUTATION   184

6. CONCLUSION: DIMENSIONAL MIND VS. LINEAR MIND 189

RAMTHA'S GLOSSARY   199

BIBLIOGRAPHY   217

INDEX   219

TABLE OF FIGURES

FIG. 1: THE BRAIN   137
FIG. 2: SEVEN SEALS THAT CONSTITUTE SEVEN LEVELS OF
         CONSCIOUSNESS IN THE HUMAN BODY   138
FIG. 3: DESCENT OF CONSCIOUSNESS AND ENERGY FROM POINT ZERO 139
FIG. 4: PRIMARY AND SECONDARY CONSCIOUSNESS   139
FIG. 5: EGYPTIAN GODDESS NUT   152
FIG. 6: ILLUSTRATION OF THE CREATION OF TIME, USING THE HANDS 154
FIG. 7: THE SWING MOVEMENT OF THE MIRROR CONSCIOUSNESS 155
FIG. 8: COLLAPSE OF THE ENERGY WAVE INTO A PARTICLE   177
FIG. 9: THE ATOMIC STRUCTURE   188
FIG. 10: THE ATOM   191

PUBLISHER'S NOTE

The teachings of Ramtha are a unique metaphysical system of thought. It requires a very careful examination and consideration in order to grasp the full meaning and impact of its content. We say that Ramtha's teachings are metaphysical in nature because they address the fundamental questions about human existence and the human person, about our destiny and origins, about the nature of good and evil, the soul, death and life, the world, and our relationship to others.

The format in which Ramtha's teachings are conveyed is intrinsic to the message itself. The teachings are not simply an intellectual dissertation on specific subjects or a mere intellectual analysis of them, nor are they a form of revealed truth that requires the blind allegiance of faith. Ramtha's teachings are not a new religion nor are they the building blocks of a new church. His teachings are a system of thought that contains within its approach to reality the elements and mechanisms that allow the individual to engage Ramtha's philosophy and verify and experience its content firsthand. In other words, this unique aspect of the teachings allows the philosophy, or the *concepts of reality*, to be experienced and become instead w*isdom about the nature of reality.*

This particular quality of Ramtha's system of thought resembles the initiations into sacred knowledge practiced by the ancient mystery schools of Greece, Egypt, and the Middle East as well as the ancient gnostic schools of the Middle East and Europe. It is important to note that this characteristic distinguishes Ramtha's teachings from the traditional philosophical schools of the western world.

What we find in the traditional western understanding of objective knowledge and truth is a fundamental assumption about the human person and the nature of reality. The scientific method limits its range of attainable knowledge to phenomena that can be observed and verified through the senses of the physical body. Anything outside this range is consigned to the realm of myth and folklore. In other words, the nature of reality and the human person are nothing more than their physical nature and materiality. Sigmund Freud's psychoanalysis and profile of the human psyche are a clear example of this trend.

The physical body and the material world, in Ramtha's thought, are only one aspect of the real world. In fact, they are only the product and effect of the real world constituted by consciousness and energy. The human person is best described as consciousness and energy creating the nature of reality. The physical world is only one of seven levels of expression of consciousness and energy. Ramtha uses the concept of the Observer from quantum theory to explain his concept of consciousness and energy. He also uses the concept of God as creator and sovereign to describe the human person as consciousness and energy.

It is easy for many sectors of society today to dismiss Ramtha's teachings straightaway due to the highly unusual way in which they are conveyed. Unfortunately, it is an all-too-common response to attach a judgment to a message based on the form in which it is presented rather than on the content of what is presented. Marketing, communications, and the techniques of publicity, selling, and advertising are sublime examples of this.

The uncommon form in which Ramtha delivers his teachings is by no means arbitrary and superficial. He has pointed out explicitly the reasons behind such a format and explained that in order to grasp his message, it is important to become aware of the paradigms of thought, the roots of preconceived ideas, unconscious prejudices, and molds in which we normally perceive and evaluate reality.

Ramtha's teaching techniques often seek to challenge the individual as well as offer them the tools to become aware of those preconceived ideas that shape and set the boundaries in which we normally perceive reality. The purpose of this is to allow as a result the emergence of a broader perspective of mind which would enable us to experience reality in a more meaningful, unlimited, conscious, and extraordinary way as well as to provide us with a greater spectrum of potentiality for our experience than was previously available to us.

One of the more controversial aspects of Ramtha's teachings

is the form in which he chose to deliver his message. Ramtha in presenting his philosophy as the fruit of his own truth and personal experience makes the point that he himself is the embodiment of the philosophy, the living representation and manifestation of his thought. Thus he says that he is an immortal God, consciousness and energy, and that he lived once as a human being 35,000 years ago in the long-gone continent of Lemuria. He explains that in that lifetime he addressed the questions about human existence and the meaning of life, and that through his own observation, reflection, and contemplation he became enlightened and conquered the physical world and death. He has taught that he realized a way in which to take his body with him to a level of mind in which his true essence as consciousness and energy could remain fully conscious, be completely free and unlimited to experience any and all aspects of creation, and continue to make known the unknown. He refers to this process as his ascension.

The fact that he is no longer limited by his physical body allows his consciousness and energy to interact with the physical world in other forms. He often refers to himself as being the wind pushing the clouds, for example, or as being the morning, or a stranger, or a beggar on the street observing civilizations come and go, or as anything that consciousness would dare to imagine.

The form in which he communicates his teachings is through the phenomenon called channeling. In fact, it was Ramtha who made the term known. He uses the body of JZ Knight to channel himself and teach his philosophy in person.

A channel is different from a medium in that the channel is not the intermediary between the consciousness coming through them and the audience. The channel does not remain in a transfixed, altered state while channeling; rather they leave their body completely and allow the consciousness coming through to have full faculty over all their bodily movements and functions. Ramtha, while being channeled through JZ Knight, has the ability to open his eyes, walk, dance, eat and drink, laugh, speak, converse, and teach his students personally. JZ Knight is the only channel he has chosen and uses to deliver his message.

Ramtha's choice to channel his message through a woman, rather than by using his own physical body, is making the statement that God and the divine are not the prerogative of men alone and that women are worthy expressions of the divine, capable of genius and of being God realized. It is also asserting that what is important in his philosophy is not the worshiping of the messenger or a face or an image — which caused the collapse of so many efforts to enlighten in the past — but to listen to the message itself. It is also making the statement that the true essence of the human person is not limited to the physical body or a specific gender. The phenomenon of channeling is made possible therefore within the framework of Ramtha's system of thought. In other words, channeling as it happens in the person of JZ Knight is possible only if Ramtha's teachings are true.

The veracity of this phenomenon points to the truth of Ramtha's message. This is an important point to consider because the advance of science has developed tests and equipment that can scrutinize this phenomenon and study it from a physiological, neurological, and psychological point of view. Scientific techniques now exist to study the phenomenon of channeling by JZ Knight and to rule out the possibility of fraud. These scientific studies took place in 1996 when a distinguished panel of twelve scholars — comprised of scientists, psychologists, sociologists, and religious experts — studied JZ Knight before, during, and after channeling Ramtha.

After they conducted their scientific research studies, using the latest technology and equipment available, they concluded that the readings taken from JZ Knight's autonomic nervous system responses were so dramatic that they categorically ruled out any possibility of conscious fakery, schizophrenia, or multiple-personality disorders.

Ramtha goes to great lengths to make his whole audience move at the same pace of understanding. He insists continuously on the importance of the students articulating and explaining to each other each segment of the teaching. This ensures that the whole audience is grasping the teaching and allows Ramtha to more powerfully address the specific background and level of understanding of the people listening to him. Sometimes he engages the audience in deep philosophical contemplation of a specific subject and at other times he uses dramatization to empower his message.

Once the philosophical aspect of the teaching has been given, Ramtha initiates the student into that knowledge so that it may be turned into personal experience and wisdom. These initiations take the form of various disciplines of his design where the student has the opportunity to engage the knowledge. Ramtha differs from other teachers in this aspect. He takes on the role of a Master Teacher and Hierophant, a teacher who has the power to manifest what he speaks and intends. This is an important aspect of the teachings that likens it to the gnostic, philosophical movement and the ancient mystery schools. Nevertheless, a close examination of Ramtha's system of thought shows a clear distinctiveness in form and content from what is traditionally known as Gnosticism and the philosophy of the mystery schools. Ramtha himself does not refer to his system of thought in these terms; rather he calls it Ramtha's School of Enlightenment, the School of Ancient Wisdom dedicated to the Great Work. The Great Work is the practical application of Ramtha's teachings where the person has the opportunity to know itself and become enlightened.

Given all these considerations, the reader must be aware that Ramtha's teachings in printed form capture only part of the teaching presentation since they miss the dynamic element of the teachings, the voice inflection, the teaching without words, and its application in action.

Ramtha redefines the language he uses to teach by coining new words. The meaning of these coined words becomes clear within the context of his teaching, and the particular teaching becomes clarified also by the use of such uncommon words. We have constructed a Glossary of terms and concepts which Ramtha uses in a qualified way to facilitate the correct interpretation of his teachings. We have also provided a detailed Index to allow the reader to reference specific topics of interest covered in this book and to encourage the research study of this material.

Ramtha uses the aid of drawings and pictures to teach and explain abstract concepts like the Void, consciousness, time, energy, space, et cetera. We have included the pictures and drawings that were used at this particular event throughout the book. Ramtha, in the course of his dissertation, points to a particular place in a drawing, using the words "here," "this," "these," or "that." We have incorporated these references to the text in parentheses. The publisher's objective is to provide the readers with the opportunity to participate in and experience the session as if they had been present.

It is important for the reader to take account of these considerations when reading the teachings of Ramtha, for in some instances it may seem at first that his use of the English language is rather archaic or unrefined. Ramtha is very careful and thorough in the presentation of his thought. Everything he does — every term he uses — has a specific meaning, purpose, and is consistent with, and representative of, the totality of his message.

The main concern in preparing Ramtha's teachings for publication in printed form has been to render them as much as possible in the context and form in which they were delivered. Great care has been taken to avoid altering and changing the meaning of the teachings by taking them out of context or by even introducing a system of punctuation that would change the meaning. Nevertheless, we are aware that the human element of perception and limited understanding is inevitable. The only way to ensure that the message will be delivered and received in its pristine beauty and originality is when it is embraced by the reader as a true paradigm. Then it bears the fruits of truth and wisdom it promises.

The contents of this book are based on Ramtha Dialogues®, a series of magnetic recordings of Ramtha in session with his students, registered with the United States Copyright Office, with permission from JZ Knight and JZK, Inc. The excerpts from the various events that were used in the chapters of this book were left in their original dialogue format as they took place when they were delivered by Ramtha. *Chapter I: Beginning the Path to Enlightenment*, was taken from Ramtha Dialogues® Tape 268, *The Plateau for Learning*, November 7, 1989; Tape 269, *The Bridge to Infinity*, November 8, 1989; Tape 348, *Plane of Bliss I*, January 24-26,1997; and Tape 355, *Plane of Bliss II*, August 8-10, 1997. *Chapter II: The Wheel of Reincarnation*, was taken from Ramtha Dialogues® Tape 336, *Only One Thing*, September 19, 1996. *Chapter III: The Last Battle Against Tyranny and*

Slavery, was taken from Ramtha Dialogues® Tape 302, *Update on Change*, January 9,1991. *Chapter IV: Redefining the Self as the Spiritual Self*, was taken from Ramtha Dialogues® Tape 348, *Plane of Bliss I — On Earth As It Is In Heaven: Our Journey Through Life, Death, and Beyond*, January 24-26,1997. *Chapter V: Death and the Revelation of our Ulterior Motive*, and *Chapter VI: Conclusion: Dimensional Mind vs. Linear Mind*, were taken from Ramtha Dialogues® Tape 355, *The Plane of Bliss II*, August 8-10, 1997.

Ramtha's teachings cover a vast amount of subjects, yet they all serve to expound the fundamental concepts of his own system of thought. On repeated occasions he emphasized that the totality of his message could be expressed in the statement, "You are God." But how are we to interpret this statement? There are probably as many definitions of the term "God" as there are people on the earth. In order to understand Ramtha's teachings correctly, it is crucial that we become aware of both our own concept of God and how it stands in contrast with Ramtha's own explanation and definition of God and the nature of reality.

What is the essence of all things? What is their source? What is their nature? What is their destiny? Ramtha's approach to these questions begins with his concept of the Void. The Void is the source from which all that exists sprang. He describes the Void as "one vast nothing materially, yet all things potentially." In the Void there is nothing — neither movement nor action. Many philosophical approaches to the question of God, including the theologies of monotheistic religions, have conceived of God as an all-knowing, infinite, absolute, transcendent, and immutable being. In Ramtha's system, the attributes of absoluteness, infinity, and immutability are characteristics of the Void. The Void is self-contained, self-sufficient, in a state of rest, and of no need. Even though the Void is seen as an all-encompassing vastness, in its original state it contains no knowledge of itself, for knowledge is an action.

The concept of God as creator, "first cause," and "unmoved mover" that we find in Aristotle's philosophy and Thomas Aquinas' theology is described by Ramtha in terms of the Void contemplating itself and knowing itself. This act of contemplation represents a unique movement in the Void that produced a point of awareness and knowingness of itself. This point of awareness is referred to as Point Zero, the Observer, primary consciousness, consciousness and energy, and God. Point Zero carries the primordial intent to make known and experience all that is unknown and in a state of potentiality within the vastness of the Void. This is the basis for evolution. The Void contemplating itself is the source and origin of the human person. Ramtha's statement, "You are God," refers to the person as the Observer, the embodiment of Point Zero, and creative consciousness and energy.

Point Zero fulfilled its nature to make known the unknown and evolve by imitating the act of contemplation of the Void. In doing this, Point Zero produced a reference point of awareness that served as a mirror through which it could become aware of itself. Ramtha refers to this mirror consciousness as secondary consciousness. Point Zero rests in the bosom of the Void and has no limits to what it can know. The reflection between Point Zero and the mirror consciousness is what produces an environment, a tangible plane of existence in time and space. The Spirit is the dynamic aspect of Point Zero. It is the will or intent that desires to know and experience the unknown. The exploration of the potentials of the Void by Point Zero and the mirror consciousness is what produced seven levels of consciousness and, correspondingly, seven levels of time and space, or frequency. This journey and act of creation down seven levels of consciousness and energy are referred to as the journey of involution. The journey back to God and the Void is called the journey of evolution. The soul is different from the Spirit. Ramtha speaks of the soul as the Book of Life. The soul is the recorder of all the experiences and the wisdom gained in the journey of involution and evolution.

The predicament of the human being is expressed in terms of forgetfulness, amnesia, and ignorance of its origins and destiny. The traveler, or mirror consciousness, identified itself so much with the densest and slowest plane of existence that it forgot its own immortality and divinity. Humanity has become a stranger to itself, to the God that lives within us and is us and searched for help, meaning, and redemption from an outside source. In doing this, humanity denies its own divinity and precludes any chance for liberation from its present condition.

It is important to note that in Ramtha's system of thought, the material world — the densest plane of existence — and the physical body are never regarded as evil, undesirable, or intrinsically bad. A dualistic interpretation of reality typically found in the gnostic traditions — emphasizing the struggle between good and evil, good and bad, light and darkness, sin and righteousness — is intrinsically excluded in Ramtha's system of thought. What becomes an undesirable condition is to remain in a state of ignorance and denial as to our true nature and destiny. It is absurd to argue for our limitations when we are, as consciousness and energy, the ones who created them.

The path to enlightenment is the journey of evolution back to Point Zero. In accomplishing this task, the person fulfills the mandate to make known the unknown and bring to the Void its experience to be turned into perennial wisdom.

All of the disciplines of the Great Work designed and used by Ramtha to initiate his students into the teachings are modeled according to, and imitate in some way, the process of the Void contemplating itself, which gave birth to consciousness and energy, which in turn create the nature of reality.

In conclusion, the four cornerstones of Ramtha's philosophy are the concept of the Void, consciousness and energy creating seven levels of reality, the statement, "You are God," and the mandate to make known the unknown. There are many traces of Ramtha's thought found in ancient traditions, although in most cases all that remains are faint echoes that have barely survived the passing of time and the loss of their appropriate context for interpretation. Some of these traditions are the philosophies of the ancient Egyptians and Pharaoh Akhnaton, Buddha's description of himself as the awakened, Socrates' understanding of virtue and the immortality of the soul, Plato's concept of universal forms, Yeshua ben Joseph's life and teachings, the works of St. Thomas the Apostle, the Hymn of the Pearl, the hymn to the divine word in the Gospel according to John, Apollonius of Tyana, Origen, Mani, the Cathars and Albigensians, Francis of Assisi, the Jewish and Christian mystics, John of the Cross' sketch of the Ascent of Mount Carmel, where the apex is placed at the top of the head of the human body, the works of art of various artists like Michelangelo and Leonardo da Vinci, the writings and mystical experiences of Therese of Avila, the works of Fray Luis de Leon, the humanists of the Renaissance movement in Europe, the Rosicrucians, the masters of the Far East, and others.

The teachings of Ramtha offer us a unique perspective from which to view the mystery of life. They offer us a framework in which the questions that have remained unanswered by philosophy, science, and religion find a new meaning. These teachings can broaden the scope of human experience far beyond the boundaries set by science and the various religions of the world to this day. Ramtha's system of thought is neither a religion nor a philosophical interpretation of reality. It is the truth that was gained and verified by the experience of a member of the human race. In this sense it is Ramtha's knowledge, Ramtha's science. And now that the path has been trodden upon, the doors are open for those who desire to explore it and make their own journey into the unknown.

NOTE ON TRANSLATIONS

JZK Publishing, a division of JZK, Inc., is the original version and only source to be used in any further translations into other languages with permission.

We would like to emphasize to the reader that rendering Ramtha's teachings in written form is a challenging and difficult task. One of the main characteristics of Ramtha's teaching format is its experiential value. It is not always possible to capture this aspect of the teachings in written form as it would be in a video or audio format. JZK Publishing, a division of JZK, Inc., is committed to rendering Ramtha's teachings in their originality and true intention in the best possible way.

CHAPTER 1
INTRODUCTION: BEGINNING THE PATH TO ENLIGHTENMENT

> *"If you don't have a lofty view of life, you are lost. You are insignificant without knowledge. Have a path. Know where you are going. Have a clear view of your personal belief. The more you want to know the miraculous, the more you get to know it. When I say be God, I am saying be remarkable."*
>
> *— Ramtha*

So what sort of person does it take to become illuminated or to begin the path of illumination? It takes the following person: one who is ready and willing to have owned all of their past. So what does that have to say about the person? The person owns nothing and is owned by nothing. There is nothing from the past that they are indebted to, indebted to not simply by gold but through grief and emotional adherence. It is an entity that is willing to have an attitude diversely different than their past.

When the person is no longer owned by yesterday, number one, when there is nothing that beckons to them — there are no dreams; there is no obligation; there is nothing owned and nothing owing — when that is accomplished, the person has a virgin attitude and that attitude is then ripe for development. And what is the third? That life is forever. When you are no longer afraid to die, then the concept of eternal life is ever-present. So if a person, as it were, no longer fears death, then what would they fear? They have no fear of public ostracism. They have no fear of social rebuke. They have no fear of being either famous or unknown. So what are the three? What are they? No past, a virgin attitude, eternal life; thus no death or fear. That is the making of a Christ.

The consciousness of the initiate, the new attitude, says, "Alas, I am finding my salvation, for indeed it is in me all along. This oppression that I feel, I know from whence it comes." And if you don't, you blow out oppression and the next part of the picture would appear until the solitary answer looms in front of you.[1] And all you have to do is bring it on — bring it on. Why? Bring it on and it will appear as magical in your life in the form of people from the past, from the present, in the form of a thing, in the form of a letter, in the form of a word. It will appear and then you will be illuminated. And when you look at this with a new consciousness you will say, "Ah, I am free at last, for now I understand." And with that glory and a great shout, it is consumed into wisdom and evermore is the consciousness cleaned out of that ageless drama.

It is not a simple measure, I assure you, to take responsibility for our life, but it is the bravest spiritual part that does, no matter

---

1 The application of the breathing technique in the discipline of C&E™ allows the student to blow out a thought, a past event, or an attitude they want to change.

how painful it may be. And do you know what pain is? The coming home of the prodigal son of energy. We call this then the dark night of the soul. All of that suffering now is full-bore upon us because it is energy returning to the source. But it is through the suffering that we are purified, because once the energy passes the barrier of the emotional body, and the emotional body is disturbed and ruffled, and the heart beats fast and the breath is shortened and the tears begin to roll, that means that energy is coming back and it is passing through the barrier of the emotional body and it is causing a storm. And, you know, you have to live in the storm. It is the nature of the child coming home. And when the storm is over, energy — now being purified through the emotional body — has returned full cycle and its coming home is a necessary ingredient in defining the self, that which we are.

And it is hard to stay in the dark night of the soul without stimulus to get you out of it. But why would you want to get you out of it? It is pulling that energy back from those painful places that must pass through the emotional body. That is where the true suffering is, but that is also where purification is. To dull it, to get rid of it, would deny yourselves purification and thus wisdom.

So at the light then we begin to see how our intentions are profoundly affected in everyone and how, if we have ulterior motives in any way in any of our actions, always those ulterior motives are the overriding and underriding crime. Ulterior motive — ulterior, the real motive behind the action — now that is where we are judged. We are never judged by surface; we are judged and weighed by our ulterior motive — ulterior. That is why being impeccable is such an important charge to the student. Be impeccable. Do not have an ulterior motive. If you do, get rid of all of the window dressing and take a look at it. That is what we must refine, not the window dressing but the ulterior motive behind our actions. Being impeccable is living from that ulterior place, because that is the engine of our life and it is the engine behind everything that we do.

And how common is this? Well, here is a common example: being nice to someone, exceptionally kind to someone, and it isn't for the sake of kindness; it has an ulterior motive to it. Now all of you have done that, and the ulterior motive is that you are wanting something from that person. You are, whether it is a relationship on any of the levels, whether it gives you something. And usually the ulterior motive is really what you really want, and we use kindness as the chariot in which to get it. So now you understand ulterior motive, don't you? The complication in a light review is that the ulterior motive is what we as a personality get to experience. The deception is what we experience as the object of our ulterior motive, the deception being the unimpeccable intention.

CHAPTER 2
THE WHEEL OF REINCARNATION

> *"If you are changing and in the flux of change the flux will manifest in your life, if you have risen above prejudice and hatred to understand the wisdom of why you are having this trial — if you can say, 'O my God, I understand that I have created this; don't let me lose sight of my purpose here' — one day you will be able to leave this place because you have broken out of the prison."*
>
> *— Ramtha*

OUR CHOICES BEFORE WE WERE BORN

Greetings, my beauteous entities. I salute you from the Lord God of my being to the Lord God of your being. Let us have a drink: the aqueous substance, that which is termed the waters of life, that which represents that which is termed the principal cause, that which is called the Void, that which sustains all things.

O my beloved God,
of this day
I have contemplated
my spiritual growth.
As of this night
I desire
to know
where I am
in my growth.
I beseech you
to send to me
a sign,
that this sign
will read to me
the level of my growth
and indeed the level
of my spiritual acceptance.
So be it.
To life.

Now we are going to have a wonderful evening this evening because it has already happened. I know it was wonderful. And the wonderful ability to be able to already know that is that I can watch several scenes unfold and, as a strategist, be able to choose different scenes from different times of this same evening, answer questions differently, teach differently, send specific runners. And

I am very happy to say it was all a success. Well, when you are on top of the mountain, you get a different view of things than when you are down in the valley and you can't see anything.

Well, I am going to start this evening off by reminding you of an event. And in that reminding, in its curious statement, it says a great deal about who you are. And after this night is over I want you to ponder this, and I want you to ponder it deeply and richly. And here is the event: The event was that before you incarnated into this lifetime — before this life, before this body — you already had the option to be here, and you elected to be here because it is part of the soul's journey. So all of you — from all times, all cultures, and all peoples — before you were born again had to have an agenda for life; otherwise the life doesn't unfold. So in that agenda all of you elected to find me in this school.

Now I want you to think about that because then we beg the question that if this was part of my soul's journey in making it here and studying, then what specifically was it that I needed to know to satisfy the requirement of the lords of karma and reincarnation? In other words, what would I gain from coming here that would satisfy this nagging problem that I seem to carry into each life, stumble through it, die in that life, and still have the same problem? What is it that the school and the teacher have to offer me?

Well, this is what I want you to know. In everything that you have learned in my audience, people, and all the runners and all the teachings that I have given you, you have made lifetime leaps in knowledge and lifetime leaps in experiences. Now let me specify that by saying that those lifetime leaps have nothing to do with affecting material form — that is to come — but have everything to do with affecting the state of your spiritual self, in evolving it through a brain-body connection in a lifetime to a level of understanding that allows that Spirit and soul to move very quickly through the veils of lifetimes.

In other words, we cannot measure yet what it is that you have gained, but understanding knowledge — an enriched experience — brings about wisdom. And I would also say to you that there are many I could sit down and parley with — and parley in terms of engaging you in a most satisfactory and eye-opening conversation — and you would be willing to keep up with me because I have taught you that well. There are others of you that cannot do that, but you will do that.

Now what does this say about you? It says that you, when given the opportunity, can rise to the occasion and address life's situations not from a common, impoverished state of social consciousness that is always blaming someone or something for the condition of people's life — in particular your own — but that you can address situations in your life without being the victim and can address it in such an enriched manner that you yourself stand in awe of the wisdom that starts to flow out of you. And it speaks of a learning capacity you have gained that you did not always have.

And why is that important? Because we — including myself, who elected in life to know everything and to find that there were no borders or parameters to the unknown and chose to live exclusively on a path that would always take me into the unknown — we were called the masters. We were called the great ones because we dared to learn more about that which is termed self than the common rabble of the marketplace did. Masters must have the ability to understand their life, to understand nature, and to understand and take responsibility for their actions in nature before the full forthwith power of manipulating mass is given to them.

That is why I tell you, you came here and you are all here because you wanted to be here. And what you have learned thus far, though not visible, is building that which is termed a bounty inside of you of tremendous knowledge. If we can continue to refine that knowledge and remove from it the silliness and immature qualities of victimization, past problems, someone else's fault — if we can continue to polish this understanding down to the present moment of self, which we are endeavoring to do — when we enter that sanctuary to where what we are is no one else's responsibility in any area of our life except our own, then when we come finally to that bare arena is the moment we become utterly and fantastically empowered as lawgivers. But it is not until we can enter that place naked — naked of our past, naked of blame, naked of envy, naked of jealousy, naked of everything that plagues human consciousness and keeps it submissive to social consciousness, particularly the Boktau group — are we polishing attitudes to a system of knowledge that blames no one, that lives in no time other than Now, and indeed from that basis grows strong roots into the Void with tremendous power.

You wanted to know what you have come here to learn. There are no accidents in life; everything is intentional. Let us say, people, that maybe the reason you have been recycled in the engines of reincarnation over and over and over is that there is one flaw in your thinking; that that flaw can be one little thing, one little event, one small attitude. And why would that be a flaw, and why would it be like a rope that anchors you into lifetime after lifetime addressing the same issue? No matter what culture you are born in, what time you are born in — no matter what color your skin, no matter if you are rich or poor — it doesn't matter; you still are plagued with this same little problem. And perhaps that is the only thing that brought you back here other than studying here, and perhaps in this study you will find the solution.

Well, let me tell you: Karma and the lords of karma, I liked battling with them because they wield an enormous power of suppression. But karma, what it really means is what you think, you are; what you think, you create. And that thinking must be that pure and that clear. Thus if you think badly and do badly to someone else, that bad will be done back to you because that is experiencing the reality that you are meting out. Now karma, as it were, can be such a suppressing concept that instead of creating masters, it can absolutely destroy minds that are in the working to greatness by taking from them every sweet thing that life has to offer: living in a monastic style of life and chartering the course of their thinking in endless mantras that mean nothing; prostrating the body; starving the body; doing every possible thing to avoid the encounter of potential karma, even with eyesight. Now that is rather extreme.

Well, let me tell you — particularly the Boktau group — that there is no one event in your life that you have that keeps you on the cycle of reincarnation that cannot be resolved when you polish the attitude and slough off of it people, places, things, events, and time. That is going naked into the center of an attitude. And only when you can do that with any problem that you have is the only time you will ever resolve it. Blaming your parents, blaming a time, being victimized by an event, all of those are actions upon a reaction that keep you coming back. And the solution is so utterly simple: See it for what it is without any dressings, including the past. And if you are able to do that, then we will know what sort of substantive entity you are that can look in the eye of your necromancer until the veil is lifted and we find that the necromancer has no face.

LIVING IN THE PAST

You know what your difficulty is and what it has always been, people, is that you live in a past hurt and past grievance. I don't know how many times I have to say this, but even my most advanced group still digs up reasons in their past for their behavior, and digging up old corpses is only going to make the situation stink. That does not resolve anything. What it does do is connect you to those same people for another lifetime to come. Why do you think that there are soul groups that work together? There is such a thing. There are groups in this very audience. And of course the larger group has a soul connection in my lifetime; we were all one time together. But in the time span from then to now, you have all had little dramas in your life that you do to one another. And whoever you lay the blame at in this lifetime for your present misery is exactly who you are going to get next lifetime.

Now think about that. Is that illogical to you? If consciousness and energy create reality through the processes of the brain and its neuronet mapping then, if your neuronet says that you are weak because of your parents and that becomes unresolved in this lifetime and they are always held issue to that, is not then consciousness and energy creating that as absolute reality? How many of you agree? Would not then that reality be carried over into another experience with the same people? Why? Because they are in your reality. How does it escape being stripped at the light? Only the memory is stripped at the light but the soul begs for resolution, you know, the page that hasn't had anything recorded on it for thousands of years because for thousands of years you are stuck in one little attitude. That is lack.

Now great beings all know this and very soon you are going to know that. You are going to know it because I am going to press to you that realization and its profound implications for your future Now. And I want to do that because as long as you play with the idea of suffering through a person, place, event, or time, then you and that suffering and that entity will be bound together for all eternity until one day you give it up.

Now this has great implications — great implications — because it shows the level of immaturity in a school of ancient wisdom. No master will ever, ever blame his or her life. No master will ever lay the power of his or her fall or rise at the feet of any other individual or any event or any time. That is how you know you are talking to a true master of the Great Work.

So is it then possible to really change the way your brain thinks by focusing on this little problem of yours without connecting it to all of these other forms that are common in association to the problem? Absolutely, because when you focus on what it is — not who made it and when it happened and who caused it and why you are in the days to follow progressively a certain way, when those are eliminated — you are looking at a naked concept in the brain. Do you not know what that causes the brain to do? Now we have an unplugging of the neurons from their dendrite stations because if we focus on what we are without association, the brain must comply to be able to understand what it is you are doing, and they have to unplug the circuitry of association and give you simply what it is. And when you stare at what it is without association, it can no longer be. It is by virtue of association that it is in the first place. How many of you understand? Turn to your neighbor and explain that in terms that are understandable to you and hopefully to your neighbor.[1] How many of you

---

1 This is an important characteristic of Ramtha's teaching technique. We have not edited out the instances when Ramtha asks the students to turn to their neighbor and articulate the teaching. We suggest to the reader to follow Ramtha's instructions and attempt to articulate the teachings in your own words, regardless of whether you have a partner or not.

understand what you just repeated to your neighbor? You understand it? So be it.

Now here is something to think about: You cannot sustain lack in any form when you have detached association from it. You cannot sustain lack in any form when you have detached associations with it. Think about that. How many of you understand?

Now the quickest road to enlightenment is not drugs, people, and it is not wine. It is not anything outside of what we are. The most rapid road to mastery is the road of detachment. And what that means is to detach from all mental, limited attitudes blame — time, people, place, events — because when you take lack and stand it on its own, it cannot sustain without blame. How many of you understand that? And hate cannot live — hate cannot be sustained — unless it has a victim. Detach the victim and there is no hate. How many of you understand? Detach from lack your job, the place you live, how much money you make. Detach from lack any perceived abilities of yours that would prevent abundance from occurring. If you detached all of that and simply looked at lack, it could not exist in your reality, because in a state of pure detachment we have the pure, present moment that is the most awesome power there is.

The Shadow Aspect of the Self

Now let's go a little further with that. Many of you have what has been referred to commonly in this group as a dark-sided character, and dark-sided means the shadow aspect of you, a filament or a thread that is rough and raw. And that thread is a thread that I would best say is a neuronet map; that you covet this side of yourself so deliciously so as to never let anything penetrate it, because this thread or this shadow self is the self that holds the burden as well as the power of victimization — reaction, hate, resentment, bitterness, jealousies, anger, all of those pitiful emotions that do nothing but destroy the health of the body — and causes you to have to come back again and to redress those issues with the same people in a future state. That is nothing to look forward to. You have this side to your character that you protect, and you relish it and you use it as a whip and a sting. And it is an ugly, ugly aspect of yourself, and I see it in you.

Now all that is, is a specific map that you have up here that you shield and protect.[2] And only a master can see what is really sitting behind that sweet little face, because most people are running around trying to put on a good face to hide this shadowy character of their personality. So because everyone is doing it, no one sees that everyone already is that. Do you understand?

Now let me tell you about that little character. That stubborn, altered-ego facet of the brain — that part of yourself that you refuse to let go of — is guarded richly by having a life of its own because it can point to circumstances in its life that made it that way: betrayal, abandonment, being lied to, being used, abused, neglected, all of those words that you use so commonly in your dialogues with one another. And, you know, this ugly little altered ego that you possess has been the most difficult entity in this school to change. And do you know why? Because you don't want to change it, and I have given you the keys to do it. And why don't you want to change it? Because it affords you a battery of protection against people that you think are out to get you or to take advantage of you. So it provides the sting, the venom, the ugliness, the manipulation, the resentment, the cleverness, and all the things that you found you need for the sake of your own survival.

But let me tell you about this dark little creature. It is going to be because of that you are going to miss the greatest message in this school that your soul brought you here to learn, and that is that when we dissolve the inner demon — that shadowy creature inside ourselves, like I did, lay down my broadsword — we do become vulnerable, but we become vulnerable only for the first moment of our fear of reprisal because we did so. And that is a useless fear in the face of knowledge.

So what holds your little demon together? Well, your nastiness of temper. You can say, "I have a bad temper because of this and this and this and this." But what if we remove this and this and

2 This expression refers to the brain's neuronet, which forms the basis of our human personality.

this and this;[3] would there then still be a bad temper? No, there wouldn't. So what do we do with bad-temper energy? It is free; it is free space.

What if then you say, "I don't trust people because I have been betrayed." Well, I would look at you and say, well, you are the first person you should trust, is yourself, because you are the greatest betrayer to yourself than anyone will ever be to you. And why is that? Because you have a guarded attitude, that you refuse to neutralize the association to that attitude to be free of it. You see, trusting people only becomes an issue when you have difficulty trusting yourself. When there is no problem in self-trust, it never is an issue because there is no association there to cling to. How many of you understand? So what we begin to do is we begin to disarm a part of yourself that is really responsible for many, many wonderful things — in the face of absolute power — coming into your life that don't come because you always have up this shield, and the shield never allows you to live in this moment. You are never really here tonight with me; you are really back somewhere else in another time.

This little creature that you have inside of you — which was appropriately called the devil or the demon, the inner demon — is that person who has a whole storehouse of information about why they should be the way they should be. And all that information is interlinked with many people and many places, many things and many events, but it is only one demon with many tentacles. And it takes a great amount of resistance to the beauty of life to feed the monster. For example, when I say resistance to life, I have people here who would rather hold onto that than to dissolve it. And how do I know that? Even in teaching the teaching of moving into simply looking at what it is without the attachment of people, places, things, events, and time, they still went back to their past. They still cling to that. Past association is an attachment. It is the only thing that supports that which doesn't really exist. Lack is an illusion. What is real is the attitude that supports it. Do you understand?

Now mastery of oneself is a noble and worthwhile pursuit,

---

3 The human personality always finds many excuses for its mood swings or bad temper.

but it is a pursuit that takes you into the inner corridors of yourself, as it were, and really makes you look at parts of yourself that so far have been your persona, the way people perceive you. And, you know, there is an element of fear there that if you get rid of that persona, then people won't take you seriously or you won't be big and bad enough to make any difference. But that is a lie, because as long as you dwell on an insignificant issue like a single attitude that has caused you to be born so many times — has ruined so many relationships, has ruined so many opportunities, has ruined so many days that came and are gone and will never be again, that ruined the landscape of life totally — as long as that remains in your life, the hope for future lives is very dim. And the ability to expressly be a master is vastly undermined by clinging to something that you just need to give up. It is a no-thing.

This is a diseasement in human consciousness. And, my beloved people, I want you to know that I am pressing you to that center arena and challenging you and endeavoring to show you something so sweet and indeed so beautiful: that all the things that you were afraid about yourself that you thought were the truth don't even exist. The only thing that exists is the association that you believe to be with them. How many of you understand? And that association is what needs to be removed. Then there is no such thing as inadequacies or indeed there is no such thing as hate and indeed there is no such thing as malice. There is no such thing as suffering. There is no such thing as lack and there is no such thing even as death. There really isn't.

So if we think about this then, our demons, your demons — ours, because I am here in the midst of it and I don't like it — are really about your need to support your attitudes in order to make you survive, and yet they are the very attitudes that cripple you from life utterly. What is on the other side of that? Well, you know, I know a brave man. All I have to do is look at him and I can see in him that substance of quality that I know what makes up bravery. Bravery isn't about being big, bad, and bold. Bravery is about the impeccable strength to cleave from oneself the cancerous thought that weakens an individual and his performance in life in every area. Now that is strength and it is also bravery.

And I can tell by looking at a woman when I know if they rest within that bosom, sincere love and affection, because sincere love and affection are the utter embodiment of God, as the goddess that is indeed the nurturer of life and never the robber of it — and is the giver of love, never the mutilator of it — and that in the woman we find God's sweetest flower. And I can look at a woman and I can tell you whether that love abides there or not. And what makes a woman beautiful is not the skin, the eyes, the age. What makes a woman beautiful is her capacity to love unyieldingly and to love without conditions. Now that I consider a beautiful woman. And why? Because when you remove from lack the association that keeps it propped up — you see, lack can be seen as a crystal ball propped up by that which is termed a triad of legs; and what is really seen here is not a crystal ball but the triad of legs that is propping it up — we could see then lack as a crystal transparent ball which we really can't see. But what we do see is the props that position it. And if we remove those props of association — and association, let me remind you again, is saying that you are the way you are because of what happened to you when you were a little girl or a little boy and then carrying that all the way through your life and coloring every day of your life with it, for that is the only way that you know how to live; that event, that time, those people, and that place are the props to lack — and when you remove them, there is no crystal ball. There was only the association. Lack doesn't even exist. It is incapable of existing in a kingdom of absolute abundance.

You know why you are insecure? Because someone — whoever you want to name — told you and made you feel insecure. And you keep going back to that time; you keep hurting over it. What if we just were to look at insecurity without the prop, there wouldn't be anything called insecurity. Do you understand? And do you know what exists in the no-space is love? Well, what is love? Love is the glue that holds everything together. That is the power.

The Art of Detachment and Unconditional Love

Now unconditional love resides in the bosom of the goddess. And why do I find that most beautiful of all? Because that means that that woman has more love than association, and in the place of association nothing but love lives because that is what you have left when you remove the props of victimization in every level of your life. And now I say that the goddess is alive and well because from her bosom flows nothing but love. It is not contrived; it is, because there is nothing else there except that. And why is that so important? Because that is the quality that makes a Christ. That is the love that heals. That is the love that binds, and that is the love that sustains. And love cannot exist in a state of attachment. How many of you understand? Turn to your neighbor and explain.

Now one of the reasons that you keep intact then this demon that you are starting to understand a little bit more about is because — let's look at it this way — if you neutralized the shadow self within you, you are afraid of what you would be without it. In other words, what would be then the stimulus behind your conversation? How many of you understand? And you are also afraid that you wouldn't have a reason to get up every morning and with blood, sweat, and tears make it through the day without having a nervous breakdown. Think of it. People are afraid to become naked to the extent of detachment, because what it means is there is real fear of what they may be or what they may become because they have shared a true and fruitful companionship with that which is termed the shadow self. They are attached to the attachments. How many of you understand?

Now that is an unnerving concept. Without going any further with this one-sided dialogue than this one statement — because I don't want you to go off of the end and then create an attachment to the teaching that I just taught you, which is always a risk — why don't you just think about then that maybe the reason you are not willing to give up your past is because it has been such a companion in your present and it would really mean having to be sort of a different person and, being the person who always wants to be in control of your attachments, then that puts you a little out of control. How many of you understand? I tell you, saints are born out of this fire — they really are — and so are masters, true genuine people who are on a divine mission to find that one flaw that has inhibited their progress for millennia. They are really after it. They really want it.

So, you know, you don't have a whole bunch of karma. What you have is a flaw — a flaw — that can be owned, and it is the most obvious flaw in your life. And it can be owned when you take a broadsword and knock the crutches out from under it and you will find it is empty. And it is the crutches that keep bringing you back lifetime, after lifetime, after lifetime. Do you understand?

So now we know that in addressing such a teaching that there are those of you who don't hear me. You have what we call selective hearing, so my teachings skip a lot. There are whole spaces of nothing remembered, and I am a much better orator than that. The selective hearing comes when you don't want to hear what I am telling you, but I tell you, you are here to hear it. You came here to hear what you did not want to hear before.

Now our first step in this resolution is that it has taken all of these years to get you to a point of knowledge beyond superstition and beyond fanaticism, to get you to a point that now we can move into the center and address this without hysteria. I am still going to have hysterical people because they don't listen. They don't hear the entire teaching and contemplate it thoroughly and see for themselves that all of these blocks are really empty and the only thing that is real about them is blame. And when we get rid of that, there is nothing else and all that exists in that is love. That is the God quality that we are after here. That is the power that moves mountains. Well, it took all of this time to get you to this little place to listen to this simple message. And it is that simple.

How hard is it then to become detached from your attachment? It is not hard at all, people, because with applied focus to lack without people, places, times and events, it cannot be sustained as lack; it doesn't exist. And when that enlightenment occurs, the brain will scramble to reconnect its circuitry to exactly that understanding. And so what happens when you realize there is no such thing in you as lack or fear or illness or evil — or whatever else you want to say — or ignorance? What happens to you when you know that that moment? The whole space of that contemplation is washed because it cannot sustain itself. And it is washed and a power moves into it. It is free-space power; it is love. And it is in that place that the miraculous takes place. The miraculous does not take place in the past nor does it take place in the future. It takes place in the moment you are present, in contemplation; that is when the miracle happens. That is the only space it can happen in. What is the miracle? The miracle is abolishing the lie and in its place the abundance appears. It was always there, always has been there.

And those of you who don't hear very well, you will continue to guard your dirty little consciousness and your dirty little thinking and be the possessors of your past because it gives you a reason to complain and a thing to work for, because you don't believe in me but you do believe in your lack.

And those of you who hold onto your torment — your imagined torment, your imagined betrayal, your imagined nastiness of reaction — those of you who will hold onto it, your life will be nothing but hell not only the rest of this lifetime but all lifetimes to come. And what is the payment for the wages of being attached to this shadow self? It is that the love of this erroneous being becomes more seductive than the love for life — and its opportunities that afford us every single day that the love of this beast is more important than the love of life — and the participation in that love in every way, in every action, and in every thought that we could say that we are truly alive and indeed that we have truly lived. Your erroneous little thinking will never allow you to experience life, and woe to you.

And you will never be a master in this school because the wages of mastership are very strict. It demands self-conquest; moreover, it demands the absolution of the divine in us. That means the freedom of our divinity. And where is that divinity? It is right in the place that you think your lack is. And our divinity is the will. It is the sword of the will that allows us as lawgivers to determine what kind of life we want. I say there is no enemy nor is there any man nor is there any woman nor is there any parent that is so great as to rob me of my life and my power to make my life what I wish. No one was ever that great in my life. Now why should it be in yours?

So those of you who have ears, listen to what I have said and interpret it no differently than the way that I have taught you. And those of you who want to know, your freedom is at hand; your absolute lightness of being is at hand. And I don't care who you are — and I don't care what language you speak and if you can read or if you can write or if you can't — we are all equal in God. And when we all have that moment to look at ourselves right in the eye and look at our limitations and qualify our lack by what sustains it and then remove what sustains it, then I swear we are enacting the divine and we all have that capacity to do that. Love is a magnet. It is magnetic and powerful. Lack is contrived, limited, destructive. Now the truly marvelous in this school is yet to be learned, but it cannot be learned until this lesson is practiced and owned. How many of you understand? So be it.

So now our first step then to engaging this began prior to this lifetime, and it was our meeting between you and I and this school. That was the first step, that you asked and demanded that the soul require of you in this lifetime a meaningful solution to your dilemma, to that one little problem. And when we satisfy the soul, then we are free to go on our way. Tonight I have satisfied the soul by giving the conscious carrier of it the information that it needs to make decisions about that one little attitude and how to eliminate it. I cannot eliminate it for you — it is not my journey — but I am your teacher and I can tell you this is the most rapid, the most volatile discipline you can do. And it will thrust you into free space faster than anything I have taught you thus far. And it is a step that is ready for those who are willing to take it.

Now it doesn't sound like a lot but, I promise you, letting go of your pride is very hard indeed to do. Being humble is very difficult for men and women to do. The act of forgiveness and the prostration of self in the act of forgiveness — prostrating, in a visual, means laying face down, spread like an eagle on the floor at the mercy of something greater, to prostrate yourself to something greater — that is the image we must do. What that means is that we be willing to give up what we are for something greater and to sacrifice it. It is not easy, but then again it is.

And you are going to find that the moment you focus on that little problem or that attitude — and I forbade you to connect it with the past in any way, with a person in any way, with an event in any form, and in time I forbade you — and if under that direction you focus on that little attitude, you will find it will be nothing. Now you are learning the secret. And all we have to do is first know the knowledge, and now you know the knowledge. The second thing you must do is to be willing to do that.

So when do you do it? When do you want to: tonight, tomorrow morning, tomorrow afternoon? You choose. And you just find it in yourself and I promise you, with a little help from your friend, that that will surface. And when it does, you have as always the election to do something about it or let it ride. If you become decisive and do something about it, all you have to do is go someplace, close those eyes— blindfold them if you can — get into a place of quiet, put that star on, roll those eyes up, tighten down and blow, and start moving energy.[4] And when you are ready, then you take that little attitude and you put it right here (frontal lobe) in your focus without any other attachment.[5] And when you hold it there for a period of time, it is going to try to be slippery, and you are going to have to blow and bring it back into focus without attachment. The moment you do that, I promise you your world is going to change — your life, your flow of energy, and your freedom — and the next time that we are together, you are going to be older and wiser. You understand? So be it.

So everyone has asked the proverbial question throughout the ages: Master, what is unconditional love? Unconditional love is that which always is. And when attachment is removed, it is most brilliantly seen. It is not something you have to be; it is what you already are. And in its place are supported illusions and

---

4 It is a common practice in Ramtha's School of Enlightenment to draw a blue five-pointed star on each of the seven seals of the body. This discipline helps the students to become aware of, and focus on, their seven seals. See fig. 2.

5 The frontal lobe of the brain is where a thought is held in focus and empowered so that it can manifest into reality. See fig. 1.

lies, and when they are removed, the love is there. It does not have to be worked on. That is the nature of our beings, my beloved people. We were conceived in it; thus we are in it. Point Zero is it, and all the power that formed all of the dimensions and all the planes and all the heavens is that very power. And thus if we are conceived in the womb of such love, then that must be the aspect of our true nature. Being anything other than that is being artificial to that nature. And that is why we have what we call the wheel of reincarnation.

It Is Possible to Own It All in One Lifetime

And is it possible to own all of this in one lifetime? Absolutely is, because if one has the privilege of moving through life as a conqueror and conquering itself, conquering the limitations and its own ignorance, then one naturally moves to an area — what I have just taught you — naturally and hopefully is endowed with enough wisdom to see the wisdom and logic in dispersing of attachments, because in their dispersal there is no threat and there is no coloration of the self, so there is no little attitude that would bind us to another life.

And is it possible in one lifetime to drink in all the mornings that Ra rises and blisters the night sky with the color pink and rose and purple and red? Absolutely. And in one lifetime can you drink in that which is termed the waxing and waning of the moon till dawn? Is it possible in one lifetime to own the experience, that the experience is always? It absolutely is. And isn't it possible in one lifetime to have eaten and reveled in the food? Is it possible in one lifetime to have drunk enough wine? It absolutely is. Is it possible in one lifetime to have grown to such an extent that not even life itself is an attachment? It absolutely is.

I would never have wanted to be on the wheel of reincarnation because the wheel then would have been my enslaver. And I will tell you, my people, the most frightening and horrific thing that has ever happened to you is being born with no memory of who you once were. That is the wine of such enchantment that it is a terror. And not to be in full faculty of what I once saw and knew and experienced, and to have it abolished from me for the sake of taking on a new child in a new body that cannot remember because the brain itself did not live in those times — to have had a brain that could not remember the mornings that I saw and indeed the evenings that I knew, and the battles that I was in and the soldiers I interacted with, and the smell of stench and blood and carnage and, yes, jasmine and olives and the color of silver-leafed trees at green-reed rivers, and wildfowl so brilliant and beautiful — the very thought of having that abolished from my consciousness is unthinkable. And yet I have watched you so many lifetimes starting over. To me, that is unthinkable. To you, you have never thought about it. That is the most horrible thing I can ever think of, because you really are lost unless you have some way — some lantern that in the night of your ignorance and your lack of neuromemory can light a path for you — that you instinctually know to follow but cannot reason with your current brain why you should. What an imprisonment. And it is not easy to come out of it.

It is possible to do all of this in one life. And it is possible to teach your children to do it all in one life when you are wise enough to understand the traps that you walked into and to teach your children to walk into them and to get out of them. And when you teach them that, you have given them life-giving spiritual knowledge that will save them in the long run from having to live a life and wonder what it was all about, only to die and to go back and to realize that one little issue you did not take care of this time. With this knowledge you cannot help but address the issue because it is the very thing that torments you. It is the thorn in your side and you know it very well. All you have to do is look at it. Understand? How many of you understand? So be it.

Now in the days that follow from this, what I do for you and what I can do for you is that I want and will raise the awareness of those little attitudes, and I will help create circumstances around them so that you get to see them starting to bloom. And they are not bad and they are not good; they are opportunities. And when you see the opportunity, understand I am pressing it to you to do something with. You can do anything you want to do with it or you can go back to your old philosophy, your old horoscopes, your own drugs, your own drinking out of control — you can go back to all of that — but you will never find resolve with it. That is your choice. Or you can become naked, unattached, and utterly and remarkably powerful. I know the way home. You are not going to get too out of control, I promise you. So be it.

RAMTHA'S LEARNING TO DETACH FROM HIS PHYSICAL BODY

Student: I would like to know when you were practicing going in and out of your body, how did you know where you were? And did you go to other levels, like the fourth, fifth, sixth, and seventh? And if you did, were you taught there? And when you ascended in front of us, did you know where you were going? And if you had a life review — I know you weren't stripped — did you still have to look at your life and then go where you decided you wanted to go? I always wanted to ask you that.

Ramtha: How I beat the light?

Student: No, because I know why you weren't stripped because of what you just said. Well, the first part I want you to answer first.

When you first were going in and out and you were laying there for the longest time — you said your body was almost dead when you came back and you would come in — how did you know where you were? Were you just out of your body in that dimension? Or did you discover ultraviolet and gamma and x-ray and be able to come back in in this lifetime? Or was that something you discovered after?

Ramtha: Can I address that before we go on?

Student: Yes.

Ramtha: The first time that I left my body, it was an accident. You remember the story in the wind, eh? And the reason that I knew that I left my body is because I found myself in an atmosphere of height that I was unaccustomed to being in. Moreover, having the point of view of which I could see my body where it was — and there was no sensation in leaving it — the only awareness that happened was being above it, which is the usual case in leaving one's body. Are you with me so far?

Now being separated from my carnal self — though I had

separated many from their carnal selves — I had never been separated from my carnal self, so it was a new experience for me. When I recognized my body and my robe and my plateau is the moment when I claimed the body as my own, was the moment I was brought back into it. Are you still with me? Consciousness and energy create reality. Understand?

Then for seven years I went out and reenacted everything — I am a patient God — for seven years. Where else was I going? For seven years I went out and I thought and I plotted and I planned, and I wondered and indeed I pondered. And what I did was I built up that which is termed an expectation, which can go nicely back to the teaching tonight. I put an attachment on an event that had no attachment. Understand? So we could say then that I built up a religious dogma about the event in analyzing it intellectually. That intellectual analysis is what prevented me for seven years from doing the same marvelous thing again. When I gave up the expectation, then I gave up the attachment of my intellectual perception of it and that freed myself to move again. Understand?

Now the next time that I moved — which was seven years and a few days later — I moved to a point near the same point of distance from my whole awareness and my body. And the moment that I knew that was my body again was the moment that I went back into it. I am very smart. I understand that every time I keep looking at this body and calling it mine is the moment I am back in mine. Do you understand? So there followed subsequently to that some wonderful lessons. I had come to the place of surrender, to where I could leave. And I knew I was gone because in various places that I left — most of which was my little hovel — I always got the perspective of the higher perspective observing a lower perspective. Coming back into my body was the recognition that it was my body, so after a while — and a while to you, well, to me it would be months and years — I understood that I needed a reference point to understand my detachment. But number two was that the moment that I recognized from where I came, I was back into it. So then the next step to the freedom was to no longer recognize my body and to no longer think about it. That took some mastery. So the first years in this art I was not a traveler in dimensions and domains. I was an entity that was remote from my body and endeavoring to learn the process so that I could do it very well.

When I entered into the tunnel, or the ladder of Jacob, I did not go into dimensions and planes unknown to me because, you understand — as I have taught you, that we all came down those stairs and from those levels, and the moment we reenter them, we are clothed in the garment of that plane — when I left my body and entered into infrared, I put on the body of infrared. When I left my body and entered into light, I understood the light because I was there. And my election to return to my body allowed me to return to my body fully cognizant of what the light meant and what I saw there. And what I knew at the light was that there were preceding kingdoms. So the next time that I visited the light, I went beyond it, and in that I was clothed in the body of Shiva. You understand? Now if I then inhabit the body of Shiva, it is the body that I once knew; it still lives. And contained within that chest of a body is all the knowledge that is afforded to me of a mind that lives on the fourth level, so I know where I am at. Do you understand?

Student: Yes.

Ramtha: Do you really understand?

Student: Yes.

Ramtha: Now let me continue. It took me until the day that I left this plane to explore all of those planes and to wear all those bodies. Do you understand? And every time that I came back to the body, I brought with me all of that knowledge. Do you understand? I didn't leave it. I carried it back with me and brought it back to my physical incarnation. That meant then that I switched, as it were, as Ramtha from a yellow-brain perspective. I became Ramtha from the deeper-brain perspective, because only in the deeper brain did I seat the memory and carefully implement it into the yellow brain.

When I ascended and left this plane, I did so because I had visited every other plane. In one nightfall here on Terra I would leave my body, and in time of another place — for example, on the fifth plane — in what was a nightfall here I lived for hundreds of years there and brought back the richness of that time frame by morning when my physical body awakened. You understand?

So to ask me did I gain knowledge and know where I was is an understatement. And by the time that I left this plane and had communed with my people, I communed with my people the simplicity of teachings and my truth that I knew and brought it forward to them in simplistic style so that they would never forget me and to understand how to live a life — a meaningful life — and that the kingdom of heaven held within its boundaries an unlimited opportunity for anyone on this plane to be a part of. But the passion has to be there. The dedication has to be there, and the patience has to be there. But that I left and did not die in their midst was an unforgettable incident.

So when I ascended that day, what I did that day was I took my body upright and put its old robe on it and walked it out in the middle of my people. And in the midst of my body I brought forward my seventh-level mind, and that mind vibrated this body into kingdom come. You understand?

THE EGYPTIAN BOOK OF THE DEAD

Student: My father passed away last year in April and I was here for an event. My family lives in India and I heard about it at a friend's house, and when I heard about it, I sort of became numb but I didn't become emotional.

This was an evening event that we were allowed to come, and this was in the morning that I heard, the first day. I went into focus and I felt that I almost went — it was an immediate feeling — where I was in the room in his bedroom, and his body was laying there and I saw him in the corner. And when I saw him, he was really afraid. These are just my feelings. I have judged them afterwards as just being mere fantasies or something like that, but I am going to go on anyway.

When I saw him I said, "Why don't you come back with me?" And I felt that he came back with me. And the focus session, I don't remember after that. But what happened is for about three days through the event I felt his presence on and off, that he was with me. Even when I was driving or whatever, I was aware of his presence.

And in all those times I would go in and out of focus. And what I did was I talked to him, and I was trying to tell him everything that I couldn't share with him when he was in his body — whatever I had thought that I had learned, whether I knew it as a truth or as just mere knowledge — to share it with him because I felt that if he could benefit from it and go beyond to ultraviolet through me, or at least know about it, maybe in the next lifetime it would benefit him.

So in the end what I had done was I felt that I was making a tunnel for him through the light in ultraviolet, and I created these blue webs, a tunnel of webs. And I told him that I would keep it open as long as I could so he could go through and see what the other side looked like and if he wanted to, he could stay there. But I felt in my mind there was a resistance and a distrust on his part, that he really didn't trust me because he didn't know. In his consciousness he had never been exposed to something like that. So even though he didn't have his present brain, the consciousness — the mind that he was occupying — did have the concept of ultraviolet. And so I am not sure if he could go through.

My question is: Can you do that for another person, even if they weren't exposed to the teachings, for your family or your loved ones or your friends?

Ramtha: Have you ever heard of a book called the *Egyptian Book of the Dead*?

Student: No.

Ramtha: Never have? I will send you a runner. It is about saying the prayers of direction for the deceased and, in particular, the deceased in elder times were the greatest entities of the dynasties of Egypt at that time. It was the sacred prayers of directing the Spirit through the passages of infrared onto the light. Now that was a science brought forward to this planet by the Gods who understood the science. So obviously there is, in what you were able to do for your father, a revelation.

When you are out of the body, what you see is perceived with greater illumination and clarity than the body could ever offer. The perception of the Spirit in an ultrafine, subtle body is much more dynamic than it is in the human body. When the human body, as an instrument operated by the spiritual self, endeavors to make contact and, in its instruction, the instructions can be received by the spiritual incarnate entity who is now discarnate — who is now in Spirit — this can provide an enormous pathway, a passage, if you will, to the other side and should never be neglected.

And, yes, it worked, but the resistance that you felt was not from your father; it was from you.

Student: And why was that?

Ramtha: Because you didn't believe in what you were doing.

Student: So was it because I thought I was unworthy of doing that, that I wasn't knowledgeable enough, or just simple disbelief?

Ramtha: You just didn't trust what you already knew to be substantial enough to make a difference.

Student: Okay. Thank you.

Ramtha: Don't do that.

THE IMPORTANCE OF CHANGE FOR THE SOUL'S JOURNEY

Now before we end this evening, there is an issue I want to address to you about change and everyone that is going through it. Change is not a disease and it is not a virus. It is necessary for a person to continue to grow and to expand that growth in one's life, to have an effect upon life. It is important for the soul that we change, and the more that we do so in one lifetime, the greater our chances are of succeeding this lifetime, not with another lifetime but an onward journey back through the ladder, back to Point Zero. We enhance our opportunity of doing that. Now there are many of you forcing change in your life in areas that you are not mature enough to change. And when I speak of a level of maturity, I mean that you have created circumstances in your life that you intentionally created and that you are in the midst of experiencing those creations.

Now there is no timeline to an intentionally created experience. For example, you may be in a relationship that has not reached a level of maturity to the point that the relationship no longer offers you the challenge by which to grow, and the challenge could simply be a matter of having the ability to respond in love. And if that is not there any longer, then that relationship has reached a maturity and it is time to change the relationship. Some of you will not find that level of maturity for years.

Now when I tell you to change, that does not mean that you are to get rid of what is in your life that you have not yet owned. It is easy to know and simple to know when you have owned something. It becomes boring, predictable, tedious. And the rewards are as little as having a roof over your head and food in your mouth, and that is the compromise. It is simple to know and easy to detect when it is time to move on. Boredom is the sign that it is time to change.

Many of you are not finished with your experiences and have no business trying to change them when they are not mature. When they are mature is when you have reaped from them everything that you are supposed to reap from that which you intentionally created. How many of you understand? You don't want to — and it would merely be impossible to — move out of love and cast it aside in favor of something bigger and better, because when love is present, that is never boring. That is ongoing and nurturing.

Now I want you to understand that the prerequisite to being a master does not mean that you have to vacate your life completely of everything in it because you think that that means unattachment. You only detach yourself from your suffering, your lack, and your victimization. And you enjoy, by God, the fruits of your focused enterprise into life, and it is your job to experience it to the level of maturity. And when that maturity is reached, it will give you up; you won't have to do anything. It will give you up because there is no longer the magnetism nor are there the dynamics involved in the continuation of it. How many of you understand?

So do not make posthaste to destroy or try to destroy what is real in your life because you have misread the teachings. There is a time to enjoy what you have done, and that is the beauty of the master in life. But the master in life can come down from the mountain and enjoy the feast upon the once-empty table that he or she, the master, intentionally created and can actually sit down and partake of it. There is a time to stop visualizing and start eating or drinking. Do you understand?

time to stop Visualizing and start enjoying

lays you are not going to want to do your focus.
ou not want to do your focus? Well, because
ning that you need to do when you wake up is
your eyes have opened to a glorious morn, and
already focused into your life is in full bloom,
the broadness of mind and the passionate aspect
olutely enjoy it." Then the discipline is the life,
ll-lived. And there are days that it is time to go
ountain and go back to work and start changing
elow. And then there will be a time to come
t. Do you understand?
ortant that you change. You should not be the
ng here tonight as you were the first time you
came to see me. If you are, we have a problem. Your life should
be like a dancing star flashing in who knows what beautiful
direction, and how long will the spike be and what coloration
will it be. You know, you should be changing and improving your
state of mind, improving and sharpening your ability to find that
center without pause to reflect about and past circumstance that
would deny you the richness of not having a problem. You should
work on polishing, and every day polish and take responsibility
for your actions and don't put it off on anyone else. And when
you can no longer find the attachment to support the action, it
will disappear out of your life and so will its effect in your life
disappear. Do you understand?

There really is an extraordinary self inside of you that in the
normal course of evolution would take many more lifetimes to
cultivate because it is just being hung-up on one little issue of
suffering. Well, we know that it is that easy to kick the legs out
from under its suffering and get rid of its associations and past.
When we know it is that simple, then it is no longer in our life.
And when we are bold enough to do that, we deserve to be that
radiant being that is no longer affected by things from the past,
people from the past, and no longer suffers under that criteria.
We deserve to be radiant beings and indeed we deserve to be
powerful in that radiant self. It is only those people that really do
deserve the honor of living for two hundred or more years, because
they are not gauged to die anytime soon because they haven't

suffered enough to destroy their own life force. How many of you understand? Polish and stop whining. Take a look at why you are doing it, at its heart, and get clean. It doesn't take a great deal of effort. Then you will understand the magical science of mastery and its effect called longevity.

And, last, it is true, before you were born in this life you knew about me, for I certainly have known you, and you made your way here and that was preordained before birth. So this school had to come into being to facilitate those whose soul choice was to find the knowledge that was at the root of the cause of their problematic behavior that kept binding them back into lifetime, after lifetime, after lifetime. And that knowledge has been addressed in this school.

So we have fulfilled a destiny, you and I, on a soul level of providing the information, inspiring you to do something about it. I am heavy in that department. But unless you want to do it, it will never work for you. And I promise you that after this life, those of you who don't apply the knowledge, you are going to find yourself back up there in another life review, and you are going to look at your silly antics of choosing to hold onto a rather sour attitude that is really despicable and unhonorable. You would rather hold onto that than release it so you can be free in lifetimes to come. You are going to look at that and you are going to be sad beyond belief at your pride and indignancy in holding onto it. After you address this little attitude, there is much I can show you and indeed much we can do. But not until you come into the center where I live can I show you around adequately. So be it.

Now I didn't come into this room tonight just to sit here and give you a brilliant teaching, which of course I did do. But I also, as the Lord of the Wind, speak as a lawgiver, that all that I should say and all that I should answer should carry the power of full manifestation, and that I did tonight. So what this means to you is what I have taught you will manifest in your life and the opportunities will come to you in glorious measure, because I want you to have a chance to see what I was endeavoring to show you tonight and indeed give your soul a chance to have a reprieve. So with the words comes the power. So be it.

I love you. That is all. So be it.

CHAPTER 3
THE LAST BATTLE AGAINST TYRANNY AND SLAVERY

"You came here in the midst of conscious collapse. It is when the programming of the personality is so intact and so ingrained that right and wrong is the nurture of your daily bread: to do right because you are so wrong; to form identities that are alien to the greater thought."

— *Ramtha*

The Conquest of Our Personal Limitations

Greetings, my beloved masters. I salute you from the Lord God of my being indeed. I am pleased you are gathered here this evening. There are things you need to relearn.

O my beloved God,
this day I have grown.
This day I am unfolding.
Change, my beloved God,
hath been a bitter fruit.
O my beloved God,
alas, it was only my fear.
Unfold me, troubadour,
unfold me.
Give me the strength
to understand
and the wisdom to choose.
So say I
from the Lord God of my being,
forever
and ever
and ever.
So be it.
To life.

It has taken a very long time in your time — from the few seeds of entities who came in the very beginning to audience — to gather unto this great place your wonderful number. It is a tribute to the possibility that God is personalized, individualized, and indeed unified. It is a tribute to truth. It has taken many arduous moments and difficult words in a meaningless language to bring you even here this evening in your time and counting. But I stand, as it were, in a body not of my kind to greet you, to deeply salute you for your courage as children to have come this far from such meager beginnings in this time frame.

This body is indeed unto me an august body, a potentially royal body, a body that can challenge limitation but, alas, only when it has challenged its own personal limitation. The blight of any one entity's growth has never been the lethargy of Spirit being weak and the body weak but the insistence upon right and wrong and being caught in such a trap.

To think differently is an alien prospect in the entity, but to think differently is to have the reward of an unlimited experience that lifts you up from the turbulence and the trap into a thoughtfulness of being that indeed allows the evolution, the wings to grow, the Spirit to grow, the body to fly. Children only imagine such wonders. For how long has it taken you to come here? But the greatness in which I salute all of you is your tenacity and indeed that small voice that rings beyond that which is termed the rights and wrongs and the thinking in this world that compels you to know. As one would put it in a more primitive aspect: to seek, to find, to realize.

There has been, you know, a language barrier between us, but that is all that has ever been between us. I am most pleased in you.

It is going to get very rough and very difficult. But like any children with an astute parent — wise and dignified and noble and profoundly loving — the child will grow, and grow not only in body but a mind proportionate to meaningfulness, purpose, to morals that supersede mediocrity, that go to the sublime; the child that can grow in the subtleness of understanding and never be hindered by fear or threats but righteously compelled on its journey. That is where you are: learning righteousness, children, and I am pleased you are home tonight to understand more. Be seated.

This is less than one-third of your numbers, so that many are not here this evening; they are abroad. But what you will reckon with, go over with perhaps to the power of the individual groups — Elohim is connected to Elohim, and Ahk Men Ra to its members, and Om Akad, the Spirit of evolution, is connected to theirs, both present and future; so perhaps you are, as it were, the consiglieri, the diplomats — you are the runners for your specific groups, for even though you are one this night, your groups do hold purpose. Otherwise I shan't ever have named you as such and ennobled that name and empowered that name for a specific shield and banner, purpose.

In my lifetime, war, as it were, was not a known science. Squabbling and sibling rivalry, neighborhood jealousies, they all existed. Tyranny and slavery were the order of the times, and so little has changed from that time. From my time, because of my intense drive, as you would term that — intent will, as you are beginning to call it — to do whatever I set my mind to do, developed in me the proponents that would allow a collapsing of the old and a beginning of the new. My life speaks of that very well.

In my ignorance of freeing people from my enemies — you know, anyone was my enemy that wasn't on my side in the beginning — it was clearly defined the law was the sword and that was all there was to it. There was no back talk, so hence the term clear-cut. I have always appreciated a no-nonsense approach to decision-making. And yet as a man grows up to be a man very early and goes through the battles of his body, the battles of his mind, the battles of his Spirit/consciousness — and then, of course, the opposing battles that are so real, the enemy — I changed a great deal. Hormones helped; being ignorant helped; being fearless was the greatest help of all. But I changed. I conquered. I did what I did and thought that I had done away with the people of the three Gods but, to my disgust, what replaced them were the ministries of worship, another form of tyranny.

I also would realize in the later part of my life that something had to be done about this forever and ever and ever, something real. Once you are a strategist and a warrior, and you bear the ever-painful wounds and the memories, and you understand the difference between the smelling of fresh blood and rotting blood, your consciousness forever after is always molded in making life better, doing away with ignorance, superstition, and unworthiness — great factors. But I understood that as long as humanity remained slaves — no better than the dog in the street or the trash from the marketplace — as long as humanity had that consciousness they were doomed forever and ever and ever because in the wake of my march, worship became the king, worshiping and empty idolism. And speaking on my behalf, no one speaks on my behalf. Perhaps you understand why, and you understand why even this hour there is none other like me worthy to hold my name, to interpret my words, to excuse my behavior, for in my life — in the wake — such came.

Vision of the Collapse of Human Consciousness

So as a warrior who is fine-tuned and addressed to this sort of life who has been converted, as you would term it, to a greater consciousness, I had great vision into the future. I made it my business to. I always had great vision. Fearlessness does that to you. Leading people develops that in you. Being the head of your family develops that in you. Being a father, a mother, develops that in you. I was the father of what you call over two million people and growing. I was their father.

In those times I knew — before the vapors of this crustacean of physical form left this place — I knew where I was going, what I would dissolve into. But before I left, I also knew generations yet unborn, the recycling of yet unborn people. And where in my day at any point in history would that change?

You cannot dispose of human will if they have got it. You cannot rebuke human will if they have got it. And if they don't, then you stand in on their behalf. That is the basis of government. That is the basis of the priesthood. That is the basis of all entities who speak on behalf of God, who speak on behalf of the people. And you will never, ever understand will until you have earned the right to possess it. It does not come easily. And do not confuse stubbornness, and hate and joy, acceptance and denial for will. Those are primitive actions on the board that eventually lead to will. When you understand will, you will understand what I am telling you. And it is with great desire that these days that are coming up in your school, that that freshening aspect hereto unrealized be closer defined, that you understand what it is and have the opportunity to possess it. It is the difference between children and adults. It is the difference between human beings, mortal and Gods, immortal. When you understand, you look and you see that it is one precious opportunity in these cycles of this plane of demonstration that cannot be erased and washed away, that it must be remembered at least every fourth generation. It must be ingrained creedlike, if necessary.

It was then and there looking upon this form of life and seeing far — yes, far — even to this very night. And who is to say that me speaking to you now are not my thoughts this very night so long ago. Perhaps it is, in a hovel on the side of a great mountain. It was implemented and willed that there would come from nowhere extraordinary human beings — extraordinary, simple and extraordinary — that would become the golden threads in the tapestry of this evolution that would glisten and never fade, when all the colors of every kingdom that come and passeth can fade in its beauty, but that the golden thread remains untarnished, brilliant, to the very end. And thus was set out in great certainty entities that were sent into the world, great beings — not stubborn beings, not liars, not cheats, not pretenders, not scholastically intelligent, not beings who think they have been chosen, but a rare consciousness — that so noble was their purpose that they would always rally at very critical points in human history, a small group of people to carry on the concept that divinity is the divine right of every human being, because every human being, as a human being, is only defined that they are from the loin and the fruit of the womb, that they possess a body of flesh and blood and sinew and tears and hair and youth and age. That is a human being, but a God can exist as a human being. And these Gods were great teachers that were sent out at critical times of conscious collapse.

What brings on conscious collapse? You came here in the midst of conscious collapse. It is when the programming of the personality is so intact and so ingrained that right and wrong is the nurture of your daily bread: to do right because you are so wrong; to form identities that are alien to the greater thought. The consciousness is collapsing. No one knows who they are except what they can tell you they are through family tradition, their pains and scars from growing up, their successes and failures. And every one of you has them and that has been your identity. That is the sign of social consciousness, and it is collapsing to such a degree that your next generation, as it were, could not fathom personal choice, the greater thought. The great schools were developed on this concept.

Who thinks of such a concept? What sort of being with far vision would make certain and put into place the prospect of salvation, not from a Christ but from knowledge rich in experience with the beginning words, "Know that you are God. You are greatly loved." It doesn't mean anything; it is a beginning. The schools flourished; knowledge flourished. It was spoken openly because honor was learned prior to knowledge coming openly.

Do you know what honor is, to be rich in honor, impeccability, to take in and not to let out but to hold an experience upon it? Few of you knew that; few of you yet have learned it. Then the knowledge came — it was free — who you are, where you came from, the ability to see backwards, to see that in the great consciousness of mind, to be able to lay the king's table out in front of them a bounty that seems to come from everlastingness, stretching all the way to eternalness and saying to them, my beloved, this is your destiny. You have walked through the light. You now belong to the ages, time. You are here to learn all of the following things: You are a spaceship in mass. You are an explorer. You are a creator, and your species will flourish. But do not flourish your species — do not give birth — until you have seen all there is to see here, until you have drank from this cup of virtue wisdom, an ennobling wine that is intoxicating and takes you to immortality. Then lay with the man; lay with the woman; bring forth the fruit of the womb, for then you will be responsible enough to bring in a God and responsible enough to rear it and one day show it its potentials.

These people learned, had the patience to learn, though they belonged to the ages. They were trapped in time. Their Spirit was free but their body was slow. They could cast their mind on yonder hill and describe a freshening brook and green reeds and a beautiful woman with alabaster knees and green eyes. And suddenly the body lurched to go beyond the hill. The mystery was if you knew that, why weren't you there? And it became obvious that the entrapment to the ages was into mass, the physical plane of acceptance. And the physical plane has its laws, its dictates, that say in order to enjoin the beauty that lies beyond the hill near the brook of green reeds, you must get up and run across the desert, and may the Gods put wings on your feet to carry you nigh to your lover's waiting nest.

Why was that necessary? Isn't it obvious? If you knew what was the beyond the hill, why can't you instantaneously be there? You were; you are, but you belong to the ages. You are now in the midst and the control of mass that can be seen as a detriment or yet a great advantage. The fool condemns his body, takes his life, locks himself in a prison, despises what he is. And the wise one says, alas, to be this, the man of virile loins, alas, to be this with a heart that beats like a great steed, to be this with the sweating of musk on a pounding temple, and to be that, one and the same, that is the wise man. The students learned that. They learned all of the knowledge that you say you are ready to learn but you are weak in learning it. Honor has not been established.

STRATEGY TO PRESERVE THE TRUTH OF OUR DIVINE INHERITANCE

So the schools flourished and the golden threads of immortality were turned out and they disappeared. They vanished into the vapor of early morn, never to be chained or whipped or abused or identified. And they live even this hour. They have never died; they have lived on. And every age they have perpetuated their great evolution because every age in which they belong to they are eating of the table that was set in front of them, from everlastingness into eternity. And in every age they are the quiet force that works on behalf of preserving knowledge, preserving truth, putting out a powerful conscious call, supporting, so that the golden thread can produce another golden thread. It was a success, as I knew it would. And then they came down upon the schools; they were infiltrated. And so the school took its knowledge into symbolism, into dance. The schools took its teaching into stones and mortar. And the weak ones were destroyed, you know, the fearful ones. So it has been.

Very, very few of these entities have any of you ever heard of.

You wouldn't, really, because there are some of them that go by several names, and perhaps one name got remembered. But who were they when that generation passed and the bones of children lay bleaching in the sands or devoured by the worm? Who were they then? This has been critical. I learned and always did I learn in my life — and I would desire it to be so, that you be the same in that richness of learning — that I gained the wisdom to understand what was in front of me would be repeated after me.

So this school exists this moment from the consciousness of the Ram contemplating this school this moment, contemplating this strategy of this moment in a very simple hovel while a fire rages on a hearth and Crosham blazes. And it is happening. It is happening then; it is happening now. So why me now? I have given runners in the past who would say this event would come and that it would be I. I have sent the vibration through the golden threads that this would occur.

And who would resonate to me? Those who are encamped outside that are contemplating a separateness of the Father from his children, for it is befitting that as grief and confusion set in on all my people, that my vision is turned far into generations untold. And to find and mark a place, as I taught you, in the Void, mark a place in the ages in which on the power of your grief 35,000 years ago, on the power of emotion — and you are beginning to understand that as a tool — that riding upon that energy, the grief of those times would set a time that the Father return to his children, the warrior to his people, the man to his godhood.

This moment is a great moment stretching forth into time as one who begins to learn remote-view — twisting time backwards and forwards and seeing it in the virgin of a moment — not caught in the past or the future but the splendidness of Now. Now you grieve and now you are here simultaneously, and with the power of that time has created me in this time. So why now? Why did the eyes of consciousness stop now? Because I am the last of the golden threads. I am the one who set them in motion tactically and strategically. That was my greatest experience, don't you know. And with the wisdom of consciousness, don't you understand I understood energy as a manifest, a mandate, of consciousness? Don't you think — ascension time and time again — I understood no-time, because Now is a point that you are referring to as critical mass?

War drums, human slaughter, the plagues, the One World Order, the mark of beasts are here. And as always it only takes a few, as it always took a few, not the world, everyone that is parleying — parleying — on the heads of the world. The greed is the world. We don't need that; only a few.

So why does everyone say that they are the chosen ones? Why indeed does every religion say they are the chosen ones of God and everyone else is condemned into hellfire for all eternity? Why does every government suppose that it is the elite of the world? Why is it that neighbors think they are better than their neighbors? Why does betterness have to do with things? It has to do with attitudes. So I am telling you the same thing. Are you chosen? I will tell you how you are chosen: You are here because I desire you to be here. But the desire — remembering, honoring will, even though you don't have it yet — is honoring that you are going to have it. And the will is that some of you — or perhaps the majority of you and the majority of those that are members of your groups that are not here — at this very moment many, many, many nights ago are in temporary quarters on the side of a great mountain. And the night has a cold wind but the sky is clear. One moon is shining in its quarter; the other is setting. And I have people who know that I am leaving them who are emotionally grieved.

Such as for a splendid few of you if I were to tell you indeed this evening, "I shall come no more; remember me in your consciousness," I assure you there would be those of you in this audience that would grieve deeply because I would be greatly missed. I know that. You are the ones that I am talking about, and you are the ones who heard my name and came. That was the voice of remembrance. You don't set into all eternity a manifestation unless it is built on the truism of willful, powerful emotion. And the greatest emotional moment was this night so long ago. That is what set the memory of this most precarious, indeed, entity before you. That is why you are here. Something had to link you present-day, forgetful beings to something immemorial, something that reaches to the core of your being of remembrance, and it was grief. Otherwise like all things that are beautiful, that are imitated and are made a mockery of, it would still have collapsed and fallen into the abyss.

There is a deep and profound binding, if you will, of you and me. For you, it is an unexplainable mixed feeling, one of confusion at many moments and, at others, profound admiration and deep love. And you know I am right. For me, you were worth your weeping women and your soulful men and your campfires and your holding onto the past and the battle cries and all of those stories. For me, it was you, my beloved people, who I detested in the beginning and came to love with such a love that passeth all understanding; it went to eternity. Now it has come together.

I knew I would select a woman. I came to love them and respect them and understand their plight and understand their curse in the times to come, understand their understated intelligence to use, as a tactician, their heightened emotional energy as power. And the greatest and noblest love was to select a woman in which this consciousness can resound over 35,000 years. And I selected well. You had best make your peace with this entity, for this entity is the hull of the ship that has its anchors in the sky — your jealousy, your hatred, your bitterness, your envy — for it may be the ship that takes you home or accounts for preservation. Wake up and understand how this is working.

Once I went into a great city — white marbled walls, beautiful. You could see them as you turned for kilometers and miles. Ruthless people lived there and beautiful people with such silken tents and awnings in the marketplace that it would even bedazzle your spoiled eyes. I went invisible, undetectable. I went not in the brazen breastplate. I went not with the ring. I went not with the headband. I went disguised, invisible. A little big, but I was there. I got the job done.

I am here disguised completely from even those who fear me because I would never stoop so low as to use such a vehicle. I have climbed high to use it and find it, and I am getting the job done. But why I? My business at this point is getting you beyond your human phase into that consciousness that is sublime and to the thought that is immortal, getting you beyond your pettiness that works so well for all the reasons why you should remain a slave. You are stupid and you are ignorant and all you think about is who you are going to lay tonight, how much you are going to guzzle tomorrow night, and how you look. Don't you know they know that? Don't be so small as to presume that in the eyes of coldness, liken unto steel, you are not worthy for consideration; your actions have given you away.

At this time in my thought, upon the bittersweet reverie of grief, was to take you further than you have ever gone in the mind — beyond the myth, beyond hypnotism — to take you further than any human being in ages has gone into the developmental processes of consciousness everlasting. That is my business. I have legions doing other things. This is my business for the emotion that this moment was created out of.

Using Emotional Energy As a Tool for Change

It is here under a Master Teacher, and I am indeed that and more, that with the gathering of a few great entities whose only reason for really being here is because something profoundly touched them, and for as many reasons as they have had to leave and to deny me — which is very obvious; I have set it up that way — they have with great tenacity stayed and clung. And if that was the only reason, that mysterious inner devotion — if that was the only reason, the hook, that you do any of this for — then that was reason enough because in the spark of love, indeed in the spark of emotion, in the height of hate, in the height of joy, in the height of compassion, in the height of freedom, that is the moment long-awaited that one moves in that energy, but not until then.

So if this mysterious devotion here has been the reason for your discipline, has been the reason for your hanging onto this school, has been the reason that you have moved here, has been the reason that you have changed, then you never had any other reason other than that to do it. You did not have the emotional wisdom to make that decision, because everything I told you the world denied. So it takes emotional energy. It takes learning how to build it and then use it at critical times to develop upon. And in this moment of flickering fires — and the murmur on that cool breeze of an old man's rumbled words that sit here this night, mute — if the only reason you did all this is for this long-lived, unraped, unstripped devotion, then that was reason enough to come here to begin the processes, because fundamentally you had nothing else to come here on except grief. So I am fulfilling a promise, not a verbal promise but a promise of profound love — an allegiance, as it were.

A greater-than-life being I am and was. I am here to use that, to take you from whence I come, to teach you methodically, patiently reiterating, working you until at some point you find another peak of emotional deliverance. And the moment you do that I will move you immediately into a new truth. I have business with you, and the business is to take a few — perhaps chosen by grief, deep emotion, transmuted into will — preserve you and teach you self-preservation wisely through all of the murk and the mire of what is really old news that is happening this hour, to preserve you from harm's way, not to send you into battle but to keep you tight and to keep you marching and to keep you learning and to keep you focused.

I never had a city that could be attacked. My people — my women, my children, my old men, and my beloved old women — marched with me, and they were in the center of the most powerful army on foot that ever lived, for they were the prize. Your business, upon my advice, is your choice — upon what I have told you nigh many days ago in your time and counting — to preserve yourselves. It is my business to get you over being slaves and mortals. And one day you survivors are going to see what has been teaching you. And in some very thoughtful moments — for this too has been seen — you are going to truly wonder why this made it its business to handle you and your kind and to come to such levels of discussion and language. And you are going to be in awe because, truly, the world is liken unto a speck of dust. And then you will understand, but you will ask yourselves why.

So I am this very moment sitting and watching the flames of a fire flicker on a great sword, shadows dance on the slanted roof, phantoms of the past. What are you doing this moment? Women, have you prepared your mead, served up the olives, the goat cheese, delicious bounty? And is the discussion this night in your camp a foreboding one? Are you weeping, because where is your leader going? Something is in the air.

And, men, are you young or old? Are you out of your hovel because you do not want to show your sadness and your weakness to your family, to your woman, who knows it anyway? Are you sitting with the old guard? Are you reminiscing? Are you trying to outthink me again, which you never could do? Is it happening? Are you there and here? Can you smell it? Can you taste it? Remote-view, there is no time.

So where are the eyes? Where are those great black eyes as they stare into the fire? Are they seeing your face now 35,000 years ago? Are they looking at this room? How does it appear? Does it appear real or is it a dream? Are these eyes moving? Are they seeing from a distant past? Well, what are they seeing? Do they recognize? Do they understand what has been said? Do they understand the reaction?

Is it possible that at this very moment there was never any history; there was only then and now? Is it possible that you never had a past? What were all those memories about your youth, you remember, your adulthood? What was all that pain about? Is it possible that in this moment you never had a past? Is it possible that you are there, wishing to be here? And if the past doesn't exist, who is to say that in your greatest moment of grief you have leaped forward to here to make it so? Is it possible? If it ever is, this will be the first and beginning instance of a revival of unspeakable knowledge.

What are all those memories? Are they like the phantoms on the fire that I see dancing across the wall? Is the glimmer and the fire that comes off of the great sword, is that the light? Are the memories just a flame flickering, casting a shadow? Are your memories shadows, and are you a fire? Is it possible you never have been anywhere other than there and here now? Because this very moment it is happening.

And there are those of you who have turned off because what I am speaking of is so bizarre — unearthly, edging on the absurd — that you haven't heard a word I have said. But those of you who have listened and are caught up in the emotional tide —

that night that is happening now, that exists now as its transmuted form — will understand what dimensional mind is going to be all about. Remember the puzzles I gave you? Someone else selected them; I instructed you to do them. What I have just told you is the greatest puzzle of all. And if you can put it together, then my business here is indeed fruitful.

Where is yesterday? Are all those memories real? How real are they? Can you verify they are real? And how do you verify the verification? Could it be that all those memories were just thoughts contemplated upon and that Now is the mother of time? Could it be that yesterday never did exist, all those memories you have? I am talking about your life. What if it is a hoax? Only consciousness and energy — consciousness in its most primitive form of fear and grief and anxiety and love and joy — those are the pregnant moments that dictate time. Those are immortal. They are the strings of the fabric of this tapestry. They are not visual; they are a hunger deep inside.

There has been, in a greater understanding, no time expedited at the same moment I sit in my hovel — and hear the moaning; I smell incense on the wind; the moon has waxed and waned — until this moment. You are here. You have the emotion. You have the memory. My business is with you.

If you contemplate what I have told you this night from the most sincere parts of your being, perhaps a greater emotion will come up — one that is fortifying, something that you can spring from to manifest, something that gives a person self-determination — because without that in you, you will never figure out the riddle I just gave you or completely understand it because you will still be a three-dimensional, captured, programmed human being who belongs to the ages and cannot fathom what I have said.

If you are determined to meet me in this moment of yesterday — and it is going to take as much effort on your part and nearly divine will — I will take you beyond this dimension in a study, a rigorous one, that will allow you the will to change your reality and affect personal destiny. But you are going to have to get responsible and wake up and understand that time is running out on the commodities. Time is running out on the freedom to be able to place your home in the earth, on the earth, and one day above the earth. And you are going to have to have the responsibility to do it. Now if that seems a bit burdensome to you, then I suggest you go back to the world and its temporary convenience, because you do not have what it takes to come to the crest of where I left you 35,000 years ago on a mountain. You do not have what it takes to go up on that mountain.

I love you people with an encompassing passion. You are my people and I was and am your Ram. The moment came as I saw and see. Take my wisdom and apply it straightaway, for I tell you this for no other reason. One day the garb, the cloak, will come off from visiting this foreign time and, because you have chosen yourself through the emissary of passion, you will inherit this place quite different than what you see today. You will have the skills and consciousness to restore and to heal. And like the fish that lives underground and the frog and the wasp and the ant, you will come alive one day and you will have an opportunity to fulfill a dream.

And what is the dream? To have seen in your lifetime the washing away of inhumaneness; to see in your lifetime a small generation of people who think in like terms — all the machines will be turned off, so the freedom of thought will be an intoxicating beverage — to know what it is to live in paradise where there is no more disease that has been perpetrated upon the species, where there is no suppression, and you can heal with the power of the touch and resurrect a seed in the impregnated earth and to make it into a tree in the twinkling of an eye. You are going to do that, but not until all of this is brought to its knees by its own hand and that which it worshiped will come back and reward it justly. And then a great legion will move to position.

In the meantime, the dream will have been realized: peace on earth and goodwill to men and women, and joy and longevity of life, and primeval urges put away in the sinful closet and remembered as perhaps only the phantoms of a dream while sitting in front of a fire. So be it.

Now for the rest of this splendid evening — while the camp-in-the-past's fires slowly go out and burn into embers and there is a restless sleep amongst my people, and I never felt so grand — you take the emotion, if you have any, of what you have learned this night, take it to the Void. And what are you going to do there with it? Be it. It, through evolution, will present itself as opportunities. Those of you who want to move out of the ages into the beginning teaching of dimensional mind, I have certainly given you an opportunity, in what are memories, to move out of the ages and be something else. The most powerful moment in ever doing that is finding the height of emotion to do it.

You have danced to the rhythm of the music and you have gone nowhere. You have had slight and great passion. The music disconnects the frequency. And first you are the music and then you begin to mutate into other lifeforms and consciousness, and you have accomplished this. But either way no one is going to sit here and watch his brother or sister either engage in the dance of dimensional mind or go to the Void. You either participate or leave. You may sit here with your eyes blinded and contemplate all that I have said — for certainly I have said a lot, but not nearly enough — and as you do, let this thought come to you: Which eyes do you possess today, those of yesterday or the projection of yesterday to today? And was there ever really a past? Maybe it was all a lie, a hoax.

I love you. Your great tree sprang but from a few noble souls. Don't you know you are their fruit? The light is coming in the sky and the cookstoves are burning. It has been a wonderful night all across time.

Love I you greatly. Do not go with a heavy heart but one filled with the potential of wisdom, and with that you can do great things. Enjoy and work hard when you return tomorrow. So be it. That is it.

CHAPTER 4
REDEFINING THE SELF AS THE SPIRITUAL SELF

"Why do hardships happen to spiritual people? They choose things the soul needs to overcome and own. They allow things to manifest that the soul needs. Battles are harsh, but the light is made brighter by this. If you are hurting inside, it is because you have compromised. You have hidden your light, not allowed self to shine."

— Ramtha

ABOLITION OF THE SELF THROUGH BLAME AND VICTIMIZATION

O my beloved God,
this night I am grateful
for my life
above all else.
Everything else
is illusion.
This life,
the blood
that pumps in my veins,
is you, my Holy Spirit,
and everything else
is illusion.
Of this night
I do celebrate
that which I am
as God manifest.
My beloved Father,
my beloved Mother,
of these days
lift me from my turbulence
and set me upon
the ground of your being.
So be it.
To life.

It is so beautiful to watch you, to listen to your thoughts. Now tonight we are going to talk about heaven — heaven — the Plane of Bliss. We are going to start this teaching tonight by you understanding an important aspect of yourselves.

You wanted the spiritual journey in this life. You wanted it. You are here because I dreamed this time and all of you — even those of you who are not here, those that are gathered in other places — a gathering place, a time of maturity, given eons to play out the human experience. But aside from that, you also had to be ready. Now this is important for every individual in this audience to understand, because from that is a springboard to understand the rest of this weekend and to understand this school and your journey in this school. Every decision starts with you. And so the ultimate reason for being here is I provided that which is termed the hub. And you came, but you had to be ready to come.

So what I want you to understand is that everyone in this audience chose in this lifetime to evolve themselves spiritually. Now that is important for you to understand because it empowers you to understand the meaning of this life and perhaps the journey of this life and that the true destiny of life, and particularly this one, is not about what you accomplish; it is about becoming. That is what is important in this life.

Now there is no one here that should ever say that they are here against their will because that is not the way that it is set up. Everyone is here freely and engaging in that which is termed the knowledge and its practices by choice. The majority of the group chose to be here in this lifetime — as hard as that may be for some of you to swallow — because when you are here and it is going well, you are happy for the journey, but when you leave this and you go out in the marketplace and you put back on your fleshy body, you find a conflict between the ongoing physical reality that you keep repeating and the spiritual reality that was really the destiny for being here. So there is a gap in destiny and follow-through of that destiny in the human incarnation. But that has always been apparent.

Given that then, I want each of you to understand that somewhere you made a choice then to be here and that you made a choice about this, about really dedicating a life, a human life, a human incarnation, to the sole development of the spiritual self, and that is why you are here. If this was not your destiny, you wouldn't be here tonight, or you wouldn't be in this school, or you would be the gray in-between entity who is not wholly here anytime they are here. They are only here because of someone else.

Now if we can take in a state of human and spiritual maturity and grasp this as a truth, then the truth empowers us. When we do not grasp this and are still wondering why we are here, we are not empowered by what we learn. We first must be empowered by recognizing that there is a self who is divine that can be empowered. That is why it is important for an entity to recognize their actions as their actions, because it is always defining self and always empowering self.

Blame, as a side note, is a disingenuous quality of the spiritual person because blame then unempowers the self. When you blame someone else, you are draining the powerful resources of self. And so what happens to self is that self then starts to be hidden under that which is termed the fog of misunderstanding. Here in this school it is important that self always be the core, and that power must always be generated from that core, and that that power from that core at no time should be ever given away to someone else. And blame and victimization — those aspects of human characteristics — are the most important ingredients in removing the place of power from self and giving it away.

In order to fulfill this journey here, self must be defined, and it must be defined not only as the spiritual self but the spiritual self must be definable within the human self. And all of this defining and polishing leads to the impeccable life, the empowered life.

Now if you chose then this life for this spiritual journey, then that empowers you because it gives the place of destiny to you, and that is where it should belong. That then is also consistent with you as a God having free will, the will that is free enough to imagine the unimaginable, but the unimaginable springing from the core of self along with its power. If we abolish then the self through blame and victimization and living in the past, we then unseat the very aspect of the spiritual journey. We disenthrone the God inside of us in favor of past incidences that we can blame our miserable, wretched and failing existence upon. That is an undefined self, a power utterly given away; that when such a creature endeavors to manifest, there is not the thrust from the core self in order to bring it forward. If no one is on the throne, the unimaginable cannot be imagined. How many of you understand? Furthermore, there is no power to do it, to do anything with.

When I then, from the first moment I appeared here, said you are God, that you are all God — forgotten, yes — it is my job to help you to remember. That is the nucleus of the spiritual journey, and you chose to be a part of that journey, to define God — to define God and to seat that divinity within self — and when we do so, self becomes definable. It is only when we have defined the self do we get to occupy it. It is only when we occupy it do we then become utterly empowered for the unimaginable. Up to that point, it is not going to work; never will. Now this destiny, before you came into this life — and we are going to talk about the Plane of Bliss — was an option seen that all of you, except for a few, were ready to take on. We are going to understand that in a deeper aspect.

But I want to at this particular point say to you that unless self can be empowered fully, then the spiritual life — that which you came here to experience — will never be realized. The walk of the master will never be walked by you until you leave no footprints in yesterday — how many of you understand? — because the past was the generation of growth that meant essentially the giving away of power to greater elements of authority. And that authority could have simply been your classmates in the first grade, the beginning of what we call social consciousness, or giving your power away to your parents and the way that you were raised. That then starts the bleeding, if you will, of a life that is disjointed and that seemingly has no purpose but to coast and to ride and to barely get by. It is a life that the unimaginable is not a part of; it is only what is in trend and what is easy. How many of you understand?

Now the spiritual walk of the master means — and for this we are going to have to manifest in your life what is called revelation so that it is revealed to you on each of your individual levels what the past and my term for it really mean — we can never abolish the memories of who we were, but what we must do is transmute the energy of what we were, a disenthroned entity searching for self. And we must take the energy that we have in the neuronet off of it and bring the power of that neuronet to continuously repeat day, after day, after day those circumstances of your past because it is up here — it is hardwired; it is happening up here — that that hardwiring takes the power and distributes it to hold in place that which the past dictated. That is unacceptable for a student in the spiritual work because, number one, there is no spiritual work without power and, number two, there is no power without a sense of self. And if self has not been reclaimed and redefined, then there is no such thing as the unimaginable, as man or woman being master of reality. It doesn't work; it hasn't worked.

So in understanding that — and listen carefully — the past means to abolish victimization, to abolish envy, jealousy, hatred, malice, to abolish that which is termed the aspects that are so degrading to the spiritual self, that literally strip it of its beautiful power and hold together the demons of our own mind. The stripping of all of that means taking responsibility for those actions and making the responsibility one of self. And when we do, then the blaming no longer is locked up in your pitiful parents — who, by the way, are spiritual people as well — or locked up in your first-grade class. It is no longer locked up in your need to be needed.

What happens is when you say I created this — I cannot tell you why I created it or when I got the idea to create it, but I did it; otherwise it would never have occurred — when you do that then, you no longer have the outlet of continuous blame focused on entities or an entity in your life. Suddenly the cord is cut, the chains are cut, and the self begins to be defined.

THE DARK NIGHT OF THE SOUL

Now this is a mournful moment because human beings by nature are cowards. They are cowards. And why are they cowards? Because they are afraid to be confronted by their own choices. And so in a state of fear we run and point a finger at someone else. And pointing the finger at someone else is our cowardly way of excusing the circumstance. When we do that, when we point this finger of power, then that means that this mind of power has focused the energy, reflected it back off of us to someone else and thus we are dethroned. It is not a simple measure, I assure you, to take responsibility for our life, but it is the bravest spiritual part that does, no matter how painful it may be. And do you know what pain is? The coming home of the prodigal son of energy.

We call this then the dark night of the soul. All of that suffering now is full-bore upon us because it is energy returning to the source. But it is through the suffering that we are purified, because once the energy passes the barrier of the emotional body — and the emotional body is disturbed and ruffled and the heart beats fast and the breath is shortened and the tears begin to roll — that means the energy is coming back and it is passing through the barrier of the emotional body and it is causing a storm. And, you know, you have to live in the storm. It is the nature of the child coming home. And when the storm is over, energy, now being purified through the emotional body, has returned full cycle and its coming home is a necessary ingredient in defining the self, that which we are. THE

Now no one is ever going to make you take credit for your life. You can give lip service to this, but the true warrior is one who does it and does it very well — it is the conquest of self — and does it in a fashion knowing full well that what they have put out is coming back home manifold. It is the one who does this that in the end is liberated.

All beings who on Bliss chose the spiritual life, they know that in making such a choice it is not the easy path, that it is a path of defining the self and polishing it, and they can't even imagine what that is going to mean in their life until they get into it. And do you know it is at this juncture that most people turn tail and run? Why? Because — it is simple — unless the divine that we are sits within the throne of this temporal body, it can never create the marvelous unless it has been divined and defined in ourselves. And unless that happens, the unimaginable is not going to happen to you, nor will that which is termed the righteous happen to you.

These measures of myth, dream, and legend always then remain that to the chronic victim. And as they remain that, we marvel at those who seem to get through and do the miraculous. We are marveling at one who has passed the bridge, who has made the journey — the journey into recalling power back to self — and has lived through it. Those who cannot face it and are cowards and run from it are never again empowered with the lucidity, clarity, and the ability to move as a master, because only until self is defined can a master then be born. It can never be born out of undifferentiated self. Did you understand what I have just taught you? How many of you understand? You understand about the core defining self and its power? You understand that giving that power away depletes the core? How many of you understand that?

Now you notice that when I refer to the past that I always refer to your greatest obstacles. And seemingly in reference to that which is termed the past, it seems as if I think that the past was all terrible. No, it was all purposeful.

Now what I want you to understand is that all the beautiful things in your life — all of those things that you did and were done to you that are sweet — those could only have occurred in a moment of self-definition, so they are always with us because they are the core of what we are. That is the reason why in religions that God is always pleading with his flock to be good and to do good deeds and to be men and women of moral and impeccable values, because there is a truth in that. And the truth is that when we elect to be that way, we have not given any power away but have been empowered. How many of you understand? And the more that that empowerment occurs, the more awesome the entity's reality; that is the way that it works. All of you are endeared with beautiful and sweet moments in your past. Those moments don't have to be thrown away because they are integral to the defining of self. How many of you understand?

So now then if those defining moments are the lofty moments in our life, they can be seen as acts of the simplest things that you did from the moment of your cognitive memory, of what was done to you, what you did to others, all through your life. Those are empowered moments. That is the true self expressing. But for the most part, you live in a dynamic society to which blame and cowardness in favor of image is a way of life here. And it is the dog-eat-dog, the hyena preying upon the young. It is success-motivated and feared, God Almighty, by the aspects of failure. These then become the dynamic in a past that is grievous, a past in which power has been given away, in which victimization and blame and the pointing of fingers begins often now at a very early age. Then we see why it is important to address the past in terms of energy and the terms of giving it away and staying confined in a mode of consciousness and its neuronet of being the eternal sufferer and the eternal victim.

No master is this, nor will you find sympathy from any master at your election to being this. Why? Because every master knows that every life's action is a personal choice and that that personal choice is a free-willed choice, and that any master who is a master understands and knows that without sympathy or empathy, very clear distinctions here in what you are learning. And the distinction is that the master now has seated the self firmly in its divine room and now from this point navigates that divinity towards a life that is based entirely upon the crucial, contemplative, meditative placement of energy. That is the master.

JUDGMENT DAY AND THE LIFE REVIEW

So now having said that just tonight and reminding all of you that you are here by choice — you chose this life; you chose this life as a life to which the spiritual will become revealed to you — now we empower you utterly. From this then we are going to back up and talk tonight about the Plane of Bliss — as some would call it, heaven.

Now over the years in your time we have discussed frequently that which is termed the interim existence, that interim existence being that which you were prior to this incarnation. And although I have not languored at great depth upon it — nor have I languored at great depth upon your past life — there is great and wonderful reason for that, for in my wisdom I understand that those who do not have spiritual maturity cling to these in the same values as they have clung to their victimization, their tyranny, and their self-pity. And it is giving more fodder to the animal within man and woman than it is that which is termed manna for the spiritual self. The focus here has been on becoming God. That is what is important and will always be important, but tonight we are going to talk about the interim place and the interim place to where all of you were before you were born.

Now I have stated boldly in the past that we do not create our parents; that is true. But also remember that we are drawn to a genetic pool that is only equal to what we are before arriving. So in that sense, subconsciously, we only become what we are capable of becoming. We can never become what we are incapable of becoming. How many of you understand that? In other words, we cannot be anything greater than what we are. So in the interim place we are talking about the third, fourth, and fifth levels. They are the planes of rest and restoration.

It becomes obvious then that the physical body has died and all of its energy from the soul that gave it life is pulling away from it. So the body goes into a slow state of decay. Without modern technology and the art of embalming, that which is termed the energy naturally would rapidly decay within a matter of a fortnight. And all decay is, is the breaking down of coagulated matter and the release of the conscious pattern. Do you understand? How many of you understand? So be it.

Now so here we are talking about the self. The self, the spiritual self, that which is not seen, has already departed up through infrared into the great tunnel of light to be met by the lords of light at the very end. And all of you went through the reading of your life. In elder times it was called Judgment Day. It is Judgment Day, except that it really isn't a judgment; it is to refresh your memory on what you did.

Now understand that you are a being that is transpersonal but still personal. You are a being that is transmuted out of a fleshy body. You have gotten out of the garment. And here, where there was such a delay in the Spirit working through the body to create reality — because you are living in a body that is mass to mass — now you are more in your own domain as a spiritual entity. You are actually vibrating in a kinder realm than this realm.

So there you watch your life. How is that possible? Because the bands that you are, that supported and gave and nourished life in the womb take back with them, as mind, everything that you ever did, because doing is an action and action is energy. And the focus of that energy is the patterns of mind. So we begin to watch the patterns of mind as they come together in a whole lifetime's effort.

Now let's pause here for a moment and let me tell you this.

Every moment — every moment — in the light of all eternity will be weighed against a feather one day. Every moment counts. Everything that you do and I did is seen. And it is seen both as the Observer and the participant, both as the doer and the done-to — everything. That is why it is called Judgment Day because most ignorant people think, or they are under the delusion, that their thoughts aren't things. Their thoughts are things. And they are under the delusionment that what they do behind their closed doors no one knows but them. That is a delusion. Everything is known and everything will be shown. And in this heightened state it is necessary not for any one being to look at you and to condemn you; it will be enough that we see it for ourselves. There is no harsher judge than the soul on Judgment Day.

Now when this occurs — and you are all at one point going to experience it because you have already experienced it — what is it that is meaningful from this? What is meaningful is how burdened are you by unfinished business? How burdened are you by unfinished experiences? If I tell you that you are God, then this life is to evolve that godhead as all. So how many experiences did you not own? And every time that you were cruel to someone, every time that you were cunning and undermining, every time that you bore false testimony against someone else, every time that you physically hurt someone, every time that your tongue lashed out in revenge and blame, every time that you meted out your fury of unrequited love to the destruction of those around you and yourselves, everything becomes you in that moment of viewing. You are everything, you know?

So then you suffer the attack of your villainy and you feel what it feels like. You become the child that you have beaten and you feel its helpless pain. You become that which is termed the abuser and the full onslaught of tempted intoxicating fury upon that which is innocent and cannot strike back. You feel what it is to be slandered upon and your good and gracious name abused and dishonored. You will feel that because you are God.

We are not separate in this hour. We are whole in this hour. We are driven to the understanding that more than any other time, it is in this passing that we realize that we are the whole web of life. We feel the abandonment that we abandon with. We feel the untruth that we are upon someone else. We feel the blame placed upon us unduly by us. We feel that which is termed the heartbreak of unrequited love, and we are the one who bore the chains of that blame. We are honored and dishonored. We are amused and bemused. We see how we prostituted our values. We become the body in its agony and in its abuse. We become the abuser and the abused. And this is judgment and we feel it full-width. We revel in the dream and in the inspiration that we had at five, and we despair in the losing of that dream at twenty-three. We become the dream and then we fade as the dream. We become the inspiration that we marveled at and then we become the boredom of inaction. We see the instigation of new ideas and concepts that we came up with and we are then the idea itself, the thought form, and we see it as an unnurtured, unloved egg that never hatches. And we see the idea that never came into fruition and the pain of its uninclusiveness into our environment. We see it all because we are all God.

The subjective element in all of this is very important, because the core of self is subjective because it is everything, so the self becomes more enriched and more defined in this view.

We see how many times we needed to beg someone's pardon, and we see all the times we didn't ask it of ourselves. We see all the times that we could have loved, but in our selfish, renegade selves meted none out, and we see the vacuous place to where love lives not and we are driven in emptiness and despair. We see it all.

And in this exposé we find wholeness even in the suffering, that rarefied moment. And how do I describe suffering without a body? Well, emotion, though it is generated by electrical stimuli from the brain, from neuronets, and then dominoed in the body through the release of hormones, becomes a living thing. It is an energy field. And it is with that energy field that we stand and we are then immersed within all of this energy. We cannot undo it. It is done. The die has been cast.

Now this is not a bad thing, but it is a necessary thing for the ignorant — and you all are — because what we do with such a vision is that we then become encumbered. We become encumbered by the difficulties in which we see. An encumbrance is a wonderful term because what it really says is all of these things that we did, we did to ourselves. And it is through this revelation that we must unencumber and give to the self love, which God is. God is giving; remember?

MAPPING OUR NEW LIFE ON THE PLANE OF BLISS

So then we walk away from this in deep ponderance. We are given any sort of image we wish to ponder this in. Some ponder on high mountain ranges on Bliss. Some ponder behind great and noble trees. Some ponder by beautiful lakes surrounded by dappled woods. Some ponder in great libraries. Some ponder floating in the midst of nothing because they can't tolerate anything to be around them. But ponderance, the art of contemplation, always follows this. And what becomes inescapable is that we have done this to ourselves because we are all the self.

Now here is the stickler. The stickler is that these acts, this life, grew out of a very slow time, that the whole focal point of this life was the human body. So no matter what you do on the Plane of Bliss, you can never reconcile there what you did on the plane of flesh. We cannot manifest on the Plane of Bliss the experiences that will bring about physical emotion because we are without them. How many of you understand?

Oh, we contemplate and then imagine, like I did by the fire in dreaming this journey. We imagine, and as soon as we imagine, all of the forms and the scenes appear; instantly they appear. And as we contemplate, we watch ourselves and how we deal with what we dealt out. And we imagine. And because we are on the Plane of Bliss to where there is no mass to mass, we are more akin to that time, which is no-time as it is referred to here. So there, the moment that we imagine something, it appears exactly as we imagine it. And so our surroundings are always changing.

And in contemplation this is ideal, because when we contemplate we can visually see the exact scene and how we would like it to happen. And try as we may, however, to get relief from that, we cannot get relief from it. What it does provide us with is our divinity. And our gift to image has allowed us to reconstruct the past, to reconstruct the past and to move from that point forward. However, this mapping, though thoroughly researched, could take thousands of years on Bliss. Contemplation on Bliss is much different than contemplation here.

And we may languor there and plot and plan, and we may seek it out in these planes. The moment the idea occurs to us that there are great beings with this wisdom, they appear. And they appear and teach us. And they help with our model of imagination. They do not change the model in the time of contemplation. The thoughts are given to you and you incorporate the wisdom into the picture. That is how it works, because it is not their picture; it is your picture.

Knowledge: If knowledge to you means then a reservoir of information flowing through a computer, a computer will appear and it will have dendrites connected to you, and then the knowledge will flow through the computer. But ultimately the knowledge flowing back to you, you must be the program that incorporates it. How many of you understand? Or you may envision knowledge in great halls of learning, in the great halls of academia. And you may envision this knowledge in a set of rare books, and so immediately a great library will appear and you will not be able to see the end of it, and yet all of the great texts appear on old and ancient shelves. And in your mind, old may mean that they are faded and they are covered in dust, and so they will be. And you look for the dustiest, faded, cobweb-covered manual you can find, because in your mind that is the one that will have all knowledge, and you will find it. And you have a table; you can sit down. You can have an electric lamp; you can have a candle; you can have an oil lamp; you can have a florescent lamp. And you sit down and you read. You read, by the way, every page, a page that looks like soft light, and letters that are multidimensional, and they jump off the page into you and you think you are reading. And it is the same knowledge.

And what you walk away from, in spending a hundred years in this library, is information on how to modulate the room of contemplation, the room of how you are going to make it different, to elongate this burden, the enburdenment that you have of being unfinished, of the error as you see it that you have done to another.

How would you be able to justify that? And how would you be able to write it? You will figure it all out.

Now it is not by accident that this is starting to act exactly like a quantum field of potential. Well, it is. The Plane of Bliss is at the quantum level. So when an entity that is spiritual — without the body — is rarefied mind, the moment occurs immediately.

So what is the entity doing? The entity is selecting paths of intentional destiny, creating them in a linear fashion with or without the help and endeavoring to find a resolve, because no one wants to live being all things punished and punishable. That realm is called hell, but one lives in it as unresolved and burdened, unfinished business.

Now, remember, keep in mind there is no one on this plane that will ever tell you are right and wrong. You are the ones that do that. There is no right and wrong. But it becomes immensely clear to us that we are of the angelic realm, and that we really are foreign travelers in an alien world, and that we really are empowered to re-create that world according to our imagination, our greatest resource. And so no one there is to say this is right and wrong. I tell you the more God you are in that moment of light review, you will feel the blow of everything measured out by you in incarnation, because how could God be anything else but everything?

Now the hall of contemplation — very important — there are beings that are still there that have been mapping a potential lifetime very carefully. They have been there for hundreds of thousands of years. They are mapping it. And they are sort of like the watcher-at-the-gate story I told you about, watches everyone come in.[1] Well, there are entities that post themselves at heaven's great gate and watch everyone coming in with all their stuff, and they learn. But what is important is it is not meaningful learning until it is applied on the level in which the wisdom was generated. How many of you understand that? So be it.

Now I am telling you about the plane in ordinary tongue that is much more illustrious, much more dynamic, much more fantastic, and much more beautiful than this common speech can

[1] The source of this story is Ramtha Dialogues®, Specialty Tape 033, *Selected Stories III: Shambhala — Leaving No Footprints.*

allow. I am endeavoring to bring it home to you, a very valuable lesson which we are going to learn this weekend about the remarkable self and understand why you chose to be here.

Now an encumbered entity — an encumbered entity — who has got a lot of unfinished business here, unless they have a physical body working in this time, they cannot finish it. They can dream it on those other levels, but those dreams will never be able to be experienced until they are born in the time to which they were meant. Did you hear me? Now an encumbered entity then has drawn out the linear path, has gotten as much help as they know to ask. And when they are ready to return, they are drawn into genetic pools that are equal to what they left off with.

In this Plane of Bliss — in heaven, as some would have it to be called; the greater planes I call them — there is no regret at being there. I want you to know never was a place more lively and more beautiful than this place, because it is the unimaginable imagined. And never was there such a state of being that utterly was free of the encumbrances of slow time and slow matter. And never was there a place to where physical beauty wasn't the most important thing, because there you could take on any appearance that you wanted, so it wasn't important. Here it is important. There it is not important because it is changeable. How many of you understand that? So then everyone is free from that, so you are floating closer to God. You are in a state shadowed by the golden realm. You are in a state to where it can be the eternal day or the eternal night. And there are multitudes there, and it seems as if there is room for everyone. Well, there is. Now it is a deserving place to be. It is the place of rest before the next battle.

So it is not unlike some of you, who are sort of prone to suffering anyway, to see it as a place to where you languor in the contemplative forests and suffer. No, but that is important as the subjective aspect of God, to be able to feel what you did. How many of you understand? But you are always objective. And from that, there is no grief about leaving your family; there is no grief about leaving your husbandmen, your wives, your friends, your neighbors. You don't have that sort of emotion because you are free of all of that.

And there is a knowingness that permeates these realms, that what is happening on the earth plane is a great big drama and you played a part. What is important is that you never finished your lines and that coming out of that thick dream, you know your children were not left behind; they always will be. And coming out of that, you didn't leave behind your love. Your love is with you, always will be — do you understand? — because when we become the subjective God, we interface with all life, so how could we be separate from it? It is in such a state that it is difficult to understand, but you have all been there. You have all been there; otherwise you couldn't be here now.

Now so stop grieving for a moment and suffering, and understand that in this encumbered state is what generates us to our greater power. And we want to design a life and lay it out and imagine it and change the patterns, the players. Anyone that wants to volunteer can move into it. We want to do that before we return and pick up where we left off. Now that is very important as well.

Now I want to back up and talk about the players involved in the upcoming drama. What has always been considered is that people who meet and have a kinship for one another met in a past life. That is not so. Try this one on: How about that you never met before and met on the Plane of Bliss, because you had both come through the same encumbrance — how many of you understand that? — that you both arrived at the same forest to contemplate the same thing? Some of these places are very crowded — very crowded — and we always gravitate to what we are.

And so, you see, the players that will play an integral part in the upcoming life don't have to be anyone that we were before. And to always delude yourselves into thinking that shows the sign of your ignorance about the spiritual life, because this place isn't everything and these lifetimes aren't everything. We will have beings that will meet in the same place of contemplation that, my God, may be extraordinarily advanced entities whose past incarnations were geniuses or great leaders and, you know, they have a flaw and that flaw brought them in contact with you. Or they may be coming from another terrestrial planet in which that flaw they can work out on this one. We meet through association of encumbrances. How many of you understand?

And how difficult is this to understand that when you sit by someone and you enjoin them in a conversation, you are bonding with them and pretty soon you are moving through the labyrinth of their mind, understanding what they are saying to you. You are into them and they in turn are moving through the labyrinth of your mind. That is what we call conversation. How many of you understand? Well, if you understand that, then you can begin to grasp the concept that association of encumbrances brings like to like and, when shared upon in that rarefied place, it is not about talking. You don't talk. Your thoughts proclaim. And so each of you engages in each other's thoughts.

It is at those times that in engaging each other's thoughts we find a marvelous and wonderful thing happens called mercy. In this wonderful kingdom then — this life that we have laid out for ourselves — we have found someone who has the same encumbrance, but the encumbrance may be that that entity had done to them what we did. And though we are both done-to-and-did in this place of contemplation, our minds come together and formulate a relationship, and those relationships then form a later meeting on this plane.

So it is not about who you knew two thousand years ago or four thousand years ago. The most meaningful ones are the ones that you meet on Bliss because they have arrived at the same place. Now these people will come in and out of your life often to fulfill the very drama that you came back here to play out. How many of you understand? And which role are they playing now? It is ultimately selective at that moment. When they viewed their life and they did an unthinkable to someone else, they can restrategize that to where the unthinkable then is done to them. And the player that will be involved is one who was the victim in the earlier existence. How many of you understand? They are learning balance. And yet they only may appear and then disappear out of our life, but that is what we are here for.

There is no such thing as chance. Everything is created from consciousness, and consciousness does not simply hold itself as sole purpose on this plane; it is all planes. And the closer we are to Point Zero, the more pure we are as conscious beings. So this great and wonderful realm — that the moment you think, it is —

is our true nature, entities. That is our true nature. That is what we are used to. What we are not used to is being bogged down and burdened down by slow time and the mechanics of the physical body, because there we are liberated from it, from all that it represents.

So now when we set out in our memorable engagement with other beings there — when we set this pattern out and we have decided upon this potential line — then we are ready to return. Those that we have blended with before, we will meet again. We won't remember them but we will meet them, and the soul will know because the Spirit recalls the conversation. The soul recalls the journey. It is just the corporal mind — the corporal brain of the physical entity — that is yet to be born will not remember this incident.

The Value of Experiencing a New Incarnation

So when we are ready, we come back because we can go no further unless we come back here and take care of this unfinished business, until we understand completely that God is one, and that when we are one — when we decide to be one — is when we have selected the spiritual journey, a life filled with that.

Now understand also that there are entities on these planes that although they too are burdened down by encumbrances, their greatest encumbrance is the lack of success because they never got to be that, so they are naturally going to formulate lines of potential to which they are born. They are born in the backwater and they have to move through this life and become a success from out of shambles. That is the way their drama will be played out. It is very important for them. And someone must be the fall guy in the play. And you know why they must be the fall guy? Because those are the entities that stepped on other people to attain success in their previous lifetime. How many of you understand? And so the meaningful minds come together for this wonderful display.

So there are people whose encumbrances are the lack of success, for example, and they are going to then lay down that potential of a whole life, a large sandbox to which they play the game for that one fleeting moment of glory, and that is all the life would have been worth was that fleeting moment. And then it becomes degenerated because it will reflect only on that one moment and it will become its past. How many of you understand?

Now that you understand encumbrances a little bit better, you begin to see then that those entities that we have met in this lifetime were not met by accident, that each person that we met along the way was actually part of a line potential that we created on Bliss.

And what is interesting about the mapping on Bliss is that it very rarely ever acts out on earth like it did on Bliss. We have a tendency to paint things very cheery on Bliss. We forgot what it felt like to have a blister on our hands from gripping too tight. We forgot what it was like holding too tight. We don't know that. That is why that in the material realm, when all of this falls into place, it is a remarkable adventure because its maturation is much different than how we planned it before, and then we held the element of the bare mystery of enchanted forgetfulness. That also plays into it and is supposed to play into it.

So all lives that come together in this life aren't necessarily recognized from before, and you shouldn't try to do that because in trying to do that, sometimes you may muddy the picture of the potential that you are endeavoring to find here. We are endeavoring to find self. We are endeavoring to do it with clarity and purity, without any pollution whatsoever, the rawest of our beautiful nature. And the more that we can demystify it, the more real it will become.

When we, in order to reconcile every situation, try to frame it in cosmic text we oftentimes muddy the picture. Relationships don't have to be cosmic; that is a joke. They only need to be relationships. And from that raw and dynamic center we are going to come closer to the plan than if we tried to take it out of context and make it into something it never was, because then we find the encumbrances of creating phantoms that only begin to bother us. How many of you understand? You do?

So in reality oftentimes every life that fulfills the contemplation room that we create — however long, however complicated, however short — our true and wonderful friends are really the emergence from the future, never the past, because on the Plane of Bliss is where the future is born. Do you understand? How many of you understand?

Now then most individuals here start out with good intentions, and their plan never comes into real fruition because they get stuck. Now this is an important message about the past. When you get stuck in the past you deny yourselves your future potential, and that is what is so grievous about your acts of holding onto your victimization, your suffering, your anguish, your parents did this, they did that. Why sacrifice what was created on Bliss for holding onto that which is temporal in the flesh?

When we give our power away to enslaving factors of yesterday, we diffuse the self to which the potential on Bliss we created it for and from. And when we no longer have self, because we have disempowered it through grief and suffering and misery and anxiety and all of that, we stop the flow of our true destiny and all we get is the garbage that we cling to for the sake of self-identity. And why not? It has served you well so far. It has enslaved lovers. It has made people to feel sorry for you. You have used it to get your way. You have used it against other people. You have used it upon yourselves. It has served you. Why would you want to get rid of it? Because unless you do, you don't get the great future that you have created for yourselves and all the marvelous beings that joined you in its creation and you with them — who will touch your lives in unimaginable ways, who will move your soul in waves of fire you have never known, who will inspire you towards your ingenious self — of which no one hereto of your past has been able to do.

You designed a destiny to unencumber yourself, and in that the great minds participated in the making. When we then release to that, we get out of the way and let it come. Our clinging nature to yesterday only is going to take us back through this process, and we are going to still be encumbered by what we have not met. And for a very materialistic term, we are going to be the lesser for the greatness we denied ourselves made in heaven. In other words, so many lifetimes are just repetitious and repetitious and repetitious — repeating the same cyclical movements that are born in the soul, the same experiences that the cowardness of the human element backs away from — and do not allow the pristine movement of the soul to finish, take its power back, and then make room for a marvelous destiny.

Now why do we do this? That "why" is a very broad understanding that takes lifetimes to understand, but I taught it to you in your first C&E™. You are explorers from Point Zero. You are making known the unknown. What is important to us is to imagine the dream and to bring it into fruition, give birth to it in an impossible, arduous, and difficult realm. The dream must exist on all seven levels in order to be fully realized by the dreamer. When we are down here casting dreams in thick time, we are down here casting dreams in a thick time that we are not used to. We are creatures of an eternal imagination because that is how we are. We are consciousness and energy. We are builders of archetypes of thought, and from that then energy behaves to form those thoughts, becomes the movement of them, if you will.

We are not creatures of the flesh. We never have been. But when we allow our flesh to give us away — to give us away — and to fracture our divinity into personalities that hold old fires, old flames, old bitternesses, unresolved and unyielding, we are fractured. We are — listen to me carefully — the self called God, and when we allow our bodies to fracture us, our power then is split as brother against brother. We are in war to our very nature. We are no longer whole and pristine. We are here to make known the unimaginable, not to rehash what is already known and to warp its sense of maturity into a state that degradates even us.

On this Plane of Bliss we get to carry with us our most recent likeness. And oftentimes it is very helpful because like the great scar on my front and my back helped to remind me always of my own inflicted treachery, we get to keep our bodies in their most recent form to remind us of what we must unencumber. How many of you understand? Or we can simply choose to be nebulous in form. However we want to present ourselves, we may present ourselves in that fashion. But while we are on the Plane of Bliss, we are in a state of bliss. We are in a state of communion with the highest levels of life, and we are ever so close to the fountainhead of it all — the eternal Point Zero, as it has come to be known — the whole unifying with the Void itself. Well, we are enjoying each other's company. We are enjoying the bliss, the harmony, the magic of a mind. We are that mind. We are that most divine revelation of imagination. As it stands before us, it twists and turns and changes at our every thought. That is what we really are, people, and always have been.

Why then would you say why come down here just to live a couple of years so that we could work out something; I mean, is it really worth it? Of course it is worth it. When you know you are eternal, playing the part even for a year, it is worth it. What isn't worth it? Our point here is that we are sort of the little Gods that tried but got caught. You know, we got caught and — in what I have been endeavoring to teach you about ever since you have been with me — we got caught in a garment, that its whole nature is so utterly backward from our very own, who has to exist in this slow-moving, slow-time, compelling existence that has alienated us from what our whole actually is.

We have to finish our business, not so that we can go home; we have to finish our encumbrances so that we can be free of this entanglement of our cowardly nature of human flesh — that we can finish it up — that the nature of the human has not been able to do.

THE ANIMAL NATURE OF HUMANITY

I want to tell you something. When it is said that man is an animal, that is correct. Man is an animal because of his animal nature: the nature of strong survival, strong reproduction, and highly territorial. Some are solitary. Predators are cunning and strike from behind; they are not brave. The weak gather together in greater numbers to protect their boundaries, hoping that someone else will fall but not them. This is the animal nature.

Now how close are you to that nature? I can tell you how close you are. The spiritual nature isn't even working when you launch an attack upon the innocent, when you flail your debtors with a cat-o'-nine-tails because they owe you, when you hate because you give, and you are territorial because you want to protect your boundaries, and you would jump at the chance to copulate. That is the animal. The body does that very well because that is the nature of the kingdom that it is derived from. And brave men and women who are acting in a role of greatness never attack from behind. Only a coward and a predator, who are both the same, do that. If that is the way that this is — and who can deny it — how far are you really from it other than that you have good table manners and you wear garments and you defecate in toilets and not on the plains? You are not that far removed from your animal nature. The first three seals are the animal nature. When that human has its way, it will always act like an animal because it is a coward. And I tell you it is the spiritual self — what I am telling you that you really are — that is the only viable aspect of this incarnation that can truly address encumbrances and is equipped to handle them. The human is not. You know, you are a coward who lived in a tarnished past of suffering; that is your cowardness. You are an animal.

If you have not been relieved from it or been strong enough to relieve yourselves of it, then you have yet to be a spiritual person, because the Spirit is what is best equipped to do this because it is after it. The Spirit is after the encumbrances because, first, it has to take its power back to regain its wholeness of self. And when it does, it is the one that says, "No more. This is finished. I created it. I am responsible for it. I forgive you. You are free." That is a spiritual person, isn't it? So what does the animal do? "You owe me," doesn't it? It does. "And now that you are vulnerable, I am going to get you." That is the animal.

So being an altered ego is not going to help you. Just because you are born down here, your genetics are not in your favor because they came from genetics that were trying to do the same thing. And, remember, you are only drawing the physical body that was closest to what you were. This is a continuing story. How many of you understand?

Now we come back here not because anybody sent us back here; we sent ourselves. We are back here not to change the world but to change ourselves. We are back here to be realized, not reforgotten. We have come back here to finish this business up.

So now I want to ask you then in the light of what I have taught you about the Plane of Bliss, it becomes monumental, does it not, that these little heart tremors of the personality carry more weight than you could possibly know. It is not the success we accomplish on this plane that is remembered in the halls of Bliss. It is not about how much money you make. It is not about how much you don't make. It is not about how famous you were here or how infamous you were here. It is not about what you look like here. It is not about any of that here that is so important. It is what did we do; that is what is important.

And it is important enough to bring Gods to human knees because our agenda is different than the human animal. Our agenda is to be unencumbered and then bring in the unimaginable. That is what this is about. That is what this is about. Have people before you done that? Indeed there have been. There have been people who have cleaned up their experiences, finalized them, and were free of them. And who were they? The brilliant people that are now scattered and peppered throughout history that were geniuses because they brought the unimaginable through. You know why? They had the power to do it because self was put back on the throne. It was gathered back together, pieced together, and put on the throne.

Very few of these individuals that are heroic in your history got there by Bliss. Most of them paid dearly for their genius. In other words, they suffered, endured, proclaimed, and accomplished. In other words, they took the tiger on, didn't they? And that turbulent life led to the one thing they wanted to accomplish here — the unimaginable — that they already knew before they were incarnated here. They got above the human drama and became Gods once again, and if only for a moment their star shined, that is all it took. It was over with then. It is finished, which brings me back to my introduction with you tonight.

You made the choice to be here and to choose spiritual learning in this life. I set the foundation and you came. Now there is one great union that all of us in this room, save for a few, have in common. We shared collectively a lifetime together, a very tumultuous, arduous, awe-inspiring, great life. And you witnessed marvelous things: the ending of an old earth and the beginning of a new one. You witnessed the dying of the Gods and the birth of men, and you marched the long march. That is what we share in common tonight. And for that, love borne throughout the pages of this march resides to this moment, which allowed this moment to have a place in the Void in the mind of God; that when you were ready to choose to know more, there was a place to come. And it is inevitable.

So why, on the Plane of Bliss in heaven, would you choose what you already are on the Plane of Bliss to realize down here (first plane) if you know it up there? Good question? Yes, it is, because what is realized up there in order to be fully known must be realized into the bowels of God, and it has to be made known here because this is the cauldron; this is the alchemist's crucible here. The shining star dancing on midnight-blue liquid suddenly recoagulates and comes down to that little ball of nickel in the bottom of the bowl again. So here we are. You have to do it here (first plane).

On the Plane of Bliss most all of you in here came through your labyrinth and your encumbrances. You still have encumbrances, but all of you had a place of love in you, a place to vacillate to. And you had something startling happen to you. You saw me leave the plane without dying. You never forgot that. Where did I go and how did I escape the decay and the rottenness of the body? How was I able to do that? You see, you got to see that. That is why the legend of Christ and the resurrection is so strong in Christian minds today. It is poignant because it is a longing. It is an unimaginable imaginable that has set its seed in the minds of many people. You will find this in all religious doctrine.

With me and my people, before all of that gibberish, I left — and you saw it and that was it — in my true style, make a point and get on, which makes you ask, "Where did he go? He is not on the Plane of Bliss. Where is he?" Well, I am on the Plane of Bliss. When you came back, before you got back, you remembered me and where I went. And love is unforgettable. It is so sweet; it is unforgettable because it lacks nothing. So in your labyrinth you asked the ultimate question, "What is the unimaginable for me?"

Now there is another group across the river asking the same question. That is the group that invented computers, because that group is just now discovering that if they can create an idea on the superplane of existence and move it right along into the timeline — that if they get it in this body they are about to be born into, and if they actually get it and it actually works — whether you know it or not those technological geniuses are starting to wake up to what you are already getting to know. In other words, they are behind you. They look like they are in front of you but they are actually behind you because they are just learning to create. They are just learning; you already know that.

So this group then says what do I need to know? What do I need to unencumber myself with? Well, you are asking a heap. But, after all, all you are asking for is unfinished business. And when it is done, what do you want? I want to go where no man has gone before. I want to know. I want to go where the Gods dwell. I want to know what it is to be a master. And when you imagined what a master was, you thought of me. When you thought of the dale of the Gods, you thought of me and created in your mind where you thought I went. And this fascinating journey — this fascinating puzzle, this exercise, this toy labyrinth that you built in your potential imagination — got you strung out on being spiritual because, you see, you don't get it unless you ask for it. How many of you understand? And somewhere along the way, there must be an ideal come into human consciousness that trips it.

All through your history you have had wonderful beings that have come in and have circumvented the system, that have been so bold, so arrogant, so pure as to stand ten feet above mediocre man. What made them so different? Because they were filled with the power of the Holy Spirit instead of the power of the animal. That is what made them different. Why did they come back? They came back to reremind you, "Never forget me. I am going to make such an impression on you, you are never going to forget me because one day you are going to want to know what I am."

REDEFINING THE SELF BY CHOOSING OUR SPIRITUAL NATURE

I am an ideal. It has been necessary to sprinkle ideals historically for all civilizations to keep them from collapsing — some astonishing thing that happened at noon, an appearance or reappearance of phenomenon; you are beginning to understand where that comes from now — something to snap us from this dream, heavy melatonin dream of the carnal life, that wakes us up and then we click on up here (the brain). When we click on, we click on as spiritual beings and click off as human beings. How many of you understand? I was your catalyst.

So now in the light of all eternity, why would you want to spend this lifetime developing your spiritual self? First you have to overcome your encumbrances, own the past, because it says to you — those of you who make it — that you really have come to understand that you have already done everything in human consciousness. My God, who haven't you been? My God, what haven't you had? My God, who haven't you hated and how many haven't you loved? How many times do you have to die? How many times do you have to get sick? How many times do you need to be successful to realize you never were a failure? How many times does it take? You know, only an entity coming back here would know that the only reason that I am coming back here is that I must finish my business. But my unimaginable dream is to be the superbeing. What greater dream is there than God? There is none.

So you included this in your potential line and remembered me from an incident I did with you. That is what brought this into being and you chose it. You want to understand what has not been you and you want to find deliverance from your burden and wholeness. And that wholeness speaks to a wholeness of the self, that once it is completely contained it will be ready for the emergence of the future that was created on the Plane of Bliss.

Everyone has character flaws; everyone here does. But what is that? To what scale of perfection do we find flaws? No one here is perfect. There is no such thing as the perfect human. No matter how damn hard you try, you will never get there because in order to be that, you are going to have to be as base as any animal and you are already too far gone the other way.

You came here through a line that you created on the Plane of Bliss to learn not what was already here but what could be here. And you came here to have something to bring up and to remind you of the experiences that you need to complete. And they can be completed as simply as you wish or as arduously as you wish and then from that be utterly and totally free to incorporate what you have already created, an unimaginable beauty. I promise you, no one ever goes backwards when they are free of their encumbrances. They are truly liberated. They are liberated from their animal. They are liberated from their suffering. They become whole. They find the self, that which they really are.

Now I told you three times this evening that our natural way of creating is instantaneously. You begin to understand why a God would become so fractured in a human, because what we get immediately has to be processed into coagulation for the human. In the human who is always protecting boundaries — always checking out victims, always looking for survival, and always needing the copulation — these are impatient qualities. Nature is the survival of the fittest. And when it comes to the animal, the animal must fit as the fittest in all of these categories. When we truly become human beings, we really fracture the holy in ourselves because the impatient human cannot hold onto an unimaginable imaginable if that dream does not directly relate to its security, its sovereignty, its longevity, its basis of copulation, and its superiority amongst unequals. The human will never hold a dream that does not facilitate its animal nature. That is the reason why the human is impatient and always riddled with doubt when it comes to imagination.

And here we are, the very Gods that made this creature. We revel in the imagination as true reality but cannot enjoy it to the root of God on this plane because the body that we inhabit cannot hold onto it and rejects it, thereby denying us access to that experience. The body is not a dreamer. It can create thoughts. It is the computer. It can hold them holographically, but it finds it tiring to hold onto them. The God is the moment. It is the dreamer. And it needs to be strong enough in the body to be able to bring the dream forth instead of emasculate it.

This is a battle because always what happens is the body wins and the Spirit loses, and so there we go into a fall, into another meaningless life; that the only thing we are going to do when we die is go back and see the same program over and have to go and readdress it in the same contemplation. Oh, we will be happy and relieved, but there is a greater calling for us even there.

We are unfinished here. The spiritual journey and the walk of the master start when very painful issues must be addressed: the nature of the human and the nature of the Spirit, the destiny, how it is perceived both human and spiritual. What is important to the human will not be important to the Spirit. What the human finds subjective and personal, the Spirit will find objective and impersonal. We also have bodies that can't hold dreams and they give up because they are prancing their territory. They have got to keep moving to keep their boundaries safe. And we have a God who is endeavoring to get the experience through.

When you choose to have a life to where you dedicate it to your spiritual revelation, you are asking for a life in which you must ride those horses of the sensual self with a tight rein. And in this life the Spirit must be developed. And the painful process of taking back one's power often means tripping up the body, its family roots — and pulling out from under it its own rug of blame and jealousy, the dynamics of family situations, pulling the rug out from under sexuality, pulling the rug out from under prejudice — and saying in an unequal yet singular tone, "I created this. It never was your fault. I made you think it was your fault because that is the coward in me. I blamed you for the lessness I feel about myself when it had nothing to do with you. I inflicted the lack of self-love upon me and indeed it is I who have rejected myself and cloistered myself. I am the one who left you; you never left me. I am the one who has wallowed in self-pity and languored in my past. You never were in my present because I was never there. I was gone. I was in yesterday. It is not your fault. It is just a habit I have."

It takes great spiritual depth to be an honorable man and an honorable woman. And it hurts deeply, but I would rather feel the coming back of the wind of begotten energy moving through the emotional body and getting purified to make us whole rather than never be whole at all.

And when we were last together I talked to you about intense clarity, pure and unobstructed, and that every thought is meted out decisively. It is never simply taken for randomness but it is contemplated so much so until the extraordinary and lofty way to think becomes the common way to think. That is hard to do, especially when your body tells you you are missing a lot. And it is hard to stay in the dark night of the soul without stimulus to get you out of it. But why would you want to get you out of it? It is pulling that energy back from those painful places that must pass through the emotional body. That is where the true suffering is, but that is also where purification is. To dull it, to get rid of it, would deny yourselves purification and thus wisdom. So be it.

But what is wrong with processing energy? Don't you think you are strong enough to do it? True, the human being is an impatient critter. It is a nasty one too when it is cornered. But are you such a coward that you can't deal with the issues that you have created? After all, they will never be greater than you because they came from you. Or is it that you can deal it out but you can't take it when it comes back? Is really what a drug is, is to numb the sensation of the return of what you meted out? I would think about that if I were you.

SUMMARY: THE SPIRITUAL WALK OF THE MASTER

O my beloved God,
unto me this day
move as my Holy Spirit,
to draw me up
into your realm
and hold me there.
O my beloved God,
let my Spirit
flow from my being
unencumbered.
I accept this knowledge
in freedom.
I desire
its revelation
unto me.
O my beloved God,
I am thankful
for my life.
O my beloved God,
I am thankful
for my body.
My beloved God,
fill me with your love
eternally,
and God bless my life.
So be it.
To life.

Be seated. For those of you who were not here last evening we had a wonderful — or I had a wonderful — wonderful teaching about self and heaven. Now let's do a little review, shall we. We will start off in the right frame of consciousness. We want to evolve this day so that we can gain deeper knowledge. So let's start with the knowledge that we had and set our minds on a righteous path to understanding.

Now what was the first teaching I gave you last evening? You chose to be here — how many of you agree? — chose to come here and to learn a spiritual understanding. No one made you come here. And you are here because this is what you want to learn. Self-choice is the beginning of self-empowerment or the redefinition of self.

Now what was the second thing that you learned last night? Defining self. Now we are still a little hazy here about self, and it is only a term. And these words that I use, they are only words. What is important is reminding you of the two evenings that we had together in your time where I talked about learning to hear and why it was important that a master teach you, because a master can teach you and, if you are hearing, what is it causing to occur in your brain?[2] Pictures, holograms. That is the way to hear. Now these words stimulate the brain to create pictures. And as you also learned last night, true self is imagination; it is the act of imaging. That is our destiny. That is what we are supposed to do. So if you listen today, you will be helped to redefine perhaps old definitions because as I talk, and if you can stay with me, your brain is going to produce the pictures that my words, properly placed, are going to occur in your brain. And if they do, then you are now thinking in spiritual terms.

The definition of self. We must go all the way back then to Point Zero, to what I taught when you first came to see me: You are God. And then of course we have to redefine what God is and remove from it the shackles of limitation and dogma. And we use that which is termed physics to be able to explain the metamorphosis of involution as well as evolution, reality. Self is a pure, creative state of consciousness and its handmaiden energy, inextricably combined; that is what we really, really are. And that self creating is none other than the godhead itself. That is what we are.

If we understand then that we are not really the faces that we wear and we are not really the garment that we wear — and,

2 The teachings of these two evening events are recorded in Ramtha Dialogues®, Tape 346, *Crossing the River Part I*, January 8, 1997, and Tape 347, *Crossing the River Part II*, January 9, 1997.

moreover, we really aren't the territories that we define — then we start to see self in its most pure origin when we understand that self is not the subjective body that we exist in but that it is the objective mind of one and all reality. With this brain that has the ability to contemplate the infinite, even on its finite terms, you begin to see then that our spiritual self has been a rolling culmination of the very experiences that it created. Now listen to what I said, that the Spirit is the rolling culmination of the very experiences that it has created in its eons of manifestation. So what that means is then essentially that the self is a broad mind — a mind, really — a mind that is made up of all of its consciousness and energy that it created, and that to move through a creation and not finish it would be a fracturing of that self, wouldn't it? How many of you understand? And, remember, that is what we are. And we then as consciousness and energy, the godhead itself, have only one real destiny — real destiny — and that is to make known the unknown. And the more that we do so to imagine the unimaginable, the greater our unity as God, as oneness, becomes. That is what we are supposed to do. We are an ocean seeping into the shores of the Void, and we should be expanding that which we are. That is what the self is.

Now if we are then an enigma, a mystifying, etherical quality called consciousness and energy, then the soul is what captures and holds forever the final experience, the final movement of that experience. And it is the soul and the holding of that experience in its finality that allow consciousness to be so broad. Without the soul helping to define mind, we would only be creating, moving through the creation. And as soon as we have moved through it, we are back where we were originally because we have no margin — we have created no margin — of static reality of which to build other concepts from. Do you understand what I have said?

So here we have then the soul of memorable experience within the conscious-energy self. It is the quality that allows our mind to grow and to expand. It gives us our finished business to which we use as springboards to create the next unimaginable. Now that is self, and it is awesome and powerful.

When we know that about what we are, we can see then clearly why a life pursued — coming out of the wilderness and out of the murk and the mire, a life that is born here in which the pursuit and destiny and goal of that life is to find out what we are — is the loftiest life we will ever live, because when we begin to imagine ourselves not in the eyes of humanity but when we begin to define ourselves in much broader terms, unimaginable terms, we start to locate what we are. That is the discovery of who we are. It is time to take a look at what is true and real about ourselves. That we call the spiritual life; that is the spiritual life.

Now to define ourselves. We also learned last night then that self is in the body of an incarnation like yours; that self, when it was on the Plane of Bliss last time and every time from every incarnation, arrives there at heaven; and that the great agenda there — the great Judgment Day, the hour of judgment — is to see for ourselves, both subjective and objective, those aspects of how we placed energy and how ultimately we affected this central core of our being — past life review, as you like to call it in its flowery, cosmic terms. And what is important about that is that in this hour of judgment, there is no one there in heaven, on Bliss, that is the judge. What we are is ourselves. And we have found then that what covers up self is unfinished business.

We learned a term last night called encumbrances, to be encumbered. When we view then our past life and what you are going to do in this one, you are going to see everything. We learned that last night. There is nothing that was ever forgotten in energy because every act was preceded by a thought, and that is what is real. The thought is real because it is what self is; it is consciousness and energy. So we review what is real. And nothing is wasted.

And we see everything that we did, what we thought we were doing behind closed doors or behind the placid face of indifference or smiling emptiness. We begin to see it not only as we who did it and were thinking it, but consciousness and energy from this point of view, as self, is both. So we not only get to see subjectively what we were thinking, but we also get to feel it subjectively as energy and where it was headed —how many of you understand that? — because we are, as we have learned, one; that God is one mind. So what we do, we do to ourselves regardless of the players.

The players are ourselves — are you understanding me? — because that is how large self is.

And we learned then last night that in doing to someone else, we have done to ourselves. In victimizing and being unmerciful, uncaring, entrapping, enslaving, being decadent, being uncharitable, being unforgiving, we have done to ourselves. So in the light review we get to feel what that feels like. How many of you understand? Well, everything is energy and therefore we are the creators of that energy. Then it is our expulsion of that energy that comes home to us. That is Judgment Day.

And why is it a painful moment? We learned last night — because we really get to see every facet of ourselves and we see the dynamics of that facet — we become the injured that we have injured. We become the enslaved that we enslaved. We are the victims of our abuse, and we feel it on every corner. We also learned why that is important is because in order to do any of these acts in a lifetime, we must have a divine quality that we can utilize to do it with. In other words, no act — again — is not preceded by a thought, and the thought is coming from the divine source inside of us. So the act is us. We learned then, remembering that, that our encumbrances are giving our power away, fracturing our God and being unwhole.

Defining self in the spiritual life is about being in pursuit of the knowledge that allows us to address our encumbrances. It allows us in the spiritual life to find out who we are. It is important that we do so. We never walk as angels in the beginning of this spiritual journey. We come humbly with our dead mules at the door — our hauntings, our phantoms, our sufferings, our anxieties — and the devil that we bring with us is our altered ego.

We learn then that the spiritual life is about taking our power back. Of everything I have taught you, the essential message is regaining coherently the power that you have fractured away because when you do, you dismantle the temple within; you dismantle the godhood within. And every block, every golden stone that makes up the temple of the self, has been given to all of these particular areas that constitute an inordinate amount of suffering, because we are separated from our God because our God is fractured around us. That is an encumbrance.

In order then to do the unimaginable, we have to rebuild this temple. We have to redefine ourselves and that is not easy. And many of you contemplated last night about — really true and sincere contemplation — where have you given your power away and what does that mean. That doesn't mean giving it to somebody to control your life, although that is an aspect of it. It doesn't really mean that. It is a finer, more mystical meaning. It means holding onto your past.

You see, the fracturing of God as encumbrances is only locked up in the past. That is where it is locked up. And we addressed this, the victims of your past experiences. A chronic one in this audience is that you have been abused by your parents, or you were ignored by your parents, or you were abandoned by your parents, and that you move through life with this sickening attitude of lack and that you point the finger at them, him or her — and these are examples — or to your friend or someone who abused you, or to someone who took advantage of you, or someone who pulled the rug out from under you. You go through life pointing fingers: It is their fault I am this way. That is the fracturing of self because what that means is that instead of taking responsibility for creating this — which is what God is about; God is the creator and, I tell you, that is what you are — that instead of taking the responsibility of that, which will define self, you fracture it by pointing fingers and saying, "They did this to me and I was innocent." No one is innocent. And the moment that you do and you create tyrants in your life, then you have taken part of the temple and you have set it over there, and its reality and its dynamic are to do this to you.

And as we also learned, it is so tempting from the human point of view to be a victim because everyone is. That is the social consciousness of capitalism is to be victimized so that they can find ways to get you out of it temporarily. Do you understand? It is easy, because it is much easier to say I am the way I am because of this and that — people, places, things, times, and events. And when you do, it works for a while. Look how you have used it. You have used it to excuse your lack of strength. You have used it to excuse your illness. You have used it to cleverly bind people to you through their sympathy and empathy. You have used it to get your way. It has served you. You are a capitalist. Do you understand? That is what you are.

And no one really wants to give that up because, as we also learned, the animal in you, the survivalist with definable boundaries, the herdlike creature, that creature demands survival. And so if every one of you stop serving the herd, what happens is the moment you say I created it — I; I is God — I created it, this is my own creation, the moment you do that you remove your power from your parents, people, places, things, times, and events. You remove it from there (outside us) and you start to rebuild the temple in here (inside us). Now that — as we also learned and some of you have contemplated about — is a very painful process.

The dark night of the soul is when we finally take responsibility for our actions. And what happens then is the energy that is coming home from poor mom and dad — and, remember, they are just Gods too — the energy that is coming home from your brother and your sister or your husbandman, your wife, or your relationship, when you start to take responsibility, look how consciousness works because if it is that and it has control of energy, when you take "I" from out there and put it back in here, then the energy starts to dissolve from mom and dad and it starts moving back to you. And it is passing through those bands. It is coming home.

Now the dark night of the soul is when the energy rushes through the emotional body. In other words, it was once sent out through the emotional body as feeling, was it not, to create? Remember we have learned that? So now it is going to come back home and impact the same feeling; that is, only when energy becomes purified is when it enters back into the physical realm of the emotional body. Simply said, when you take your power back of making someone else your tyrants, then the energy starts coming back to you in the form of a tyrant. That energy is a thought form. It is tyrannical, and it hits the emotional body and it is like a reverse charge. Instead of the energy coming from here (inside us) and being affected hormonally, it is coming from out there, passing through the energy band and hitting the body as a direct charge. It is a reverse charge into the brain. How many of you understand? When it does, it activates the field and it causes suffering. This is where tears come from. This is where wailing comes from. This is where anguish comes from. And if someone says to you, "What is wrong with you?" "I don't know," well, this is what it is: Your chickens are coming home to roost. Do you understand?

Now this is very hard to do because I have taught you so much to have joy and I will continue to teach you to do that, but we must be free of our encumbrances. What we started we must complete, and we must bring the energy back to the temple here (inside us). And we have to build it within ourselves; that is the self. That is redefining it, and it is painful. No one wants to take responsibility for something that all these years has served them so well. They don't want to take responsibility that really they are the one that lived in the past of a circumstance, that the people who were connected have long gone. Nobody wants to admit that that is how they lived their life. It is hard.

But when energy passes through the dark night of the soul, then it is home and the self starts to be defined. This is pure judgment. And I will tell you something I did not tell you last evening that will become self-evident through this workshop, that the spiritual path is the path of purging and it is the path of cleansing. It is nothing about cleansing the body or the colon. It is not. I am not speaking in those terms. I have to be very clear.

Now energy between two points of consciousness is defining time, its velocity, its momentum; that is defining time. Now we have two levels of consciousness in this body. We have body/mind consciousness and we have God consciousness; therefore, time bounces back and forth between the two. But if we then take that and understand it as a momentum, the body is continuously under emotional duress. And that means that if it is, the emotions that are moving from within the body are draining the storehouses of hormones and energy that govern them. And those fundamental building blocks of the tangible physical are being used up every day by reminding ourselves of something that we used to get away with in our youth but has taken its toll in middle age. So every day the emotional trauma of your past eats away, and that is time. That is why when the encumbrances of the past are owned and the power is taken back, the past reaction ceases. How many of you understand that? Getting back then to ascension, all ascension becomes then is the natural apogee for owning one's encumbrances. The master truly is walking on the face of the earth at this point.

So the true spiritual life then is about a life that we are born into to understand self and to heal it and to make a life dedicated to the art of healing it. And what begins to happen that is so different than the group across the river, that is inventing computers, is that the spiritual life is an eternal one so that when we do heal it, we belong to the ages; we belong to eternity. When we focus on what has given us life and what we truly are — and we endeavor to become it and understand its methodology and its science and the mechanics of how it works — when we dedicate a life to doing that, then that Spirit is our reward in a never-ending existence. How many of you understand? So be it.

Now this school is defining that self, defining it. We only make it hard on ourselves. Isn't that an interesting phrase, hard on self? It takes on a new light, does it not? Now what was the third thing we talked about last night? What was the third thing that you learned? Last night you learned in the orientation about going to the light and the Day of Judgment, and you learned about being all things in that light review, the subject as well as the Observer. And we learned then that after we have this light review, as troubling as it is, we are nonetheless closer to our natural element on Bliss than we are here in this foreign land, and therein we have a place to which we can go into contemplation. And we learned about the different areas of contemplation, from pizza parlors on the fourth plane, sitting by a great and beautiful placid lake — instantly appears — sitting in the midst of the Void somewhere. We call it the halls of contemplation — now this is important — in which we have the ability of contemplation. We have now been removed out of our altered ego.

We can retain the likeness of our former body if we wish to help to remind us what we need to do, but we have been removed from it. We don't really care who we left behind anymore. And we don't really care about what went on with our personal property after our death. We really don't care. As much as the lawyers tell you, we don't care. And we really are very different than what we were in that human existence, but we are close to the existence because we have to now go and, taken from what we gained from that existence, we have to be able to contemplate — knowing that contemplation is our natural order — because as soon as we do, it appears. We must contemplate on how to finish the business that in yet another lifetime we were unable to do.

And we all know when we are in that place how cowardly the body is, the human is. We know that. And how do we yet move into that orb of experience and be able to impress what we want upon a brain that clearly is not going to remember? Now as long as we understand the unity, God is one, then the sweet things of our life are going to be carried on genetically. If we bore children in that life, then one honorable thing that will happen is that we have started a bloodline to which we helped produce, and here is the advantage of that. We know that our attitudes become flesh in the next generation, and what better place would we want to land then and to work on unfinished business but in the very genetic pool that we are endeavoring to address concurrently. How many of you understand?

So in this place we are endeavoring to figure out that line of potential and create our future, to be able to finish this business up, because again let me tell you it is not about being a good person or a bad person; it is about what we do with opportunities and which level of consciousness do we approach them with. Do we approach them with the human that is instinctively a coward, or do we approach them with the Spirit that is all-prevailing? It is about creating, experiencing, so that the soul has yet another block, another tool to build another reality based upon that wisdom. That is why it is so important.

We know all of this, but we know that our unfinished business, as we learned last night, can never be finished on Bliss. Oh, we can see the end of it. Why, we can see what we are in other realms. We get the opportunity to play there. We get the opportunity to instantly see what we would be if we were this life or that life or some other life. You understand? We are only limited to what we know. And we get to do all of that. We can take our next incarnation and we can go all the way through. We can visualize for ourselves the most idealistic life, but it isn't really going to happen for us.

We are not going to gain the substance of the wisdom unless we come back to the place of its origin, down here, the plane of demonstration — the thick, gooey, syrupy plane. This is where we have to be defined at and we have to make it known here.

So how do we transfer our sublime and sparkling consciousness that immediately imagines and it is? How can we get that magic into that body? Well, we know that the only way we can get it there is if we lay a course ahead of time on Bliss of what we want to have accomplished down here. Now how are we going to get into it? Well, we are going to permeate the bands that surround the tissue of the child in the womb. The child in the womb is going to feed off of those bands. But more importantly we have laid the program in the soul, the one who remembers. And the soul is what is going to give life to the child in utero. The soul is going to create the rhythmic beating of the heart. It also, because it is called the lord of the body, has got jurisdiction over how the genes play a part in manufacturing the body. It is going to do that. But it is not going to make the brain have memory of which it does not yet have. How many of you understand that? It can only store it away in the lower cerebellum. That is the only place it is allowed to store it. Now we know that. We know that when we are on Bliss.

So what is being a spiritual person about? It is about being the self utterly and totally; that the self is all things and all beings, and that the self — if who we want to be is spiritual — will never, ever hold a grudge against anyone, because if we don't do it on Bliss and we have instantaneous manifestation, why do we insist on doing it here? And, second, we should forgive everyone, because in doing so we forgive ourselves. In forgiving ourselves, we take the monkey off of our back and give the power back to us. When we learn that everyone is us in the way that we are, then we are being spiritual because why can we not be on earth as we are in heaven? We simply have to choose to be it and we have to look at the conditions of being it. If there is no cheating in heaven, why do we do it here? How many of you understand? And if there is no doubting in heaven, why do we insist on doing it here? If there is no malice in heaven, why do we insist on doing it here? How many of you are beginning to understand?

Let's have a drink. To more freedom. Isn't it so that the truth does set you free? It does. God, let us always wish for that freedom. So be it. To life.

RESOLUTION

Now what was then the next thing, the next point that we learned last night at the close of the evening? Resolution — resolution — a very nice word; sort of sounds like revolution, a spiritual revolt.

Now already we have discussed today in review what unfinished business is. And although I have put out some very harsh examples, it is the irony that those are the examples that are always put forward because, as I have said to you last night, there are things about our life that will always be with us. They are the sweet things; they are the true godhead. Those are the great acts that we do that really transcend the normal course of business. There are aspects of ourselves that we have earned the right to be defined by. And these aspects, as in human consciousness, we could say, well, those are the good things. Well, they are the virtuous things. They are the virtuous lessons. They are the virtuous deeds. Now there are things about aspects, about colors, about dimensions to all of you here that are really quite spectacular and you have earned the right to keep those. Those are not disingenuous to your nature; they are quite genuine. And those we don't need to talk about because when we do acts, when we impart the extraordinary from ourselves, we are not fracturing; we are defining. And those qualities all of you have.

Everyone in this room at some point in your life has been called upon by a friend or a desperate neighbor, or in a time of chaos and misery, that something greater has risen out of you and you have acquiesced. Now these are the great defining qualities in our lives that will never be taken away from us because they echo what God is. And you know, my beloved people, there are certainly many incidences in nature or through intentional human destruction that all of you have been participants to.

And whereas only days before you may have been griping

and complaining about your neighbors — because like I told you last night, there are stinkers in this group and you know who you are — but isn't it interesting how the humanity part of us is quick to recognize that in someone else because that is what is in ourselves, isn't it? That is where our energy is, isn't it? That is the fracturing of us. And then the next day a terrible incident could befall those neighbors in a very, perhaps, life-threatening way and suddenly without even thinking we are riveted from our comfort zone of conceit and arrogance and we are transported into a venue of thought that seems to spring from somewhere deep inside of us, and we rush to their aid and we help. We hold back the waters; we move the food. We take raggedy, smelly children in our arms and where two days before we couldn't tolerate the sight of blood, we are there cleaning wounds, holding them dear to our breast where our soul lives. And we are helping. And when two days before we were complaining about our lack of revenue or lack of funds, suddenly it doesn't even become an issue. Your hand reaches for your pocketbook and you pull it out and you give, and you don't even think about the consequences of giving.

Now that is our nature, our true defining moments of self, and that when we do help, no matter the cost — and sometimes the greater the call, which would demand of you the greater the cost, the greater the effort — it is in those moments that we are defined as God. We truly are. Or as some historians would say then, those are the defining moments, the crowning jewel of human existence. These are the great points about us. There is not one of you that really hasn't, in a small way or a large way, riveted from the hypocrite to the God in a matter of moments. Those kindnesses, that thoughtfulness, those areas of generosity without thought to the repercussion to yourself, when you do that, you are God. When you pause and reflect and think, then you redefine your boundaries and the moment passes, and that defining of God has missed its opportunity.

This act of emergency that we arise to is what helps to not only define the self but it also binds us to the eternal self. Now these are the great things that we have done, you know. Someone who loses their purse and has all of their life savings in it and you who are working on fabulous wealth find it, it is a great temptation to say that it is your manifestation. That is the altered human instinct to survive. The honorable God, without question, would find its rightful owner because in that rarefied moment we are back on the Plane of Bliss because, you see, on the Plane of Bliss there is no need; there is only the expansion of knowledge to make greater forms of preexistence. That is when the God kicks in. That is when we are at our best. That is when we are at our most ennobled.

How many opportunities are you placed in to where the living truth of the Spirit is able to speak instead of the cunning of the flesh? Why, you are in them every day. How many opportunities are there for you to shine what you are nobly when it would be easier to hide and to become pale and run away? You have all done this, and this is your beauty. This you will never have to be ashamed of in the light of all eternity. And it is not something that you have to own in this lifetime; it is the fabric of the construction of self. And you all have that to your credit. It takes a truly remarkable man and woman to be in the fire of social consciousness and suddenly, in a blinding moment, know the right path and to take it.

Resolution is sort of taking then those splendid moments to your credit and applying them in the areas that you are encumbered in and not to apply it with human logic — because it will always have an ulterior motive, as you know — but to apply it forthrightly from that which is termed the spiritual self that created it somewhere else.

I tell you it is a finer thing to walk away from the emotions that rip and tear you apart. It is a finer being who can get up off of their knees and dust themselves off and walk away. And they may have nothing when they do, but they are finer, more ennobled, and more spiritual in that moment than in the fray of who is right and who is wrong. It takes a very powerful person to do that, but those are the acts that give us this defining quality of God.

You chose the spiritual learning. That is why you are here. I set up the format. You chose to be here to learn about that which is not completely tangible. You learned in this life to help to define you instead of living in the fog of life after life which, on that plane before you were incarnated, all of you here found a central core of something that needed to be done. You needed to study. You needed to define what it was that has been forgotten instead of going over those same meaningless experiences and never finding resolution to them. So you chose in heaven a part of your linear process, and if you hadn't, you wouldn't be here.

There are no victims in this audience to the spiritual teaching. It is here by design and by choice. You are following your soul's journey. And what higher life could anyone live than to live the life that defines God, because ultimately that is what everything is. And you chose to be here in this learning. And, remember, you obviously thought that I knew what I would be talking about and that it was important enough for you to tarry with me for a time and to dedicate a part of your life to gaining this. In that potential you created; you saw its value, of course, and you remembered the different road I took than the one you have taken ever since. You remembered that. And so you are here then to be dedicated to the knowledge that I am giving you and to teach you how to think, not as a fractured God but one that is whole, and to keep showing you through processes which, though very difficult, can be very simple. And you chose to be here.

The spiritual godhead is the resolution to everything, because it is in it, that when we learn about self, then self is no longer cloaked in mystery. Although it is much bigger and broader than any painting that we could put forth, we still begin to have a sense of its presence. We begin to study our tracks and we begin to look at the tracks that we have made. And when we do, we will be closing in on the invisible presence that has made them, and you are here to know that. And when we do, we will find all of the answers that resolve the encumbrances that you are all dealing with. You have heavy ones that you obviously haven't been able to get out of and so you have gone to the fountainhead itself on this plane to find your way out of them and free of them.

So how do we resolve? Resolution is so simple it can happen in a moment. It is the same moment of clarity that happens when you finally give up your past on the field and you lay that focus in clear water, and then it happens. It is a dynamic, showing you that all we must do then is to be able to move above our past and no longer affiliate with it. We must do the work as the human — to forgive in every quarter — that we can find forgiveness, because only then are we forgiven. It must come from ourselves. To do it out here gives permission for the God or the prodigal son to come home, and the tears of joy are passing through that emotional barrier. At every area in our life we must look to see what bothers us, what infringes upon our peace, what drives us and who drives us, and why we keep thinking in terms of the past rather than the present. And we must get rid of it by taking our energy off of it. When we do, we become whole.

That is not to say that the drama of tangible reality doesn't continue to play; it does for a while. This then brings into full forbearance the teaching of looking at the table and seeing it filled, even though it appears to the eye to be empty. Forgive, forgive, forgive, forgive, forgive; release, release, release, release; allow, allow, allow, allow. At every act of the way we become empowered. Remember, we want it all back, and it is locked up in the past. We want it all back.

Now here is the frightful moment of doing that. When we do that, we sometimes cut the lifeline to our own sovereignty, don't we? In other words, our sovereignty, our boundaries, our definition of love and companionship are all based in these places we are about to cut out from under us. We are literally pulling the rug out from under our carnal life, aren't we? Well, that is what the spiritual journey is about. We want to do that. We want to do that. We want to take the box and shake it up and throw it out there. Yes, we are going to fall on our face. Yes, everything ceases for a while. Yes, it is going to happen. What else do you expect? Well, the cupboard is empty but I am empowered. Yes, yes, you are. But if you even dare to regret that the cupboard is empty, you are not empowered because isn't regret also an empowerment of the godhead? Isn't it? You have to stop regretting. There cannot be any regrets, none, because if you do, you are fractured. And what we want is not to save face but to become empowered again. Do you understand? How many of you understand?

Now in the sense of the term that I have talked about, that makes us naked and vulnerable, it seems, and we get the shakes and we are nervous. But if we can hold that pure place, it is the same place that finally happens when you break down and finally tell the truth to that fool. You know, you don't even care any longer what the repercussions are. It can't be any worse than what you have been experiencing. How many of you have had those circumstances? And when it is finally done, you feel so light, don't you? You don't care if the house falls down around you; you feel light. That is spiritual; that is the Spirit. You understand? Well, the Spirit then is starting to float. It is coming together again. And that is where the training on how to start applying pure power to what you are doing starts to become so important.

Now when we have resolution and we get to work on this in our life, how is the best way to work at it? Well, you have to stay conscious, you know. Now you can work eight hours of the day unconscious, but let's dedicate at least two hours of the day being conscious, being so conscious and so aware that we really influence the other eight hours. How many of you understand that we really do make an impact; that in those conscious moments I train you how to first release the energy from the first three seals, which is the grounding place here?

It is the first discipline you ever learn to do, to pull that (energy) up. I teach you the discipline, and it is proved by science that it works. I teach you to do that. So first you have to get out — out — of this plane and you have to be able to become mobile in the Spirit. So you have got to take the energy out of these places and they have got to come up here (upper four seals), and that is what C&E™ does. And then if they are up here, you can shoot on into the Void, and you should go there. You should allow yourselves to dissolve into nothing — to nothing. I taught you how to move to points of light, how to become mobile, and how to turn around and how to be literally in the Void itself. Remember, consciousness and energy are creating reality. This is our natural place, on Bliss. We are imagination. It is our product. So we have to go home to our natural self, our productivity of imagination, and the Void is where we dip into to be cleansed, to be purified, to be free of our attachment. And then when we are ready, when we are unattached, then we can move from the Void back into Point Zero again. Then we move from nothing into God — from nothing to God — and then from God we are at the pinnacle of our spiritual self. How long does this take? It is dependent upon the master. Some of you for an hour of blowing, you still won't get there; others of you two breaths, you are there. There is no standard. It is all individual. It all means how deep are you ingrained in the first three seals and do you want to get out of them. Some people don't like to get out of them. Some people want to feel tired in the mornings and they want to feel this and they want to feel that, so wherever their want is, is where they are.

So the closer we are in working spiritual, that that becomes our prerequisite, then we want to wash ourselves of this body, and we want to go and take a swim in nothing and then come back to the godhead absolutely pure. We are at the spiritual head. We are now in the Observer's point of view. We are getting now to take a look. As we start to fall from Point Zero and we fall into the fifth, fourth, and third levels — which we are going to do when we start imagining — we are going to come back to a very familiar place. This is the place that we created the opportunities in this life from, and we are going to fall into them. They are going to become very familiar. We are going to fall into those, and as the Observer we are going to allow the review of this life and what we want to accomplish to pass before us. The line of potential has already been set up for you to do. It is easy to do.

So what do you want to work on? You want to become unencumbered by your regret. Today it is regret and it will just come on you. And what you are to do, you take regret and you blow it out three times, just like the next thing I taught you to do, until it is clear. What will happen, you will know when you have affected it because there will be an incredible beingness of lightness in the fourth seal. Then what is going to happen is all of the people, places, things, times, and events that regret is attached to will start to pass in front of you, and each one of them you do the same thing with: You address it. You are now consciously addressing it.

Or it may be forgiveness. Remember, I told you you can tell who you have run into from the Plane of Bliss. Who you have made a deal with is going to be the most difficult person to forgive, and that is someone that agreed to play that part for both you and for themselves. And you are going to have to root it out and you are going to find them and you are going to have to address it. And when it comes to your parents — a most precarious relationship — you can no longer sit as judge over another person's actions. And so far in being the victim, you have been their tormentor. You can no longer sit in that place of power to hold them responsible and blame them for everything in your life. You are going to have to set them free, because only in doing that do you get the power back that is no longer rooted in blame. Then you are free. My God, you are free. And you can feel it as it starts to wash you.

And you may spend the next six months doing that same process until one day it is a no-thing. You will wake up in the morning; you will look out that window and it is not there anymore. God, be it that we are so empowered. The moment that we decide to do this is when we start the true spiritual path, because it means that we are reaching for a higher and loftier order to refrain the lower order of ourselves. How many of you understand?

Now how many of you see the value of taking thus what you have learned here by choice? Remember that. That is empowering to you. You came here by choice, to learn this by choice, so you already had a head start, as it were. How many of you see then the value of addressing the retrieval of your power, and how many of you can see clearly that attitudes, all based in the past, are where the power is locked up? And how many of you see the value of applying the discipline on a conscious level daily? How many of you can see the value and what it will bring as far as ripening fruit in your life? Do you understand that?

Now that is the means. That is how we are going to get it accomplished. The sticky part is we can take care of superfluous things that really aren't deep in our core. But we have got to reach down and find those issues that we talked about last night when I said to you, when you face now the fracturing of your God and heal it now, there will be nothing to look at in the light to come. Do you understand that? How many of you understand that? And with that we begin to see more that self becomes more identifiable.

It is really a God that once it is freed up from its encumbrances, its burdens of finishing up its creations, look what is standing in front of it that has an enormous wealth and revenue of reality to bring forth. And because it is not cluttered, it brings it forth quickly, not in a long period of wait.

The only reason you haven't gotten everything that you want is because you have too many things standing in the way of it. What you want is the future; what stands in the way is the past. How could you possibly make room for the future when you don't have any because it is cluttered by the past? And simply wanting it isn't enough. There has to be power to instigate it, power to imagine. How can you possibly imagine an unimaginable when your thoughts are always riveted to some little emotional trauma that you are feeling? You are not going to imagine the unimaginable if you are thinking about food. You are not going to imagine the unimaginable if you are sitting there suffering, if you are sitting there regretting, if you are sitting there wishing you could be someplace else. There is no room for it. There is no God for that to happen, so it won't work. That is why it is important that we do this by sheer choice because then we give ourselves enough power to follow through with what we are learning, don't we? We never, ever have follow-through if we don't want to be here. Runners don't come; nothing happens. You have to be open for it. In resolution we become clear of our past, and it is no longer there and we don't have energy on it. The master hunts it down and digs it out and roots it out and confronts it, confronts it for the sake of self.

It is really incidental what anyone else does. If you have made the move to retrieve your energy back, if you forgive them of something they can't quite let go of, then the rubber band bounces back in their face, doesn't it? And the energy of it comes back to you. Do you understand? Then it is their issue. So it has nothing to do with you anymore. And the way you will know that is that no matter how much they try, they won't arouse a response because there is nothing there to arouse. It is as if the incident never happened. Do you understand?

Now this makes for sort of an interesting day, doesn't it, when we continue to have resolution. And it should be your focus, because what are we going to talk about then? What do we have to talk about? It is sort of the same thing about what do you bring to the table to a master. Why do you think that you deserve to be in their presence? You don't, any more than what do you have to talk about if you have resolved the past with someone, someplace, something, some event? What do you have to talk about? There is nothing to talk about, is there? Are you understanding what I am saying here? That is when you know you are free of it. You don't have to have an appointment to go back and to rehash it. And sometimes people just like to dig up the past because it takes them out of the present backwards, because they think they have to do that. There is nothing to talk about, is there? That is when you know it is finished.

Now why languor there any more than why would a master want to sit there and talk about you to you? Why should they want to do that? Well, it is the same analogy. Isn't that what we want to be? Then why do we want or have the need to go back and have a conversation if the conversation was always based upon the dynamics of regret, resentment, failure, heartbreak, loss. And we could put that in all kinds of categories: jealousy, envy, betrayal, all of that. If we have resolved that in ourselves, there is nothing to talk about, is there? So what kind of conversation are you going to have? Are you going to try to regurgitate it and get it back up there and start working it back up in a frenzy so that you have an equal playing field? Cut its head off.

And this is what then becomes — as you are going to start to see very clearly this is called — enlightenment. You begin to see why you have grinding relationships. They grind on you, things that grind on you. You know why? Because it is over with and the only meeting ground that you have is to meet on those conditions. You don't know when to leave. You are a little confused on obligation here. You don't know when to give it up because the only thing it is giving you is this friction back here. You have grown. You don't fit anymore. Do you understand? That is when you walk away because that part has been played and it should be finished. Now what does that do? Is your human intelligence going to tell me does that mean that you just kick your friends out? They are not a friend; they are a God. You have no beholding to any God but giving them freedom. That is the way it is.

True friendship doesn't grind. It grows together. It is Gods growing in ultimate freedom together. There is no grind there. That is why I tell you there is no lack in it. So why are you going to go back, go back and keep rehashing it, because that is the only premise that you can meet equally upon? Tell me, my beloved people, is that resolution? No, that is regeneration of fracturing; that is what that is. We must walk away. We have nothing to talk about. Think about the basis of your conversations every day. What are they based on? It depends upon the person, doesn't it, the place, the thing, the event. It depends upon that, doesn't it? Well, why revisit it? It is over with.

Now there is grace in that. Isn't it grace to have a community of individuals as family but that in that greater spiritual family that there is no dominion, and that there is no agreeance in that family to meet on the conditions of any past, and that the family are each individual Gods — there are a forest of them that are growing — and that as the energy grows and changes in one, it is spread to everyone else? That is what we want.

You are confused about friendship. We made friends in paradise. We made friends only because they became closely associated with us in our journey here in integral parts and we have met them along the way all through our lives. And we have yet to meet many more who just wait for their part they are going to play in the potential that is yet to be unfolded, when the self has been healed. And they are yet to come too. How many of you understand?

In God we are one. We don't have to make that clear delineation. When you helped your neighbor, you didn't think whether they were your friend or not. You helped them because it was something urgent in you that did it. That is the sort of relationship I am talking about. Do you understand? How many of you understand? So be it.

INSTRUCTIONS ON THE PRACTICAL APPLICATION OF
THESE TEACHINGS

We have now a list here of four things: free will and choice, defining self, unfinished business, and resolution. I want you to take each of these four things and separately image them. For example, resolution is going to be a little difficult. I want you to draw pictures of it. I want you to draw a choice to be here. What does that look like to you up here?[3] What does free will and choice look like? Because if you have to think about that, then you are going to have a new definition on its meaning, its performance.

Defining self, well, how do we draw self? One of the most endearing symbols, of course, is we can use the blue star. But I like the heart, because God is love and the heart also sits by the fourth seal. So what if we start out with the premise that the self is a heart. Let's begin with that concept and then let's tear it apart. Let's fracture it and break it down and move bits and pieces of it over here to demonstrate that a piece of my heart, a piece of my God, is empowering my victimization, or over here my tyranny, or over here my greed, or over here something else. Then it is up to you to meticulously create your past and where your energy is locked up, and don't leave anything out. And take a piece of my heart to show that the only reason that that past is in place is because it has been sanctioned by divine energy.

And if we can show that effectively on a drawing, we get then a great visual — inspired by the master and followed through by the student on a great profound teaching — that if we can put it into a picture and draw it, it will be one of the greatest mandalas we will ever do because it is ours. It is real and it is about us and our journey.

Then we make another drawing on defining it. Well, defining it is going to encompass these two aspects right here. First we have got to get the energy back, so we start to see in picture after picture what we must do to bring our heart back and to put it

---

3 In other words, how do we visualize what we desire to manifest in the frontal lobe of our brain.

where it is now perfect again. And so we have to see measure by measure what we must do to get our energy back. And you must draw those pictures of it.

Those pictures then are going to also include number three, unfinished business, because the unfinished business is the encumbered self. It is the past self; it is the past unfinished. And we are going to have to draw pictures of those. What is unfinished? What have you started that you are in the midst of and can't get out of? Where are you still human and where are you not God? What seems to be in this life your great learnings? Where are your weaknesses? That will point to the unfinished business and the encumbered self. And I want you to draw not a caricature of some fictional entity but a caricature of yourselves and what lies unfinished. And however you depict that, it is going to be all right.

And then I want you to draw resolution. Perhaps the greatest way to draw resolution is to redraw the heart. Radiant and shining inside of an undersized body, there is an oversized heart that talks about a place of spiritual peace. Or perhaps we can draw the body and mimic it as the temple and that shining through its spires and its windows is the radiant light of spiritual power. Perhaps that is how we see it. Or perhaps we see resolution as the rolling up of some ancient scroll long left undone and seeing it rolling up. Or maybe we see then a cage opening and the flight of a dove. However we picture it, it must be a picture that is meaningful to us. And when we do it correctly, then we will understand our own journey. Mandalas should not be made en masse. They are personalized aspects of one's own journey. They should be created by ourselves. Do you understand?

It is important for the master to be a master but not an intimidating one. It is important for the master — whose greatest phenomenon will be the endless show of wisdom; that is the gift of the master — not to intimidate but to encourage. And I tell you, I do so ask that you feel encouraged by what you have learned today and that you feel that you are in a place that is safe enough for you to address this and that you are safe enough to be encouraged to want to change because, I tell you, you are never going to disappoint me. Oh, I have left these events and at moments had to go refigure my dream, keep downsizing it, but you are never going to disappoint me because I am not at a place that I could ever be disappointed, thank God. And so with that, you see, you have the freedom to be yourselves and the freedom to go and change, and my love is not going to change for you. It does not float in and out on the tide. It is not fickle. I love you. I desire that you feel comfortable enough to be inspired by who I am and what I am, even though you can't see me, because that is the kingdom of the Spirit. That is what is radiating out here in front of you that is so beautiful, and that perhaps in this ideal you will want it enough to be impassioned enough to take a stand and do it. I want to give you the room to do that. I just thought I should tell you that. So be it.

If you are utterly self-empowered, what any man says about you will never move you from your center and it won't fracture you. And then that is just a state of radiating love. And when you can still love them and bless them for their opinion, then you are a true kindred of the highest order. But you should not move down to their level for the sake of kindredship. You have to bloom in their midst in spite of them and for them. And I promise you that one sweet hour they will call upon you, and you will have the power in that need to do marvelous things. And therein lies the gift of being your own master.

I expect for you to apply diligently what you have learned here because it is given from a greater and more priceless place than this place that we know. Use it. If you don't, you have nothing to complain about when your life, instead of getting greater as a result of the teachings, seems to become diminished by them. So be it. Be happy. I love you.

O my beloved God,
I awaken to your presence
in the present.
O my beloved God,
deliver me from my past
and reclaim my kingdom.
O my beloved God,
bring forward in me
the great virtues
that I shall be deservant of.
O my beloved God,
God bless my body
and change my life.
So be it.
To life.

CHAPTER 5
DEATH AND THE REVELATION OF OUR
ULTERIOR MOTIVE

"When you are not creating the outrageous, you are going to get old and die. You know, our dream is to be free, people — free, free. That is the ulterior motive; that should be the motive — freedom."
— *Ramtha*

REVELATION OF OUR ULTERIOR MOTIVE

O my beloved God,
manifest straightaway
my created day,
and let me marvel
at my simple power.
So be it.
To life.

The Plane of Bliss, as it were, is that marvelous golden place that I taught you about to where after passing from the physical body, if you are fortunate enough to then go on — some don't go on, but if you are fortunate to go on — then after going to the light and being stripped, you then see everything from your conception in the womb to the day you passed because, remember, all actions are the direct result of conscious intent, aren't they? And so the action is actually the energy of conscious intent. So conscious intent becomes a living, viable concept through action, energy. When I tell you that consciousness and energy are inextricably combined, it is a truth, because in what you do is the doing of what you know, and we call that doing the experience of reality.

Now all of those experiences, you have logged up here (neuronet) and are in those bands that surround your body. Those bands then that surround your body are governed, if you will, by the soul, which you are going to learn more about today. And it is the soul in a light review that gives up her knowledge. In other words, the Book of Life is opened, and in opening the Book of Life one then sees what we cannot talk about in references of linear time, but we must say that the time that it takes to see this is a brief moment, yet a million years; that when you review this life lived here, you are both the Observer, the participant, and the receptor. Interesting, because that statement goes back to say that we are all things in our reality, including all people, and that those people and our affection — indeed that which is termed our magnetism to them — they are aspects of them that we are. That is where we are bound with them. Just as things in our reality are reflections of us, where we are is a reflection of our reality. So everything around us is really the action of the thoughts that we have up here (neuronet) being realized.

Now human beings have a problem because they see this in their life as something separate from what they are doing. They see themselves separate from the things in their life. They see themselves separate from the people in their life. In other words, we say that is a fine individual, and that individual is a sovereign God, but the fineness that we see in that individual is equal to the fineness that we are. So the reason that they are there in our life is that they reflect perfectly and exquisitely an aspect of ourselves.

Now the royal road to perfection is to trash our life of imperfection and fill it only with the highest pinnacle of reflection that we beseech in ourselves. To do otherwise is to live a lie — a hypocritical lie — or a life in which we have prostituted the lofty aspects of ourselves for the common denominator of simply being accepted or the common denominator of survival, which is certainly the human drama lived in the first three seals: sexual activity, birth, pain, power, and victimization. If we seduce our lives to live here and abash our loftiness here, then we are going to see exactly what that is in a light review. Now a master trashes his or her life and gets rid of the dross, the imperfect. It gets rid of the seduction, gets rid of the lie, the hypocrisy, the victimization, the tyranny, gets rid of all of it and puts only in its life — if only one bright and beautiful thing — that one bright and beautiful thing that mirrors exquisitely the apex of the master's ability to perform reality; that it is exactly what it is up here (neuronet).

Now you are all, as it were, simply learning to do that. That is what the talk last night was about, about change, but change in the context that it is fruitful, that it is letting your life fall apart and letting go the dross, the heaviness, working too hard to keep something together that does not bring joy, but only when you glue it together here (neuronet) forms a crack over here (our reality). How many of you understand?

Well, coming back to a light review, in a light review then what becomes exquisite is — because the way the soul plays it out in energy — the drama is more than three dimensions. It is actually seven dimensions because we are seeing it from the godhead, which is every player in the drama. We are seeing it from the Observer, which is the Spirit in the drama. And we are seeing it from the soul's perception, which is the personality-individual in the drama who thinks they are an individual. So we are seeing it from a holy place on all levels. And what begins to happen then is the whole life starts to play out in front of you. Every thought creates an action. You become the thought. You as personality feel the action. But then as the godhead, as the Spirit, you then are the reaction of that action to the whole environment, so you are experiencing it on every level. And isn't this where true learning is, is to actually know what our thoughts and actions do to others, other lifeforms?

This is a painful process, but the God in us holds us steady with love and keeps all of the multifaceted vision in place so that we don't break down and weep and get caught up in our individuality, which begins to see the drama to which it has created. It sees the suffering that it has created in another individual, in another lifeform. It sees the difficulty in the environment that it has caused for its selfish reasons because it wants to be acknowledged as an individual. It sees its power and how that power warps and bends. But that God, so loving, keeps all of our perspective together. It keeps the Spirit intact at this review, keeps the soul intact — which is the personality in this review — and the God; all stay together.

So in one moment we weep and we can hardly bear to see what we are looking at. But then the love of God that is all things flows right to us and gives us the strength to continue to view and to continue to view it from different reflections; otherwise you would never make it through it because it is enough in this life that you have created such regret. It is going to be a very difficult problem in the light review to see your intentions on others, the environment, lifeforms. And, subsequently, who is ultimately crippled? You are. And every one of you has had this happen before and you are going to have it happen again.

Once you get this well-rounded of what the great self really is, you really are something much more extraordinary than the isolated human being that you think you are. You are really more. Remember what I told you last night: What makes great initiates? What is it that makes great initiates? How many of you remember? Turn to your neighbor and tell them. Were you listening? Well, if you don't remember, then you didn't hear me. I am not going to repeat it because when we get together, you gain from this audience and from these teachings what you want to hear, and if you didn't hear that, it is not what you wanted to hear. So we will go on now. This individual body that seems so isolated is only a splinter of what you really are, because the great self is ultimately everything.

Now there are people who take that teaching and prostitute it in a very fanatical and unfortunate way. All is the one and the one is the all. Well, that is philosophy that has not been actualized except to a point that it is self-serving. How many of you understand that? If it is self-serving, it is actualized. If it isn't, it remains philosophical. So, in other words, people toy with a spiritual life because it is advantageous to them at certain times. It gives them an advantage rather than a stability to which is the bread of their life to which they live by. They have to have a greater understanding than that. So at the light then we begin to see how our intentions are profoundly affected in everyone and how, if we have ulterior motives in any way in any of our actions, always those ulterior motives are the overriding and underriding crime.

Ulterior motive — ulterior, the real motive behind the action — now that is where we are judged. We are never judged by surface; we are judged and weighed by our ulterior motive — ulterior. That is why being impeccable is such an important charge to the student. Be impeccable. Do not have an ulterior motive. If you do, get rid of all of the window dressing and take a look at it. That is what we must refine, not the window dressing but the ulterior motive behind our actions. Being impeccable is living from that ulterior place, because that is the engine of our life and it is the engine behind everything that we do.

And how common is this? Well, here is a common example: being nice to someone, exceptionally kind to someone, and it isn't for the sake of kindness; it has an ulterior motive to it. Now all of you have done that, and the ulterior motive is that you are wanting something from that person. You are, whether it is relationship on any of the levels, whether it gives you something. And usually the ulterior motive is really what you really want, and we use kindness as the chariot in which to get it. How many of you understand? You do? So now all of you understand ulterior motive, don't you?

It is the ulterior motive in us that we must refine, and we must refine it and it must be refined without emotion. In other words, it has already got an emotional attachment to it. To become its emotion then is to become it again. We must refine it without people, places, things, times, and events. When we do that then, we have changed the substance of our being. Now we become an impeccable person. We do exactly as our ulterior motive says. We are our ulterior motive. There is no confusing of signals out here. We are what we are.

The complication in a light review is that the ulterior motive — the ulterior motive — is what we as a personality get to experience. The deception is what we experience as the object of our ulterior motive, the deception being the unimpeccable intention. Do you understand? How many of you understand? In other words, we simply get to be the person that you are being kind to: that we get bottlenecked into giving something away; that we feel used; we feel betrayed; or we were a pawn in a game, and that when we gave of ourselves through true kindness, we realized that we were moved as a pawn to get something from us, that the kindness was disingenuous. So we get to experience that betrayal of a disingenuous move. How many of you understand? And how is it that you can understand that? Because there have been many of you that have been on that receiving side of a disingenuous person who gives you what you want in order to get something from you.

And we can get very basic with this and we can talk about then the power of women over men. Women have an absolute power over men because they rule a man's loins. They do; make no mistake about it. They do, and that is their power. Is it love? No, it is seduction. Well, what is seduction? An ulterior motive for something else, that the activity is given as a power to submit the male energy to a governing force that has a whole different agenda. Now this is where we get to see it in its rawest, most animallike nature, and we see the abuse of it. We see the ignorance of man — the ignorance and stupidity of man for his loins — that his brain is really in his penis, and we see a powerful and skillful operator, a femme fatale, and in the light we get to be all of that. We know what it is to be used.

You see, we can take that example then to levels of pain and suffering — pain and suffering. A suffering person has power over a well person. A powerful person — a demonstrative, powerful person — has charge over lesser people. That is why we have principalities and kingships and states and countries and local communities. Politicians are power over the people. It is the same seduction as we go back to men and women. How many of you understand? And for what? Because a man has an instinct. And we talked about instinct last night. Instinct is that evolution from the sensitivity of original polarization: We are sensitive to what we are not. Do you understand? We are sensitive to what we are not because when we get it, we become whole, and in wholeness we bear the children. We do not bear children out of unwholeness. In nature the law is very simple: We are attracted to what we are not, and when we come together with that which we are not, we form a unity of oneness. In oneness we have no polarization. When we have no polarization in oneness, we have analogical mind. In analogical mind the seed is planted in the womb. That is what the ecstasy of the experience is all about, that moment that your mind is in such a convulsion — your nerves have put you into such ecstasy — that in that moment of orgasmic experience there is no time; there is only the experience. The experience in and of itself is a powerful, energetic, analogical experience. That analogical experience is wholeness, that only from that can bring forth the child, the child in the womb, by natural law.

So why are men suckers? Because they are sensitive to what they are not, and their serpent power is awesome in their member because their sensitivity has led to an instinct that propagates the species. Men, at the bottom of their motives, have an instinct to propagate. That instinct to propagate is to propagate women in season to bring about more children. It is a struggle in the base animal for unity, or for God, in that moment that propagation can take place. Remember, here is propagation (first seal). Here is how we create: The polarities come together analogically. The idea that collapses into them becomes reality. How many of you understand? That is the highest order. That is the fountainhead of all nature. In its basic stratum it comes down to copulation and that is a powerful place.

And women are not motivated to the degree in instinct that men are for orgasmic experience. Their true motivation is not the orgasmic experience, but their true orgasmic experience is the powerful surrender of their mate. That is true orgasm. That is how women see it. Even though women orgasmically can be fulfilled, their modus operandi, their instinct, is the surrender of their mate. That is their greatest joy they get. That is why the oldest profession in the world is still around. That is why it has been such a success. They never get involved with these people, but they know how to bring them to their knees and get what they want out of them. What is it they want out of them? Money, gold, survival, luxury, a way to live. How many of you understand? You do?

Now so on the Plane of Bliss, whether you are a woman or a man, you are going to see that too. There is no editing of your life. You get to see all those times you were copulating behind the door. You see all the fantasies that you used to do that, because they tell a story and they tell a story of what it takes for you to be submissive. And fantasies warp and warp and warp and warp until finally we have children who are preyed upon because the warping fantasy in the sexual act creates the mental imagery, that orgasmic experience is the rape of innocence. And that is why we have predators today — never in my time, but today — who prey upon children because they have fantasized it into being. They weren't born with it; they made it. How many of you understand? You do? Excellent.

So this explanation goes back then to ulterior motive. So what is the ulterior motive behind every action? And when I taught you about the seven seals in the body — the seven levels in the body — and what energy pours out of them, what glands are activated, we can say clearly that the brain lives in those seals.[1] We can see very clearly the hardwiring of an individual because even though the brain is sitting up here, it is actually hardwired by this (first three seals), and we see so clearly the actions of an individual. And what is their ulterior motive? Their ulterior motive is the energy. That is what they really want.

So on the Plane of Bliss it is embarrassing to the individual aspect that is viewing it. It is not embarrassing to the Observer, and it is simply reporting the facts by the soul. So when you have to observe it, it is going to be embarrassing because the personality-individual of yourself is going to see it. And you know your God has been watching the whole time, and your soul has been busy — oh, my — and you think, well, this has got to get better. But we see then that the ulterior motive just keeps running through every one of your lives. Every day of your life there is that ulterior motive, and you are going, "Oh, my God."

And it is saying, "Yes?"

"This was really me? I thought my life was so adventurous and so fruitful. I thought all those people that I had in my life, it was jolly friendship and all of this and all of that. I really thought I had made much more progress."

I don't care who you are. You could have been the king of the world and had all the world as your subjects or you could have been a pauper down on the street of the cheesemakers begging for cheese, and the reality will be the same if every day the same ulterior motive existed. No matter how many people came into your life, how many people left your life, how many things you got, how many things you didn't get, they were all the result of a modus operandi of the personality self, the ulterior motive. And you will say, "My God, I thought I did so much good." Well, wasn't the ulterior motive behind that the same one that you used when you were twenty-two years old? How about when you were seven years old and you thought you were a victim? No, you became a victim and it gave you power. That is the ulterior motive behind that story.

So what did you end up with? Every day of your life was just

1 See fig. 2.

the same-ol'/same-ol', and it is embarrassing. And we see that as you start to get older, you get more fanatical and so you get more cunning in ways of control. In other words, you may soften in your old age, but has the ulterior motive left? No, because it was never looked at and it was never recognized for all of its equal parts in your life: all that it does, all the drama that it does, all the pain that it inflicts, and all the sickness that comes from it.

The light review is a horrific experience. That is the reason why the great Gods of old that became the priest Pharaohs, their object in their rule was at the end of their life that their ka and ba could be weighed on the scales of Osiris; that their heart placed on the scale and a feather placed on the other scale, that there would be no difference; that the heart, which is intention, is weighed against a feather. And so their entire time of rule was very precarious, and yet those who were ruled by them were blessed because they were truly a royal godhead struggling in a place of power to be the ultimate servant, the ultimate priest, the ultimate governor of people — the ultimate. There is no politician today whose soul could be weighed against a feather. And wouldn't that make a new interesting, political campaign motive? I will lead you, if you vote for me, in such a way that by the end of this life my intentions will be weighed against a feather. We would all vote for him. Now what does that mean? Without prejudice — prejudice — an important word. You see, there is a lot that goes on in this life review, and we begin to see its entanglements in ulterior motives, prejudice.

These beings, which I am endeavoring to teach you to be, then in a light review must understand that when you see it, that somewhere along the way it will become obvious that there was needed a meaningful change and the change was not necessarily an environmental change. It had to happen first within the self.

Love yourself and you will be free. What does that mean? That means dig in here; find out. What is your ulterior motive in degrees of your prejudice? Very simple. Men are turned on by beautiful women and beautiful women know that. They in fact strive to be that way so in turn they can have the power to have a place, to have commitment, to have children, to have survival.

And if it doesn't work out, they can always gussy up, as it were, and go after someone else — that is their place of power — and leaving the poor man holding his member. You laugh because it is the truth. Or the other way around: When the woman has gotten so comfortable and beauty begins to fade and the man's interest is no longer there, she exchanges it for guilt, children, and your rightful place. And he starts wandering off and looking for new excitement and so she is left holding the burdens. But she has got the power still; it is called guilt.

So he can go out and be submissive all he wants to, but it is his prejudice that has led him astray inasmuch as it is her prejudice that enticed him, kept him, or let him go. How many of you understand? Got to understand the rules of this game, and they are pretty sticky once you get down in here. You see all of that, and it is not a pretty sight. There is not a woman here that is going to be proud to see what she is about to see. And there is not a man here that is going to be proud of what he has to see. That is the reason we come back — that is the reason you come back here — because the only way you are ever going to be released from the plane of Terra and the human experience is to conquer it. And how do we conquer it? By the revelation of our ulterior motive and the degrees of prejudice at which we use it. That then tells the whole story.

So what then do we glean from this very painful, yet most extraordinarily, revealing life? Why, the soul is looking at it in sheer fascination. "I can't believe you did all of this." You know, when it is over with, the soul is your best buddy. "I can't believe you did that."

"Well, you kept me up late at night."

"And I kept you up late at night because I kept bothering you right here."

"Oh, yeah, I remember that."

"Well, you know, when are you going to learn? You know, we have been on the same page for all these days that you had this life. I have written this. I am bored. I have written the same thing down every day."

Well, once it is over with, you get a very clear picture of how primitive you are or how advanced you are. And even the most advanced think they are primitive. That is so beautiful because it is that longing to return to splendid perfection that they come back and they bring back with them gifts of that ennobled existence. And their energy just can't be found in the normal ulterior-motive realm. They are just somewhere else. They are utterly and totally unique. Now that is a substantive person.

So what happens on the Plane of Bliss? Well, after that exhausting life review you go and you get to eat for two or three thousand years anything and everything you want — you know, lots of wine, goat cheese, olives, sweetmeats, turkeys, you know, all of that sort of thing — and then this beautiful kingdom that you get to dwell in is called the Plane of Bliss. It is the golden, beautiful, exquisite plane called paradise. And you get to go to school there. And in school you are essentially studying, as it were, the very origins of your difficulty, and you study them in a way that the light review showed it to you. You are actually studying the friends that you had that you perpetrated this on and they perpetrated it on you — the lovers you had, the children you had, the family you had — and that is what your school is about. But you can never move to a higher school or a greater hall of learning there unless you know how to ask the right question. And so all you are really doing there is learning about the unity of God as a whole, and that God expressed through the individual is impacting the whole of what God is and the greatness of what it is. And we learn that.

Then we go off and you have what is called the long season of contemplation, and the long season of contemplation on this beautiful place can be anyplace that is tranquil to your mind. For example, whatever you call tranquility will appear instantaneously in front of you. To some it will be a tranquil lake, quicksilver ripples on the top reflecting weeping willows and an occasional flower drifting by on a slow, lazy summer day. Now that is contemplation. And there you are going to meet other beings who have the same likeness, and that same likeness is that they manifested the same sort of place, and you get to share that with them. If you want absolute solitude, you will get absolute solitude: same place, no visitors. Everything is respected there; nothing is cast out. Or if you see that your place of contemplation is a high mountain place with the great white snow, so it will happen. If your contemplation is riding a great steed in the throes of battle and that is where your energy and your adrenaline are at its greatest, then you get that whole scene.

If your place of contemplation, wherever it is, is around children, then you get to be around little children there. And why are they staying little children? Because that is the place of their greatest innocence to where they can contemplate, so they come and come back to Bliss as little people, little children. And they really died perhaps in this experience when they were eighty-two or one hundred and forty or fifty-two years of age or twenty-nine. And yet where do they rest? As a child, and maybe you want to seek their audience. And in that they are learning to be that simple, that when they come back it is their simplicity that overrides everything. And in simplicity we do not have ulterior motives; we are simply simple. How many of you understand?

Do you understand? Let's take a moment and turn to your neighbor and explain what you have learned so far before we go any further. See if you have been listening. What a beautiful conversation you are having, aren't you? Now we are getting somewhere. That is the kind of exchange that you need to enrich your life, and if you weren't having a very fruitful one, well, that is self-explanatory too, isn't it? This is beautiful. This is how you are getting it. If you are able to articulate it and understand, you start uncovering your own ulterior motive. How many of you see that? Now listen. Ulterior motive is the thunder passion in your life. That is where your real passion is. That is where your real powerhouse is. When you uncover that, then you have uncovered the great energy storehouse of your life. And when you can bring it to the surface simply, then we can do marvelous things with it.

That is the reason why whenever I address an audience, you can hear particle dust hit the floor when I talk about sexuality. You know, we are looking at ulterior motives here, and everyone has rapt attention: money, rapt attention; or extraordinary phenomenon, rapt attention. It is ulterior motives. And isn't it interesting that all three of those are used somewhere on different levels? They absolutely are, aren't they?

Well, this is the reason that you go to the light: We have to review what truth did you bear in that life. And the whole problem is the only reason that we are doing this is to review our progress in making known the unknown and where we are so trapped that we cannot expand.

FREEDOM FROM THE DECEIT OF THE PAST

You know, our dream is to be free, people — free, free. That is the ulterior motive; that should be the motive — freedom. Freedom from what? Having to use anyone, any person, place, thing, time, or event to become it; just to be it. The mastery is to wrestle it out of people, places, things, times, and events, isn't it, because aren't people, places, times, and events what a light review is all about? It absolutely is.

Think about it: This very moment millions of souls are crossing over and getting a light review. Now there are a lot of fireworks going on somewhere, aren't there? Millions of them are passing right now. Someone just died a few miles from here. They are gone; they are out of here. They are on their way. Someone else got shot not too far from here in a city, and you know what they are doing? Why, they have just slipped out of their body and they are turning around looking at that phosphorescent skin laying there and they are panicking. You know why? Because that is all they ever thought they were. They are trying to get back in a brain that is no longer firing. And they are trying to get back in the blood in the body to where the blood isn't flowing. They can't; they are moving in and out of a dead body. It is gone. Well, what are they doing? Their whole modus operandi was a physical life. Why, the reason that they got shot was because it was all about physical dominance. That is what it was about. How enlightened is that soul? That is not very enlightened.

Or a woman dies of rape. What kind of fantasies did this woman have? Where did it ultimately lead? What kind of a flirt was this woman? What kind of an enticer was this woman? What was the ultimate fantasy? And now it is out of its body. What is its worth? What is your worth if you don't have a body? Look at the person you are with. If you didn't have this body and you were in another body, would you still be with them? Think about that, because it is coming. Age and time do that work wonderfully. Excess does that work wonderfully. Think about it. And if you look at your partner, the person that you say that you love, and if they looked any other way could you still love them? If you can't and couldn't, then who are you? Why, you are nothing more than a body. What is going to happen to you? You are going to have a lot of problems.

Remember, not everyone that passes gets a life review. A lot of them are stuck between here and the moon. They are floating around above the ground. They are in the fog. They are in the atmosphere. They are the moon shadows at night. They hang around bars and taverns. They hang around places of excess. They attach to you when you get onto their level. People, not everyone gets a life review. Most of them can't find it because their ulterior motive was all about the body. And I tell you this because I don't care who you are in this audience, and I don't care how beautiful you are or how ugly you are, if that has been your ticket, you are a loser — a loser.

The great school of ancient wisdom is not about ancient bodies. It is the development of the invisible, the substantive aspect. We get there by understanding the modus operandi, the ulterior motive. When we have built spiritual substance in ourselves is when we love who we are. That is transcendent of the body. Those are the lofty ones that get to go on, because what they really are is that substance and they can detach from the body and have no other dealings with it. Easy; why? Because most of the days of their life they are out of their body, meaning not that they have vacated it but their thought process isn't spent solely on it; that during their everyday life they are thinking in terms of different realms. Their passion has not to do with the body; it has to do with life. It has to do with God, and that is manifestation. To come down from that lofty high and to have to fix the body is a downer for these people. It is a downer to them.

This is not an ancient school about bodies, but it is a school that trains the great self to be dominant over them. And it is that great self that ultimately is going to be reviewing this life: this life, this body, a garment in the closet of lifetimes.

And what was the fruitful experience? Remember why we are here. Remember why we are here: We are to make known the unknown; not to hold onto the known but to be the unknown; not to be the known but to be the unknown. That is why we are here, people. That is why the Spirit starves in the cadaver. That is the reason why the personality can't get a clue of what it is and it suffers so much, because it is so based upon flesh and blood and bones and the way genetics threw you together.

Now I know that this is philosophical, premium stuff. But the fact of the matter is, it isn't practical in day-to-day life unless one has a passion to understand its truth enough to be able to live it. And therein they get the keys to the kingdom of heaven because it is something that must be lived. You are not the sum total of the mass to which you are made from. You are not it. And for you to sit out here and say, "Well, this is just the way that I am," fine. When you get tired of being just the way "you am," come see me. We can fix it. We can change, because the nature of us is the divine.

Now there are so many variables that work into this life review. I mean, there is not a person in this audience that isn't going to be brought to your knees when you see it, because there is nothing in your life that you have done that is without shame. You have done many things with shame and most of it when you knew better. That is when the true shame comes and that is when the working — the working — of that conscious action starts to fix the personality and fixes the hardwiring up here, and then you are going to find it is a very difficult hole to crawl out of it. But it is about rewiring. It is about today you are learning knowledge, to which that knowledge will become apparent in your life when you have infused it into your neuronet and start to make that knowledge the goal of your thinking process every day. Then we will see the results of this knowledge. Now we are starting to see the action of the divine starting to take place in your life: fruitful change, miraculous.

There is no one in this audience who cannot change — no one. Now what things do you change? Think about if you were to review your life right now. What if today we got to spin out those bands and you got to see everything from every point of view — from the godhead, from the spiritual point of view, from the soul personality — what would you change today? Because if you know the answer to that, then you don't have to die today and be reborn ignorant again. If you know the answer to what is it that you would change in yourself — when you are everything, everyone, and all the environment in your life, what ulterior motive are you going to change — if you know the answer to that today, people, you will never have to die in this life. People die because they don't know the motive of their existence. That is it. And that, when we look at the other side, becomes so apparent. This is where the training of being the Observer is so marvelous, because the Observer becomes detached from the personality and the emotional body. It can observe from every angle one's intention — intention — the arrow, where it goes. It can observe it and see it and be it at all places.

And to be detached and be the Observer is difficult. And why? Because we ourselves are most afraid of our own criticism — we ourselves. It is you who are afraid of your Observer. You can deceive other people but you can't deceive yourself. And you are afraid to switch modes because the moment you do, you are going to see what you have really been. And it is from that point of view that the light has its most profound effect. How many of you understand? You see? Know yourself and you will be free. When you can become the Observer and observe your actions this life and find out your modus operandi, your ulterior motive, it also means that the personality will become criticized. It becomes threatened, and it will. As the Observer you can freely admit it. The moment you switch back and become the personality, you are going to suffer emotion from it. You are going to cry and weep and deny — it is all your imagination — but these are the qualities that do the review, and indeed these are the qualities that allow us to go on to the Plane of Bliss.

But you don't have to die to do that. You can do it here. What is then the process of that? Long contemplation and being acutely aware of how we are with different people; what is our agenda? How are we with nature; what is our agenda? How are we in our work; what is our agenda? How are we in our family; what is our agenda? What is it? How are we in our sexual life; what is the agenda here, the real agenda? Look at it. Don't be afraid to look at it, and when you do and you can find it, I tell you, beautiful people, it will become real clear.

And it is simple; it is not complex. You don't need a psychiatrist to figure this one out, and they never do figure anything out; you just need to know for yourself, and it will all be individual. The moment you know that, that is the one thing we must dissolve in the crucible. It is that motive; that is what goes into the crucible and must be dissolved. That is the place we change, right there, because to change surfacely is not to change its nucleus.

We can change surfacely. We can switch partners, like so many of you do, go through each other like flies. You know, you can switch partners. You can move, move around a lot. You can get rid of things, get new things. You can go out and throw away the old clothes, buy new clothes; throw away the new clothes, get old clothes. You know, it doesn't matter. It is all surface. But that doesn't affect the nucleus. The nucleus of you and your job here is the ulterior motive. That is what must be changed. When it is changed, it in turn will affect profoundly the entire environment around you. That is when the dross of your life starts to drop. And here is the true test.

You know, God doesn't test you. And everyone here uses the words, "Well, it is a test." Well, there is no test. There is no one keeping score somewhere; it is simply choice. And if you call choice a test, then so be it. But, you see, there are no tests; there is just choice and opportunity. The moment everything starts to fall apart because you have disrupted the nucleus and changed it — if you start suffering from that outward effect of that nuclei change in the self — the temptation is to go paste it and put it back together because you can't handle, personalitywise, emotionally what you have done in a loftier venue, the Observer. You can't handle emotion because the Observer is not emotional, and you are not going to know what you have done until you move back into the personality. Then all hell breaks loose. Then you see; you see?

Now everyone says, well, it was a real test. Now what am I going to do with this? Am I going to run back? Well, I can't bear it. I feel such guilt, and I don't want that person to have this person. I can't fathom him sleeping with this person. I can't fathom it. I can't tolerate it. I can't this; I can't that. I can't lose my children. I can't lose my home. I can't lose my point of view. I can't. I can't. I can't. I can't. And, you see, what has started in a nuclear reaction coming from Point Zero into a biophysical reaction is — it isn't a test — can you carry it all the way through and let it fall apart? Can you do that without pasting it and putting it back together?

Now here is the warning that I always tell you: Don't go back to your past. That is exactly what I mean by that. Once we have changed, don't go change the change. Don't go glue it back together. The temptation is because you are emotional, personality creatures is to do exactly that and to draw the line in the sand, territorially speaking. And so what happens? You go back to your past through emotion. What is emotion? Guilt, shame, fear, insecurity, envy, threat, power. Those are all the emotions that cause the swing all the way back. And if you hold that emotion and go back and paste it together, then we are going to have a problem, aren't we, because the nucleus change that has occurred is not reflecting the physical one that has now been put back into place, is it? So now we have great contention.

Some of you might know this, that when you went back to your past and you did paste it up, it was never the same. Why wasn't it the same? Because something fundamentally had changed. Even though you went back and put it back together, there was a change that happened. And what happens in those situations? All emotions become heightened — heightened. Why? Because the ulterior motive is changed; that is why. An emotion has to stand on its own. It doesn't have the fundamental support of the ulterior motive any longer, so emotion is hysterical. Turn to your neighbor and explain. How many of you are learning? You are? Are you enjoying this little dissertation? Aren't you beautiful. All of this understanding is a prelude now to an action graphic that you are going to draw a little bit later today to understand then what is intent coming into reincarnation. We are going to understand that.

BEING AN HONORABLE AND IMPECCABLE PERSON

Now here is where I want to pause for a moment and let's make mention of then what is honor. Everyone — everyone — cherishes that word honor; to be honorable, isn't it? Everyone wants to be somehow honorable. It seems to be a noble and befitting way to be. But I will tell you what honor is. Honor is when you don't play games and simply are your ulterior motive. That is being impeccable. That is not necessarily beautiful, but that is impeccable. That is being honorable. That is being up-front and the way that it is. There is no mishmash. There is no gray area. There is no maybe. There is no hot and cold: one day you are on, the next day you are off. You know, there is no instability. When you are what you are at this time in your time, as it is known, that is being honorable and indeed impeccable. To waver off of that is to be unimpeccable. How many of you understand? And so do we not then find truth in the axiom that there is honor amongst thieves? Isn't there? Yes. And cannot then be your enemy — the enemy, your most awesome enemy — closer to you than your lover? Absolutely. Absolutely.

This then is what I call an impeccable person. That impeccable person, I will jolly well enjoy their presence. And I am very picky about who gets into my presence, you know, because you always have to deal with the soap opera with people who have ulterior motives and you are always having to deal with them. Like a soap bubble, they are changing colors and they are filmy and they never really want to really know. So you always have to entertain them or not talk to them at all because they are not impeccable people. They are not who they are. They are pretenders. They are an imitation. They are not genuine. And there are a lot of disingenuous people sitting in this audience hearing this message. You are disingenuous because you don't live in your life what you have learned here. You are disingenuous because you take what you have learned here and use it as a pretense while all along coveting a rotten nature, covering your ulterior motive. That is why you are not consistent in this school.

Now you can be consistent as a scoundrel out there. Scoundrels find their cards all the time and lofty people don't find their cards all the time, and vice versa.[2] You understand, it is the ulterior motive. Where are you with this? And so these soapy, soap-opera people are never genuine. And genuine beings I enjoy, I engage, because with them we have a true interaction, for they have nothing to hide. And so when we engage, they engage from a truthful place. When they learn, they learn truthfully — not soapy learning — real learning. Now how many of you understand that?

This is no different then than at the light, because at the light then everything is uncovered and the soap opera is shown right in front of you, and you are all players and you see how disgusting that is. And the one thing that you walk away from it feeling, as the personality aspect of the great self, is that you dishonored yourself — flat-out dishonored — and as a result manipulated other people because of that, were insincere and untruthful.

Now I used to call lies creative truths, and they still are creative truths. Creative truth is the avoidance of the motive. When you are what you are, you never, ever have to protect what you say, and you never have to worry about what you say because all of your thoughts are written — written — in the energy around you, just as if they were written in the sky above. And you never have to worry. If one hundred thousand years from now those thoughts come back to you, that ulterior motive comes back to you, you will feel no shame for it because the motive was not disingenuous. It was a motive evolving. It did not make a lot of people succumb to it. It wasn't usive and it wasn't abusive; it was genuine. That is true evolution.

Now if you dig up fossil remains of present-day animals, you will see that there is a modulation, a change, in who they were ten million years ago versus who they are today. If we look at those remains, we do not say, oh, that is bad; that was a mistake; we are much better off today with this one. You do not see evolution in those terms. You simply see the fossil from where it was in its past to where it is today, and you see through geological age the evolution of that species. And we celebrate that it changed. It gives us hope for ourselves. But we never look at what it was

2 See Fieldwork™ in the Glossary.

and condemn it. We only do that if we are disingenuous.

When we look in the light and we see, if we are honorable people we are going to see our honor. We are going to see that we lived forthrightly what we were and had clear boundaries about it. It is going to become obvious who we were and how it affected everyone. Most certainly it took unique people to live in your life as an honorable person, but by the same token you to them were the spark of honor in their life. So what are you going to view as God when you look at the consequences of every action in the light? Think about this. Then you are going to become the person who you mirrored to them that honor, and in that moment you are going to feel their honor. It may not be the epic point of evolution, but it is the point of evolution of that life. It solidified; it was real.

So in honor, those that are around us can only be with us because we are that way. And they can only love us because they love in us what they love in themselves: that poignant truth, that honor, that nobleness. And it may be backward but it is real. It is tangible. It is substantive. It is not illusionary.

Illusions: When you love an illusion, it says that you are only one yourself. That is why it never lasts. Relationships based upon illusionary love are an illusion and both participants are illusionary. They never last. It is like the vapor; when the sun hits it, it dispenses. When real heat comes into the relationship, it dispenses because it is an illusion. It is ulterior motive to ulterior motive and soap in between. Nice lubricant.

COULD IT BE THAT YOU ARE ALREADY DEAD?

Now this I am telling you: You have seen before — many times before or you wouldn't be here — and you are going to see it again. What I am telling you — and when you see this in life review, when you see today this is the grand, grand booby prize of this school — is that you get to live it over again, after you die, every class you ever attended. A little extra on the side for when you cross over. You see, right now — listen to me; now can you think this way? — right now you are viewing what you are doing right now from the other side. You are viewing it. It is already happening. You are the entity being viewed. Think about this. Don't get linear with me. Think about this. Right now you are dead and on the other side, and you are viewing this life. And it is happening right now, people — right now.

So what are you hearing on the other side? Yes, what are you hearing? What am I telling you? What are you thinking? Well, you are seeing it right now. It is unfolded. It is in your time flow. What am I telling you? What are you hearing? It is happening right now. You are watching this and you are already gone. All you are is remembering this participation. Could that be? Could it be? Now wait a minute. Is this the only reality you are living in or are you a multiple-reality being? If you are, you are already there and you are living what you are viewing right now. Remember, in God we are eternal. We are the past, present, and future simultaneously. When we are a human being, we are only the past struggling for a future, but in God it has already happened. Turn to your neighbor and explain.

Are you thinking? Are you thinking? Are you visualizing without time? Can you do that? If you can do that, you are what great masters are made out of, because they also possess the ability to disenfranchise time; that means to actually remove time as the dominant factor.

So let's go over this again. Could it be that you are already dead? Yes? It is true. Am I speaking to an audience of the underworld? Why not? Why can't you entertain that? Because if you can entertain that, then you are very loosely tied to your body. If you can't, you are going to have problems. Why can't you entertain that, that maybe you are really already dead and maybe this class that is being held is being held right now in the light review and this is one of the classes that you are attending? Keep scratching. You are going to get it.

Why not? Now what kind of a Master Teacher would I be if I told you that it wasn't so? This is how a master God thinks. Don't you understand I have just given you a dynamic secret — a dynamic secret — and that I have just made you a dimensional mind. I have just made you for a moment become a dimensional mind. And all along you may think that you are really alive. Maybe you are just dead, reliving a moment in the light. Don't you give me that business that, oh, that is not real. It is more real than you think this place is.

You are in school today. Why are you here? You are learning about the very thing that you are watching right now. You are learning about it. And you want to know, "How do I flip this? What do I do with this? Where do I put this?" It is wonderful; you have no place to put it. You have no place to put it; that is even more beautiful. If you put it over into your imagination, then it doesn't serve you. If you put it over here and just say it is a potential trick question, it will serve you but, you see, both have not been integrated.

Here is the idea: You are already dead. You are in the light and you are viewing this and you have come back and you are reliving this experience. Why? To understand the key of being red in the rainbow, to understand why are you having to do this again and, when I find the key, what can I do with that.[3] Tomorrow morning, if you find the key, you have flipped back into this life from being dead. You have flipped back into this life, and you have a new agenda. You have been reincarnated in an immortal body, because we are going to talk about immortality in context of the living, vital energy called idea. Turn to your neighbor and explain.

Now I want to remind you that between life and death there is no distinction in the Spirit. There is none. There is no life or death in the Spirit; there is only life and death to the individual personality and its cohabitating body. But to the Spirit and the godhead, there are no clear distinctions between the two. But I want to remind you that what I have told you could be happening right now and is — is. So why are you here? To learn something, a key, understanding something, to understand a key, a bit of knowledge, to know what to ask, to know what to suddenly turn on and to know, because this is what the Plane of Bliss is all about.

You see, there is a real reason why true masters gain the stewardship over the physical. They die to the physical, first off.

---

3 Being red in the rainbow is an expression that explains the common inability of individuals to recognize their own limitations and shortcomings. When we are red in the rainbow, we can see every other color but red.

Somewhere in their initiation they die to the physical. What that means is that they are no longer concerned with the physical. They die to the world. They are reborn into the life of an initiate, a master, where there are no clear lines of life and death. And they can flip right into such a scene like this and review it and relive it over and over and over without ever having to die in the body.

Who is to say of all the potentials that exist, do you know that you cannot exhaust the ideas, the things that can be manufactured from atoms? You cannot even exhaust the probabilities of potentials that they can become. And all they are is coagulated ideas in the form of energy. You cannot exhaust it. You cannot think long enough in a lifetime to make them become everything that they have the potential of becoming. So who is to say that you have not flipped already back into this (Plane of Bliss)? And let's say this: Who is to say that you are one of those masters on the other side that is this close — this close. You have flipped back into this time. You have died to this life review. You are reviewing it — you are reviewing it — something you have missed. You have the power to do that.

Why then would you want to do that without going through the ability just to die? Why not give up this physical body? I mean, it is certainly a trap. It is a prison. I don't care how you look at it; it is a prison. Why not just give it up? You have the power to leave your body, to get out of here. Why then do real masters learn the art of longevity and immortality? Why? There must be a reason that they want to preserve this. And it isn't about their looks and it isn't about how many orgasms they can have and it isn't about how much food they can eat. They want to preserve it. It is not about how curvaceous or uncurvaceous; it has nothing to do with appearance. They died to that a long time ago because when they were born spiritual, they could love nothing but spiritual.

Now why would they want to preserve this? Why are they here? Why are you suddenly — some of you, not all of you I can tell you, not all of you; only a few of you are real masters — flipping back into this death scene? You are on the other side and you are living this. Why are you doing that? Because there is something you are going to know about yourself that you are going to have a passionate fire about, and that when you unlock ulterior motives you will have unlocked the power of the nucleus. You have absolute radiant, atomic energy. That is what is locked inside ulterior motive. Why then would you want to flip back into this scene that you are dead, viewing this in an incarnation? What would be the reason? Because if you can gain in this school, in the light, something that you are revisiting over and over, you are going to pull out of it the question, that only you have the answer to, that is going to unlock immortality in the body on the other side of this light review. And you want that.

Why do you want that? Because in order to make known the unknown, the immortality of the body is as much a mystery and a desire as any desirous, seductive food or entertainment to the lifetime of the body. We want to master the longevity of the physical, and only a powerful Spirit can do that. Only an enlightened being can do that. Only an entity with fortitude and will and intent can do that. Why? Because that is the true manifestation of the image of God, and it is through such beings that the great and marvelous deeds of God are revealed.

All masters are immortals. Does it mean then that they are caught forever in this body? Just however they want it; they have it on their own terms. They can flip that body into its rainbow body, into its golden body, into its Blue Body™, all the way back to its flesh body, into its lightbody, into its infrared body. They are lord of the entire ladder, of all dimensions. They never have to die; they have conquered it. And what comes with such a powerful spiritual intent? Why, the seeds of immortality itself. We cannot have an ulterior motive of immortality from a spiritual intent and not have the substance of it in our life.

There are some of you here that have gone backwards in time and are dead, reviewing this moment that happened a long time ago right now, working to understand what was not understood before — knowing it is an opportunity — that in this moment if in the light you are participant, Observer, and God, then that master brings back to this the entire self on all levels. And that self has no problems seeing this conjunction of time happening right here. They have no problem seeing it. A truly physical person will have a lot of problem understanding this, not a spiritual person because to them manifestation has nothing to do with its coagulation in time but has everything to do with its coagulation in thought. That is a spiritual person; a material person, just the opposite.

So I already know who is going to come out of this school. I already know my place with them. I already know; that is a certitude. But in revisiting this, does revisiting this then afford what wouldn't have come out the opportunity to bloom from it? Yes. Why do we know that? Because if that were not true, there would be no law of incarnation. There would not be reincarnation; there would not be the transmigration of the Spirit and the soul, and yet there is. Why? Cannot time double up on itself? Of course, it can. And what, I tell you, bends time? Mind; that is what bends time. Mind is the subject of God, that between the two, time exists only.

When we revisit the light in this life, are we given another opportunity to polish, to improve, to pick up what we didn't hear the first time, what we didn't feel the first time? If we revisit the same situation with improved knowledge, is the scene going to change? Always. That is the law of making known the unknown. So how many times do we have to go back to the light and review the same source material from the soul until we change it? We understand that knowledge and its integration into mind is the fire that changes it. When we revisit our weakest point with knowledge is when we change it.

How many times have you heard this message from me today? Does anyone dare to guess? How many times have you revisited this session in the light? How many times has this teaching happened? This day, the way you look, the way your neighbor looks, how many times have you seen this? Don't you get a feeling of déjà vu a little bit? This is the only time today ever happened? You think this is it, this event came and went? How many times have I stood up here and given this event? How many times have I taught beginners? How many times have I taught about Point Zero and the great vast nothingness — how many times — in your short career in coming to this school? Well, I have done today more than those times. I keep saying the same thing. I vary it. Why do I vary it? Because you have been varied. You are ready to hear. You are ready to see. You are ready to feel. If you are not, you are dead; you are dead.

I want you to draw a picture — put it down in an abstract graphic — seeing this in the light, and that you are already dead and that you are about to be reborn, and you thought you were alive all along. You draw that. Draw it and color it. Why do I want you to do that? Because I want this knowledge to be up here (brain). Why? Because at the end of the day you are supposed to know something that the soul knows. And unless you can draw it and color it, you are not going to know it and you are going to have to revisit this day again. So be it.

THE VOID, POINT ZERO, THE MIRROR CONSCIOUSNESS, AND OUR HUMAN INCARNATION

God bless,
embrace,
and allow
all the voices
of my total self
to be heard
and be seen.
So be it.
To life.

Sit down. Now I want you to take out those drawings and I want you to turn to your neighbor as the Observer and explain the drawing. You may begin. Remember, I told you last evening that I was going to have to consult with some sort of dictionary in order to endeavor to explain nearly an unexplainable? And we have done a marvelous job so far today. It still is wanting, because the words are very much needed to blow the mind. You need to have your perspective blown in order to understand the last statement I said to you. So I have chosen the words well. I endeavor to keep this very simple so that you can grasp what it is that you are here to understand again.

FIG. 1: THE BRAIN

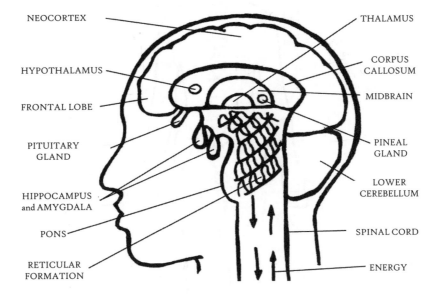

NEOCORTEX

HYPOTHALAMUS

FRONTAL LOBE

PITUITARY
GLAND

HIPPOCAMPUS
and AMYGDALA

PONS

RETICULAR
FORMATION

THALAMUS

CORPUS
CALLOSUM

MIDBRAIN

PINEAL
GLAND

LOWER
CEREBELLUM

SPINAL CORD

ENERGY

This is the original two-dimensional caricature-style drawing
Ramtha used for his teaching on the function of the brain
and its processes. He explained that the different aspects of
the brain in this particular drawing are exaggerated and
colorfully highlighted for the sake of study and
understanding. This specific drawing became the standard
tool used in all the subsequent teachings on the brain.

FIG. 2: SEVEN SEALS THAT CONSTITUTE SEVEN LEVELS OF CONSCIOUSNESS IN THE HUMAN BODY

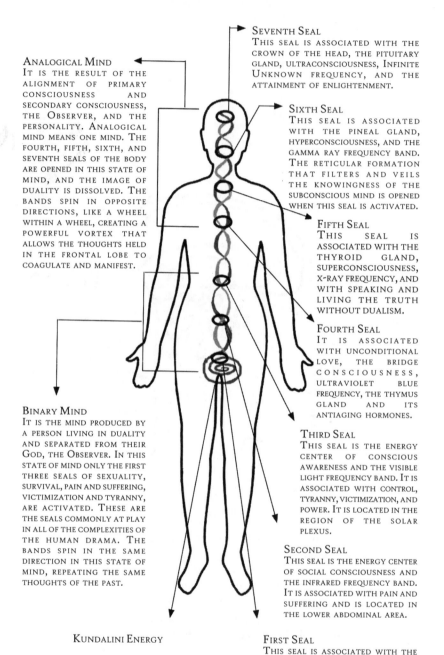

SEVENTH SEAL
THIS SEAL IS ASSOCIATED WITH THE CROWN OF THE HEAD, THE PITUITARY GLAND, ULTRACONSCIOUSNESS, INFINITE UNKNOWN FREQUENCY, AND THE ATTAINMENT OF ENLIGHTENMENT.

ANALOGICAL MIND
IT IS THE RESULT OF THE ALIGNMENT OF PRIMARY CONSCIOUSNESS AND SECONDARY CONSCIOUSNESS, THE OBSERVER, AND THE PERSONALITY. ANALOGICAL MIND MEANS ONE MIND. THE FOURTH, FIFTH, SIXTH, AND SEVENTH SEALS OF THE BODY ARE OPENED IN THIS STATE OF MIND, AND THE IMAGE OF DUALITY IS DISSOLVED. THE BANDS SPIN IN OPPOSITE DIRECTIONS, LIKE A WHEEL WITHIN A WHEEL, CREATING A POWERFUL VORTEX THAT ALLOWS THE THOUGHTS HELD IN THE FRONTAL LOBE TO COAGULATE AND MANIFEST.

SIXTH SEAL
THIS SEAL IS ASSOCIATED WITH THE PINEAL GLAND, HYPERCONSCIOUSNESS, AND THE GAMMA RAY FREQUENCY BAND. THE RETICULAR FORMATION THAT FILTERS AND VEILS THE KNOWINGNESS OF THE SUBCONSCIOUS MIND IS OPENED WHEN THIS SEAL IS ACTIVATED.

FIFTH SEAL
THIS SEAL IS ASSOCIATED WITH THE THYROID GLAND, SUPERCONSCIOUSNESS, X-RAY FREQUENCY, AND WITH SPEAKING AND LIVING THE TRUTH WITHOUT DUALISM.

FOURTH SEAL
IT IS ASSOCIATED WITH UNCONDITIONAL LOVE, THE BRIDGE CONSCIOUSNESS, ULTRAVIOLET BLUE FREQUENCY, THE THYMUS GLAND AND ITS ANTIAGING HORMONES.

BINARY MIND
IT IS THE MIND PRODUCED BY A PERSON LIVING IN DUALITY AND SEPARATED FROM THEIR GOD, THE OBSERVER. IN THIS STATE OF MIND ONLY THE FIRST THREE SEALS OF SEXUALITY, SURVIVAL, PAIN AND SUFFERING, VICTIMIZATION AND TYRANNY, ARE ACTIVATED. THESE ARE THE SEALS COMMONLY AT PLAY IN ALL OF THE COMPLEXITIES OF THE HUMAN DRAMA. THE BANDS SPIN IN THE SAME DIRECTION IN THIS STATE OF MIND, REPEATING THE SAME THOUGHTS OF THE PAST.

THIRD SEAL
THIS SEAL IS THE ENERGY CENTER OF CONSCIOUS AWARENESS AND THE VISIBLE LIGHT FREQUENCY BAND. IT IS ASSOCIATED WITH CONTROL, TYRANNY, VICTIMIZATION, AND POWER. IT IS LOCATED IN THE REGION OF THE SOLAR PLEXUS.

SECOND SEAL
THIS SEAL IS THE ENERGY CENTER OF SOCIAL CONSCIOUSNESS AND THE INFRARED FREQUENCY BAND. IT IS ASSOCIATED WITH PAIN AND SUFFERING AND IS LOCATED IN THE LOWER ABDOMINAL AREA.

KUNDALINI ENERGY

FIRST SEAL
THIS SEAL IS ASSOCIATED WITH THE REPRODUCTIVE ORGANS, SEXUALITY, SURVIVAL, SUBCONSCIOUSNESS, AND THE HERTZIAN FREQUENCY BAND.

FIG. 3: DESCENT OF CONSCIOUSNESS AND ENERGY FROM POINT ZERO

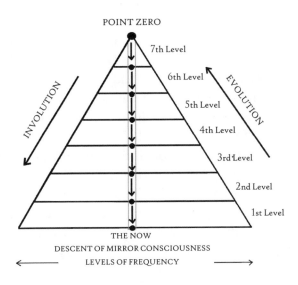

You all remember this from your beginning C&E™. What is it? Point Zero, primary consciousness. Would you just color in a black dot. Over to the side write primary consciousness — a very simple little drawing here, one of my better masterpieces.[4] The purple dot is secondary consciousness. Now you notice that I have a green extension there. The green dot is the soul, and the soul rides along with secondary consciousness. It is the recorder of events. The red dot, or circle or blotch, is the incarnation, the body itself. And here we would say body/mind consciousness — body/mind consciousness. In other words, we have to credit the body with having its own intelligence, which it does. It is a conscious intelligence, a biophysical, sentient being.

FIG. 4: PRIMARY AND SECONDARY CONSCIOUSNESS

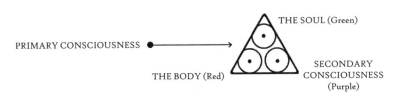

---

4 See fig. 4.

Now this is the order in which they come. The great self is constituted by the integration of these four right here (see fig. 4). And whether this body is a sixth-plane body, a fifth-plane body, a fourth-plane body, a third-plane body, a second-plane body, or a first-plane body, it is a body. This body then is held together by that which is termed the spiritual body or secondary consciousness, and what holds them all together is called the Holy Spirit, which is the spiritual interaction of the complete self. So then this is where we get this idea of a triad.[5] So we go back to the beginning event to understand better your incarnation from the Plane of Bliss or perhaps your present revisiting to this school.

I want to ask you a very important question: Why would you not believe my last statement that you are already dead and you are in a light review right now? Why wouldn't you believe that? Why isn't it believable? It is a very powerful question because it has everything to do with the intrinsic knowledge that you have incorporated about time and space and consciousness. It tells you the degree of that knowledge that you bear up here. This body/mind consciousness would never believe what I have just told you. They would see it as a fanciful imagination, a paradigm — a monad, if you will — but they would never believe it because they can point to their body and say, "Look, I can pinch this body and it hurts. Look, I don't know what that person is thinking. Look, I visited the graveyard and I am not buried anywhere — yet." Correct?

Now I want to tell you something. Listen to me. Then if this becomes the choice factor of which we determine reality by, then we will wholly disbelieve the potentials that we can exist in. In other words, we have sided with our body, haven't we? We really have. We have sided with the body because we cannot quite believe that this is possible. Well, what does that tell you? That tells you then if you side with the body, then the joke is on you because you continue to live and you say, "See there, I am continuing to live. One day, I am going to die." Is it possible then that in doing that, that we are living in a delusionary illusion? Is it? Absolutely.

So why would you want to side with your body? What is the

5 See fig. 3.

upside to this? What if you sided with this right here, these two, primary and secondary consciousness? Why secondary consciousness? Because it is the Spirit in the body, that contains the spiritual body that the soul itself rests in. And, remember, the soul keeps track of who you have been. It catalogs what you are, so it is the carrier, if you will, of the memory of personality. And let's face it; if you have looked at a cadaver of recent or of late, you wonder where the person is. You know, you look at the mouth you kissed and the eyes that used to dance and the animation in the hands, the softness of the touch, or the athleticness of movement of the body. And you look at it and it is stiff and it is hard and it is lifeless. Listen to me. It is lifeless; it is. What left it? Secondary consciousness, the soul personality; that is what left it. So is that really you? That is really a part of you.

Now if we were to think in terms of, as an example, if you could accept today this teaching that you really are in a light review right now — and that you are actually reviewing who you are in a classroom that has to do with exactly the subject matter in which you are involved in, ironically — if you could believe that and have room to accept that, that speaks of a great graduation of evolution of your own personal consciousness. It means then that you are so lofty, that the idea that you are actually in a light review is not astonishing at all.

Why would that be to your advantage to side with primary and secondary consciousness on this issue? Obviously because those are the selves that remain when birth and death go on as cyclical reincarnation; they remain. What other advantage is it? Well, here is the advantage: If you really believe that what I told you today — I mean, you really believed it — by the end of this day you will know your ulterior motive. And because you will know it, you will change it. And what sort of dynamics are going to spin off of that change? What are they going to be? It must be as real to you as the denial of its reality is to you. It must have that same equal thrust. It must be as real as denial is real, and if it is, then think of the possibilities of what we are looking at here. You are actually in a moment of observable participation in which you have been here before, and you are back and so much of this sounds familiar. And it starts to come to the surface of your mind.

And when you reach back to try to look at it, it disappears like vapors. There is a familiarity to this.

And why is it important to believe that it is possible? Because in the cyclical reincarnation — the linear process of birth and death, afterlife, new sojourns — the whole process is to be able to see a life from the vantage point of the all, not just the singular, which is so indigenous to how human beings are. They are very singular and very separated. They cannot see through the mind of God, only through the mind of the body's personality. It is very self-evident in the way you live.

And if that were so, then in a light review you would get to see all and you would get to see where your problem is. And in that light review you would be able to take and learn a lot about that problem and then meet people on the Plane of Bliss who share the same problem or who share a splintering of that problem. Maybe — maybe — one little area that is of no importance to you but is still a splinter is a logjam to someone else, and you meet on the Plane of Bliss because you gravitate towards each other. And in gravitation towards each other, you work out a relationship that exists there before it exists here, a relationship to which you want this person to come into your life here, and you want the memory and the bonding of it to be so strong on the Plane of Bliss that there is no denying the recognition; that there seems to be an instant acceptance of that individual — a harmony, if you will; even a disharmony — because all of those factors, if we have done it correctly, then are incarnated into a life to which as blind men and women we struggle to uncover the mystery, the great unfathomable mystery, of what we are doing here. What is this person trying to tell me about myself and what indeed am I trying to tell me about myself, because all they are, are reflections of what I am. They are here to teach me lessons, or maybe we are both here to gain a lesson to various degrees. Why do I need that lesson? Well, because it is daunting. This subject matter keeps reappearing. And so everyone becomes a player in everyone's life.

Now the only difficult thing is — and I always said this, and here I part ways with New Age thinking to some degree because they don't have all the information — it was always broadly understood that you choose your parents. Well, in the naiveness of the human culture, they simply think that you go to that big parent garden in the sky and you say, "I will take you and you," and that they know beforehand who those parents are going to be. That is not correct. It has truth in it but it is not solid, substantial truth.

The way it works is that whatever your issues are, whatever you have decided on Bliss that is the next level that you have to work on — which is really the same thing you worked on two thousand years ago and through successive generations and technological changes you have made little progress — you are still in a problem. The whole world is. You are still dealing with this issue that is two thousand years old. This is not something of the twentieth century, technological-based, rapid-growing, artificial-life century. This is an issue that goes way back. And what is so frustrating about it is it is a very simple thing. But what is simple to the Spirit is so difficult for the human because the human is complexed by its emotions.

So what happens is that once we have formulated what we come to learn here on the Plane of Demonstration, we don't pick our parents. We are drawn to a genetic pool that is no greater than the question we asked. Why should that not have continuity to it? God only knows what you know. Why should you be drawn to a genetic pool that knows more than you? You are not going to be. You will only manifest in reality — whether it is atomic structures, cellular biology, whether it is environmental, whether it is thought, ideas — you are only going to manifest what you are equal to and what accommodates the learning here. You do pick your parents on an issue of like begging like, but as far as descriptiveness, no.

Now there are people who have an issue with bodies and have always had an issue with bodies. And they always vacillate to those who can produce to them the best bodies, but that is body/mind consciousness. And that is self-evident too, because the greatest asset is that and nothing else.

Well, what about geniuses? My God, don't you know the most brilliant — brilliant — minds that ever came, came from very simple stock? That was amazing, wasn't it? It was almost as if the genetic stock itself was not complex but was simple. In other words, the genes had clear windshields so that what you brought through to it could clearly be brought forward, into a life, a mind to grow and flourish. We can grow and flourish as exquisite flowers in a simple garden. If it is cluttered, we get choked out by weeds and other shrubbery and the like. How many of you understand?

Now then you are born — and I want all of you to know right now; you think about your body — you are born exactly with the genetic body that is the utility to match and to work through your altered agenda, your karma, your lesson, finishing it. Now this is quite amazing because then we begin to look at bodies, and it becomes very clear who chose what and for what reason. Everything is a story. Ulterior motives can be seen in the body, literally can be seen in the body.

And you are born into a family. Well, who are these families? Does it mean that your brothers and sisters that you share an incarnation with came from the same place on the Plane of Bliss? No, because, you see, the genetic pool to which they came through offered primitive or advanced opportunities. They are different levels, but the body suits them. How many of you understand? You do? So be it.

Now I want to ask you this question again: Why would you disbelieve that you are in a light review? Why would you want to do that? I will tell you. Victims want to do that and materialistic people want to do that and carnal people want to do that because when they can deny this possibility that I have given to you earlier — don't go to sleep — when they can deny this, then they have no threat to change their life, no excuse. They say, "I am what I am and I can't change. I like what I am. I like to hate what I am and so I don't have to bother." So that is very secure ground, isn't it? It is secure, isn't it?

Tomorrow morning you are going to wake up; you will still be in school. But the day after, you are going to wake up and you are going to someplace else. You can count on that. In a body-physical life, you can count on every day waking up and every night going to sleep and in-between having fun. That is a sense of security. So you have pragmatic minds that will disavow primary consciousness and say that doesn't exist. You will never die? What a fool. Who do you think you are? Go to the graveyard.

But there is a little problem with that, you know. Science is starting to wake up with, as you have learned, the quantum theory of all potentiality existing simultaneously — all potentiality. And remember what I told you about cosmic atoms, atomology? What that means is that you cannot exhaust the potentials utilizing atoms as building blocks.

Now here is something else I want to ask you, a very important question: If you did accept this and believed it, how would your life change today if suddenly you said, "Oh, my God, I am in a light review. I am dead. I am actually viewing as the Observer how I lived it. And thank God I came to this school, because I wouldn't be awake to acknowledge that I should be thinking about this in the light." It is: I am calling out to you from beyond the grave. What are you thinking watching this? What should you be thinking? "My God, this very moment I can change my life because all I am expecting is to see what I remembered that I was."

You know how hard it is to remember the rest of your life? Not very hard. Think about it. If you didn't work in lofty thoughts, how hard will it be to remember the rest of your life? It is pretty predictable, isn't it? Isn't it? You look forward to those nights that you go out and do this and that, and then you go to work, and then you do that, and you have little problems with your family, little squabbles here and there, but you know they are going to be resolved sooner or later. You have a little problem here but it will be all right there. And I am a year older and I am this and I am that. How could you not remember what is yet to come? It has already happened because it is predictable. That predictability is powerful security, and there are people who will deny the opportunity to change for the sake of predictable security. It happens every day.

Now why not believe this? And what would happen if that great big beautiful orb sitting on top of those shoulders finally clicked and said, "What if I am; what if I am dead? Here is my chance. What will I do different in my life? What do I come away from this with? What is it that I want more than anything? If I get a chance to live again, what do I want? Oh, my God, I never want to forget this moment. I don't want to be born ignorant. Somehow I want to maintain this moment. I don't want it to be elusive and fly away. I don't want to lose it in the birth canal, and I don't want to lose it in youth, and I don't want to lose it in reckless adulthood. How do I remember this?"

Think about that. "This moment can change my life. Nothing is set. It is a light review and I am in the midst of it. How do I want to see me right now?" Shine, my beloved people. How do you want to see you? You want to see you as primary consciousness sees you; that is what you want. You don't want to see you as body/mind consciousness sees you, because if you do, you are a dead ringer to come back again. Everything is up for grabs; the whole life is over with. I just thought I was going to an event. Marvelous thought, isn't it? Is it real? Is it? Only you know that answer. But if it is real, it is absolute freedom. My God, what do you do with a treasure? How do you want to be from this moment on? How do I want to see me? How do I want to see me? What is the great reflection that I must shine back to my eventual observation in the light?

Now think about this: You are going to die. Those of you who are body/mind consciousness, you are going to die. You are going to go to the light because you know about it. You are going to see this day again. Why would your soul leave this day out? Why would it leave this day out? Why would it leave this morning out? Is it going to remember all those things you did behind closed doors and forget about this one? No. It has recorded everything. Just like those of you who are taking notes, you are writing the same words your soul is writing. But your soul is doing asterisks down here, footnotes, soul notes there at the bottom. Soul notes are the Observer observing the notes being written. Are you with me? How many of you are still with me? So be it.

So now if this day is going to come again — and you are standing there with your Holy Spirit and your God and it starts to come on you — and you have been the great self in every view of this lifetime since the womb on, why would this day be left out? So how important is today? How important is it? Very important. Why? Because what do you want to tell yourself today? What do you want to tell yourself? It is going to be replayed. What do you want to see and hear? Turn to your neighbor and tell them. What do you want?

Now I want you to take your paper, your pencil, your writing instrument. Now this is no joke. What do you want to be remembered today — that has already happened and is being reviewed now — about yourself? Come on, what do you want to hear and see? Anything goes. You would be very wise if you included in this what you have found your ulterior motive to be and be able to say it. Write it down. What is it, and how has it served you? It is important that you remind yourself what it is, what you have been, what is the hook that keeps bringing you back here. It is important that you say it.

And having said that then, you must also add to it, being utterly impeccable, if you are willing to give it up, because if you are not — no matter what you see, no matter how many people are hurt, no matter how many people are used and abused, no matter what you have done and how clever you are — if you cannot give it up, you are doomed to relive it again. You are doomed to relive it again. So you have to cry out to that which is viewing this now what one must change and what one desires to be, and then the great pronouncement, the great question, the great desire must follow. What does this have to do with the Plane of Bliss? Everything.

NEAR-DEATH EXPERIENCES AND THE EGYPTIAN RITES OF PASSAGE

It is reported that entities who have near-death experiences, when they fully have one, that the experience enriches them and changes them marvelously; they are never who they used to be. Who they used to be will never be recaptured again. Why? Because in a single life they had a heart attack, they drowned, they were electrocuted, they took a fatal dose of something, and they got out of their body and they went so far as the great life review. Some of them went all the way through a life review and they got to see the self from all perspectives. They got to be the self from all perspectives, except that aspect called God, that great being that poured out unconditional, profound love. They all say that they were connected to this being, and yet this was God. They weren't advanced enough to know that the great radiating being was them as God. They didn't know that but they suspected an interconnectedness with everything. And they got to look at who they were married to and their children and their problems and their issues of success and failure, their prejudices, their ulterior motives.

I mean, how great is the ulterior motive of someone who wants to kill themselves? People who kill themselves do it out of revenge for other people. That is the way to get back — it is — make someone sorry. What is the ultimate trip you can lay on someone? That is the ultimate trip. Now that is an exaggeration, but a heart attack is the failure of living. It is the failure of expression. It is holding things together that should be let go of. It is, in its way, a suicide.

Well, they get there and they suddenly see all of those things, and they see the impact that they have created in other people's lives. Now don't go to sleep. This might be your next experience. They see that and suddenly become so understanding of the importance of life. In other words, they wake up in the light review. They wake up in the light review. That is why they get to come back. That is why they get to come back and resurrect that dead body laying on that table, that machine starting up that heart again or those chemicals being thrust into the body to cause brain-wave activity to occur. They get to come back to that body. What a deliverance. And when they come back and they awaken, they are not the same people who only moments earlier lived in that same body. They are different, profoundly different. Their views on life are so drastically altered as to make one suspect that this cannot be the same person. Why am I telling you this? Because all that they get to experience, you get to experience today and tonight in the same manifesto. You have to know this day is inevitable. Know it, because it is.

So why is it so important? Because maybe it has already happened. Maybe this is the opportunity to see in a review what has doggedly plagued you all of your life. Perhaps it is the day that you wake up and realize the value of what you get to have on the other side of this day. What is the difference? Maybe you are already dead. Do you think I will wait and worry about that when I die? Maybe you already are and the joke is on you because, you see, you should live every day consciously and not postpone it. Every day should be primary (consciousness) — not secondary or body/mind consciousness — primary, because that is what fires the Spirit of secondary every day. Well, why do you think then that this is something that you can wait and play around with? How do you know how beautiful your life is about to be? How do you know? What did you just say to be remembered? You are going to be saying it tonight. You are going to be talking to yourself tonight and it will be remembered and it will be played back. And what are you going to want to hear?

What is going to make the difference? When you are doing a light review, are you going to tell your body — you are going to tell your life — look, I am your memory. I was in anticipation of now. Let me tell you what I want. I have been dead. I have been uninspired. I have lived as a human being struggling for the rapture of spiritual countenance. I have desired it, but I haven't done it yet — yet. Remember me, I am telling you this. What do I want? I want this day in my life to be remembered as the day I fell apart and was reborn to a change — a fundamental, ingrained change in me. I want you to remember that, because whether it is today or the day after, this day has already happened and surely will come.

What do you want to say? Wait, you have time. You, I want you to resurrect my body. I want you to go back, but I want you to go back with this knowledge. I do not want to be born again in another body. I get to say my piece. Listen to me. I want another chance, but I don't want to forget. I want to know and remember. Thus you go back to the body and you revive it and put me in there consciously altered and changed. What do I want to be altered? I don't want to be a limited human being again. I don't want the value of myself being based upon my body. I want the value of myself being based upon the consciousness of what flowers from within me. I do not want to play games anymore. I want the reality of the manifesto of the great arcanum. I want to be a living-fire master. You go back to that body and you wake up.

No one told you to say that. I am telling you to say that because you have already died. I am telling you we must be immortal in an incarnation. We don't need to incarnate. We only need to wake up now.

So you say what is the problem? I am not getting this now. You know what the problem is? It is because you haven't realized what has held you back, where your power is coagulated at. It is coagulated in your ulterior motives. That is where your real passion is. Passion is power. And if you are trying to start something new and it isn't in alignment with your ulterior motive, you are not going to have the passion to bring it to fruition. This has to be your passion. And if you were as passionate about today as you are about your ulterior motive, you will live forever consciously — ever. You will live forever. How do I know that? Well, because I am that, because this primary consciousness and this entity here (secondary consciousness) must agree. The agreeance is the Holy Spirit and the power of the Holy Spirit. These are who you are. They are going to live anyway. But what about them; why do we need this? Because we are unfinished with this stage of exploration. And the truth is we cannot be this (primary consciousness) fully and richly until we have been that in this (secondary consciousness), until this mirrors that. When you do, you will only have this (primary consciousness).

Now who says I dare you, that such a command would not be hastened to? Who is going to stop you, God and his angels? You are God and his angels. Who is going to stop you? The only person that is going to stop you is you. You know why you are going to stop you? Because you don't believe that; you only believe this (physical body). That is why. That is why.

But I am telling you, you are going to put the message down because this day is going to be played again, and someone has to remind you what do you say in the midst of a life review. What do you say? When do you wake up in the dream? And when do you command the dream? What is going to happen when you say to you — you turn right around in the light review and you are looking at you and you are going — I know you are watching me now. I know you are watching me. You, who went on, I am giving you a message now because you are going to see me again. I am you. I am what I look like in the body. You are viewing me outside of that body. Let me tell you what I want you to do: Remember me. If I am buried, so is your wisdom that you have learned. You are not going to pick a genetic child that is going to be fully opened. You remember me. Come back after me and bring this knowledge with you, that I am resurrected into life, that I command you to resurrect me today. What do you think is going to happen? Consciousness and energy create the nature of reality.

What is initiation? What is resurrection? What is the resurrected death and rebirth? What is that initiation for? It is to prepare you on how to act. What is *The Egyptian Book of the Dead*? *The Egyptian Book of the Dead* is to teach the sovereign what to do the moment it is out of its body: what to say, where to go, who to say, who to see, what to do. They are enchanted with it. Why are the priests saying prayers twenty-four hours a day reciting those passages, reciting them over and over and over? Because that priest is in the light review of that sovereign. That priest is praying for that sovereign, and that sovereign in the light review is hearing the priest from the other side. Don't you understand? Why is it necessary to pray for the souls of the departed? Well, don't pray unless you have something to tell them.

But what if such a command was in the hands of a skillful arbitrator, Aleph, who has one hand in heaven and one foot in the earth. That is the supreme arbitrator, that can reach into heaven and reach into the earth. That is a master. What if then a master arbitrator knows exactly where to reach and find you on the other side and what they want to say to you? Then the chanting is going to be seen, and they chant over and over and over and over, riding Nut all the way over until the weighing of the heart, the weighing of the soul.[6] Over and over and over the weight must be

6 Egyptian Goddess Nut. Her appearance is that of a woman whose body arches across the sky, wearing a dress decorated with stars. Nut was the sky Goddess whose body created a vault or canopy over the earth. Nut was the sister/wife of Geb, the God of the earth. She was also the mother of Isis, Osiris, Nepthys, and Seth. The ancient Egyptians believed that at the end of the day, Nut swallowed the sun God Ra and gave birth to him again the next morning. In the light of Ramtha's teachings, the Goddess Nut represents the interim place where the soul rests and reviews its life after death.

to a feather — over and over and over. How much is that sovereign going to see that is not going to be featherlike? A great deal. What is it that he is going to keep seeing though when he sees the scale? A feather. How is it going to be weighed? Against a feather. Who is weighing him? Himself.[7]

FIG. 5: EGYPTIAN GODDESS NUT

Is this getting into any of you? This is all happening at the same time, the same moment. So who is going to say the chants for you in your passing? Who did say them? Who is the greatest arbitrator at that vulnerable moment? You are. What are you going to say? Get back here and be enlightened. For God's sake, dig me up and let's get on with this.

And you say, "I don't want that body any longer. It hurt too much. I am so happy to be free of this cumbersome prison." And you are going to say to it, "I know what you are thinking up there" — you are saying this to you in the light — "I know what you are thinking, how good it feels not to have me. You feel so great because you don't have me anymore, because I don't have a headache and I don't have a backache and I am not this and I am not that and I am heavy and I like to eat. And you are thinking you are better off without me. Listen to me. We will be better off together if you come back for me and make me the way you want me. Make me in the image of God. If you do, you will never have to die again and you will never have to be reborn again." Turn to

7 See the *Papyrus of Ani*, commonly known as *The Egyptian Book of the Dead*, where the heart of the individual is weighed against a feather in judgment after death.

your neighbor and explain.

One day when you have the opportunity — one fine morn or one splendid evening — to sit down with a gathering of masters, you know, you will have earned the right to be there because you will have for a period of time changed enough to literally think as they think. And today's teaching is how they think.

To a Master There Is No Birth and Death, Only Creation

You see, to a master there is no birth and death. There just isn't. That is an illusion. There is nothing but the continuity of their ability to dream states of reality. And in order to hold a meaningful dialogue with a master, you would have to hold it on such levels of thought, like this one, because to be anything else, to become contracted and to go back down into the selfish human would not be a conversation that would be attractive to them. They are not attracted to soap bubbles; they are not attracted to soap operas, and they are not attracted to fickle people.

But how would that be possible then? Is that possible? For example, today if this is a light review, and you are in the midst of it and you have been given a powerful orientation — and if this is meaningful for you and if you believe that this actually could be — you have credited yourself with a quantum leap in evolution, because you have actually set up what has already been and will become, and you have given yourself instructions and directions, exactly what you want. Now those are the proper things to be able to do.

How many people go to the light every moment and do not know this? How many people could not fathom that they are already dead and they are just reviewing their life? How many people can fathom that; do you know? Not very many, eh? It is not a conversation that you have in your salon or in the meat market. It is not a conversation. It is a rare conversation, isn't it? And yet everything should be done as if it is being done in the light of all eternity. So now you cannot prove to me that you are not dead — you cannot — because then you would have to prove

153

the existence that you are alive, and how do you do that?

Now how would then you get to gather with eagles? How would you get to gather with masters? What brings that into fruition? Now this is the part that we are going to study in depth tomorrow. We are going to introduce it tonight.

Remember at your beginning event — which is so vastly important to begin this school, because without this knowledge you are lost — remember we started with this little Point Zero, that was the child of the Void and one vast nothing materially and all things potentially? How many of you remember that teaching?[8] Exquisite, isn't it? You just don't know how exquisite until you are finally alive again and that here is primary reality. I tell you, it doesn't get more simple than that. Here it is. And the only way that it can do anything is to create the stage of something. And it certainly is not going to have that interaction with the Void because the Void has no parameters in which to fundamentally set up the stage of time. Time is important because it is what allows energy to become a coagulated force in an idea.

And isn't it interesting that you had to go within to contemplate to become expanded? That is the greatest law that has set into motion all of life on all planes in all spectrums, in all planets, in all pasts, in all times to come. It was this simple concept here. Now look at that. Remember when I had you look at this?[9] Show me time. Show it to me.

FIG. 6: ILLUSTRATION OF THE CREATION OF TIME, USING THE HANDS

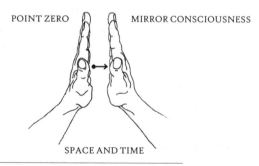

POINT ZERO   MIRROR CONSCIOUSNESS

SPACE AND TIME

8 See *A Beginner's Guide to Creating Reality,* Revised and Expanded ed. (Yelm: JZK Publishing, a division of JZK, Inc., 2000).
9 See fig. 6.

FIG. 7: THE SWING MOVEMENT OF THE MIRROR CONSCIOUSNESS

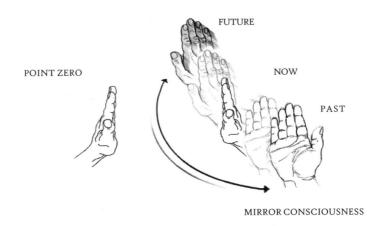

Now what was the reason that we had these two, that between them was an atmosphere — rarefied atmosphere — just like the earth's atmosphere? From the earth to the sun, there is an atmosphere that is shared between the two. Well, between primary (consciousness) and secondary, there is an atmosphere which is exactly like the atmosphere you have here.

Now this is what is so important that I want you to remember: How do I know you are God and how do you know that for certain? Because you came apart right here (see fig. 6) and began contributing to the atmosphere of life. Well, what I am saying is from your side (primary consciousness) issues the energy to the brilliant mirror that you also are, and from side to mind this energy exchange is moving to and fro. The energy that is being exchanged between primary and secondary is, like I also explained to you carefully, that the energy wave — and we can determine this wave by how much time we have — we can determine what frequency exists on what level by the anatomy of the frequency itself, how short it is or how long it is. We have a good understanding of where that energy is coming from.

For example, superquarks, as it were — transient tachyons that only appear for brief moments in time, that are so brief that you can't even put down here — must come from an extraordinary atmosphere. And what is an extraordinary atmosphere? Remember this: Atmosphere is that which exists between two points of consciousness, and the only two points of consciousness there are, are primary and secondary. So a tachyon is a burst, a brief moment, in time but comes from a different time, a different atmosphere, and so it is elusive down here. It is elusive in this atmosphere because it is an alien; it belongs somewhere else. I also taught you that although this is a linear drawing, this is actually an enfolding and an unfolding. This is an enfolding and an unfolding from the Void, from primary consciousness to secondary consciousness. And what happens? It is carrying an intent, consciousness, an idea — you got that? — so that when it collapses, it has the intelligence to become something. Now don't go to sleep. Become something? Wait a minute. I thought this energy was coming out of me. It is. I thought it was bouncing back in the mind of God. It is, but when it engages from God to you and you both agree, then you give life to the thing. How many of you understand that? You do?

So in the beginning, the atmosphere between primary and secondary were the children of primary and secondary, the atmosphere. And what was the atmosphere made out of? It was made out of energy and particle potentials. Who puts the idea, riding energy? Who is responsible for giving energy the notion to collapse and formulate into a concept? Who does that? You think that just happens? Do you think that there is some big pot in the sky in which this stuff rains out and you are not responsible for, that someone else is responsible for? You think it is the sun's fault that this happens? It is you. It has always been you.

So what am I telling you? Who created this earth? Who created that tree out there and who created the insects, and who created the fishes, and who created the worms; who created the bacteria? Who did all of that? Where did this abundance of natural life with an intelligence — by God, even rocks have intelligence — where does the intelligence come from? There are only two places it could have come from. Right here between these two (primary and secondary consciousness). You mean that a rock has intelligence? Yes. Well, where did it get the intelligence from? It got its intelligence by a primitive form of polarization. Well, where did the polarization come from? From two points of consciousness. Well, what were the two points of consciousness? Primary and secondary. Well, what in the world were they doing? They were creating. And what was it they created? Thoughts. Well, where are the thoughts? They are in the rock. Now all life we are and we have been.

I used to tell this wonderful story in the Dialogue days — sounds like something ancient, doesn't it — wonderful story about what it was and how we created flowers, how we created animals, how we created insects, and how the symbiotic relationship was only a reflection of the symbiotic relationship we, as mighty divine creators, shared and that this life was just spewing from us because every time we had a thought, that the thought was automatic. We didn't have to think about making a rock; the rock just came out of our head. It was this side; it was a result of our movement. It was a result of this.[10] When we pulled apart, we have started to coagulate things. Well, what are these little things? What are these little creatures? Well, these happen to be those intelligent thoughts that were divinely given birth to when we went analogical.

Where do you think analogical thoughts go? Do you think we just have a copulation of primary and secondary and that is it, and everyone feels terrific and we separate and we are friends forever? Well, that analogical union, what happens to it? What is the reaction from analogical union? An atmosphere. What is the atmosphere? Well, the atmosphere is the coagulation of analogical union.

When we were here, we created a plane of existence. Who created it? We did. How did we do that? By doing this.[11] And every time we did it, something was happening: The atmosphere was getting denser; things started coagulating; thoughts and ideas started to take form. What was a form? We had never seen a form before. We didn't know what form was. This was a reaction from an intention that was natural to us. The phenomenon that occurred became reality. We didn't know that. No one told us that. It was the way time worked in energy, and it is exactly where thoughts and ideas went with time. And they only spewed forth in an

10 See fig. 7.
11 Ibid.

analogical fountain, and we were that.

So here is what I am trying to tell you. I am trying to tell you that as we descended down this ladder, we left these vast continents of beautiful, pristine environments. And just think how pristine they must be because those were the ages of innocence — those were the ages of innocence — true and pure divinity. Those planes must be indescribable. They are. And where did this place come from? From the indescribable. Every time that we affected energy, every time we got separated in the primary course of involution, we began to affect all planes with our ideas. It became impregnated.

So where did the earth come from? Where did any of the planets come from? And where did the black holes and white holes come from, those quantum tunnels of unfolding and enfolding potential mass and gas? Well, they came from analogical mind and the intelligence from all of you that are in this room and all of those that aren't in this room, and all of those that are visible and invisible, all of those that live in other dimensions, on other planets, in other galaxies, in other forms, and in other stratums. It came from all of us.

Should we consider ourselves then to be in this descent, into a fall? Because there is a multiple of us, should we consider ourselves a spark or a raging fire? We are a raging fire. Never consider yourself a spark; that just isn't good enough. I would never consider myself a spark; I am a raging fire. And that is what you are. How do I know that? Because you can only inhabit the environment that you gave analogical intelligence to. You cannot inhabit an environment that you have not contributed to. What did I just say? You are always where you are and should be.

Now it hasn't occurred to you yet — but I am very desirous that I have still got you blown open here, because this should be also impactful — that the only reason you are in this earth incarnation is because it is the only place you have contributed to. Got that? So where else are you going to go from the Plane of Bliss? Think you are going to go to Venus? Think you are going to go to the twenty-third universe? Well, my great school there is producing remarkable beings, and they were in the march with you a long time ago. How is it that they got there and they are not here? Because they believed the story that I left them. They believed the story that I left to them, the one hundred and twenty days of communion. Well, what was the story? I told you where I went, an unfathomable, unbearably beautiful place. And to those who could understand, understood. And they contributed to that place because therein was where their longing was, their real passion. Now do you know where your passion is? So you know why you are here? Because it is the only place you have contributed to.

Those people went because they dreamed a passionate dream of following me, and they went there. And yet they used to be creatures of this world and they are somewhere else. And they have also had reviews. They already know what I just taught you, and it was not too far after that that true masters emerged, and women were amongst them. They got it. They understood. They grasped it. It was there for them to have. And they never let go of it. They wrestled with God until they got him down. Do you understand? Now they are warriors, so that is all right for them to do that. They were a marching army. They understood siege and they didn't give up, so they grasped hold of the concept and conquered it.

So if you only get to where you belong, then now take a look at your life. Just take a moment and look at it. You cannot be victimized any longer by anything in your environment and anyone in your environment. You deserve exactly who you have got. You deserve them. You deserve exactly what you have in your life. You don't deserve any more or any less. You have exactly what you are worthy of. That is what you have contributed to. Your opportunities in your life, you are only going to get those opportunities because it is all that you have contributed to. And you may not even get them, because somewhere you haven't believed them into life because you have been too busy taking care of physical business over here. Do you understand? You can never go where you don't belong. It never will happen. It is against the law of primary and secondary consciousness creating the nature of reality.

Now the environment that you are in, you created it all. What about the lowly worm? Well, how do you think the worm got intelligence? And intelligence then speaks of a soul. Does a worm have a soul? Yes. How did it get a soul? When you became it. When you became it. Where does a worm get its intelligence from? Yes, it is a remarkable creature that works off instinct — but what have we come to learn about instinct? — and that instinct was a sensitivity, a sensitivity that grew into an instinctual, genetic memory that then creates a sentient being. The sentient being then has intelligence and where there is a sign of intelligence, there is a remarkable soul caught into that intelligence. Small, insignificant, yes, but nonetheless intelligence. Where did it get it if there was only this and this (primary and secondary consciousness)? Where did it come from? You. How were they given life? Through incidental creating ideas — ideas, people. That is all you had to do was have the idea. Did you have to fire the engines of genetic evolution? No, all you had to do was have the idea. You see, that is how it works on the Plane of Bliss too, that remarkable place that is detached from the physical. Everything appears immediately as you wish it to be.

And can you say is it real? Well, what do you call real? What is the determining factor of reality? Well, can I touch it, smell it, feel it? Absolutely. You want it to be real, don't you? Well, go jump in the lake, in the lake of tranquility, and see if there are fish in there; there will be. And see if you get wet; you will get wet. See if you can drink the water; you will be able to drink it. See if you can crawl out of the water and get warmed on the grass by the radiant sun. Will you feel the heat? Yes, you will feel the heat. Then is that real? Is this real? Where are you? Aren't you starting to wonder that now? Where in the hell am I? What am I doing here? Who am I? I don't even know anymore. But that is the way you are supposed to think. That is the making of a great initiate. I don't know where I am anymore. I don't know what is real and so I am going to act like everything is serious business now.

So here is the truth. The truth is the environment in which you exist is the one that you have contributed to. And so all of nature around you is a reflection of you, because at one point you have made a visitation to it. How many of you understand that? Absolutely. Absolutely. Now isn't that beautiful? It is like out of our side gushes life. Out of our mind gushes ideas that we don't even have to do anything with them; they are the lawgiver to the atomic world. And so where does the atomic world get its intelligence? From us who have created it as atmosphere. I tell you — I am telling you — it is so, and it is consistent all the way back up to Point Zero.

Now here is what I want you to think about. If you get what you deserve because of what you think, then when you are talking to yourself in memory in this light review, there is something you are going to have to remember to say, and that is, "My passion, you are to make my passion be a passion of the unknown. I want to belong to the abyss. I want to belong to the potentials. I want to exist in an environment to where ideas start manifesting like raindrops around me. I want that because the environment that I come from is already fixed and coagulated. I want a new environment."

Now the way that you get to dine with masters is you have to think like them. Well, when we start talking about such a lofty concept and then ponder if it is or it isn't, how are you going to convince yourself? You never will. But this day is going to be seen again; that we are certain of. What perhaps I want to impress upon you is then that when you begin to ponder in contemplation these things, there is something wonderful that starts to happen, people. Listen to me.

Let's go back to the beginning event of these two (primary and secondary consciousness). In contemplation we are doing this (see fig. 6), aren't we? Now let's take a look at this from a beginner's eye. You are down here at the first plane, aren't you, living in the carnal Hertzian body, aren't you, down here? Right here (first plane). The thoughts we are having today are reserved for great minds who usually exist about here (fifth plane) and here (sixth plane). And what does that say then? That means that you certainly wouldn't be having that conversation based in these seals (first three seals), and you may be having it in the fourth seal. But more than likely this kind of a conversation is going to be happening in this seal right here (fifth seal) and this one right back here (sixth seal). And if you contemplate why this one and this one, it will become self-evident to you.

So this is what I want you to understand. If you do then, right here, then we actually are starting to think on the fifth plane, aren't we? When we think like we think today, that is how long it takes to go analogical — got that? — versus try and get that pendulum to stop right here (the Now). I mean, that is a mess. You are right up here (sixth plane); you are right here (fifth plane), that close. Now what does that bring you? That brings you right into a rarefied atmosphere again. In primary/secondary consciousness, we don't care about the body because this is not body talk. This is God-Spirit-soul talk and we are right here (fifth plane). When we are, we are brought into a rarefied atmosphere. How many of you today felt that atmosphere in this room? Didn't you start to know something? How many of you were suddenly on the brink of realizing what I was saying? Raise your hands. Well, that is the atmosphere and we are coming into it right here (fifth seal). It gets supercharged.

Well, if you learn to stay in that atmosphere for a while, you are inevitably going to be doing this (alignment with Point Zero). And if you do, then you are going to be moving into a very changed reality. It is not going to be uncommon that in a moment of talking, suddenly you are going to enter into a tunnel. You will see it and you will look around, and you will not be able to see out of your peripheral vision; it will get cloudy. And you will look directly at the mist and you will say, "Something is wrong with my eyes." No, you are leaving. You are moving into a rarefied reality.

Now you can get back to this one by rubbing your eyes and insisting on being back here (first plane), and it will clear up. "Whew, I am glad that passed. I thought there was something wrong with me there for a moment." You want to stay in it because then you are going to start to see flashes of blue and brightly gold-colored lights flashing. When you see them, you are in a rarefied atmosphere. You are on the fifth level. You are in a place to where the atmosphere coming off of your mind is going to start manifesting. The abnormal will start to occur as normal. Then is when the master will walk out of the mist because they are already there. How many of you understand?

Now it is at this place of consciousness also that we do the Great Work — that we do the really Great Work — that we impregnate life with the atmosphere. We have to live in the atmosphere, this energy, with ideas all around us just pouring off of us. All we have to do is be in it, stay in it; the manifestations will roll off us like sweat. And yet with every drop of sweat, there is a realization. There is the precious, aqueous substance that is coagulated thought, that is an adventure, something wonderful and marvelous. That is how we get to a new stratum. People say, well, how do you do this? How do you apply that? Just go back to the principle: Consciousness and energy create reality. If you can ask the question, if you can beg a greater knowledge, you deserve to live in that knowledge.

In the light, if you can beg to differ with the status quo of the mundane existence and call a halt to the whole show and ask for a reorganization and insist on that reorganization, in the midst of that, then the light and everything else will disappear and the new life will appear as if like a dream, and you will be changed but you will remember the dream. And you will wonder was I dreaming or is this the dream? Where am I? Who am I? What part am I playing here? How have I produced this? And with that kind of mind, then we start the true evolution.

Now that then also says that then everything — things — have a lineage back to primary consciousness. Everything has a history going back to that momentous moment, doesn't it? In other words — listen to me — perhaps the alchemist knows more than what is first perceived. Perhaps the alchemist is endeavoring to reach way back to this point here (seventh plane) to capture the atmosphere. And perhaps the philosopher's stone is the captured atmosphere of the seventh plane. And if it is, if it is induced into the electromagnetic body, it will rocket that body back to a seventh-level being and it will preserve it for all time. After all, shouldn't the prima materia be you?

I want you to do the List — but the List you do is what you wrote to your God today — over and over and over. And you are to go back into sleep with that List. How many of you understand? In other words, we are going to start to distort reality here (first plane). Sometime when you are laying down, you are going to have to surrender and simply say, "Maybe I am dead. Maybe I really am. So what do I need to do? What do I need to do here to remedy the situation?" And when you really believe it and you start speaking this, talking directly to yourself — because one way or another, people, that speech tonight in the covenant of your cape (Twilight™) is going to be revisited in the light; it already has and it is yet to come — well, what do you want to say? And if you totally surrender that maybe it has already happened, perhaps with such fortitude and intention and will and strength, tomorrow morning you may wake up and you may be born again. So be it.

OUR HEART WEIGHED AGAINST A FEATHER

Greetings, my beautiful masters. I salute you from the Lord God of my being to the Lord God of your being. Let's have a drink.

O my beloved God,
bless me this fine day.
Awaken my soul
and my conscience to hear.
God bless my life
and all the changes
set forth
therein.
So be it.

Now how many of you last evening had a very meaningful dialogue to that which has already been and will come again? How many of you felt the passion? So be it. How many of you see the purposeful good? So be it.

Now everything that you do — every thought that you think — should be weighed in the light of all eternity. Every thought, every feeling, should be weighed against a feather. Why? Because the soul sits right here in the chest. Why do you think that the heart sits off to the left of the breastplate? There is a cavity there and a very powerful gland. How many of you know the name of the gland? There is where the soul sits. And how oftentimes have you thought something and had a reaction here? Raise your hands. You did?

Now it is interesting to try to explain that reaction because if you have ever analyzed the reaction, when you get the feeling here, it is the same feeling whether it is guilt; it is the same feeling whether it is shame; it is the same feeling whether it is fear; it is the same feeling whether it is uncertainty; it is the same feeling whether it is hesitancy. Think about that. Remember this feeling you have had here (chest) felt the same way when you were afraid; felt the same way when you felt guilty; felt the same when you were ashamed, felt bad. It is the same feeling. So who determines the emotional state of this feeling right here? You do.

Now when you go against this (soul) by thinking something, when you go against this, what you are actually feeling in your chest is what you put together on the Plane of Bliss. On the Plane of Bliss — just like you did last night and we studied yesterday — we are viewing a life from the great self, from the God, the Holy Spirit, the soul, personality. We are viewing it from all different perspectives. And in the total view we get to become the bruising we do to someone else, because suddenly we feel the injustice we have done to someone else. We feel that. We feel the pain that we inflict upon others. We feel it first as the self, who feels totally justified in what they are doing, but they also get to perceive the feeling of the soul the moment that they do it. Their brain is wrestling with their soul, or heart as it used to be called, and they dish it out. When they dish it out, then they feel justified. So the self is seeing that in the light review. Then the God feels the reaction of it because we create reality. Our job is to create reality. So what is the intention and what did the intention deliver and add to the bounty of experience? We get to feel that, so suddenly we feel what happened to the other person. We feel what we have done.

Now in that review the soul has recorded that and so we take from the whole light review a collection of feelings, subtle energy ideas, intentions, and we have to hold that bag and take a look at it. What you do to others, you do to yourself. And we take a look at that and all of that then is recorded, and we walk away from the experience with a mixed bag of goodies because we also see what we do to others.

We see our thoughts. When we choose kindness and compassion and understanding over the rebellious nature of the human being, and fit for the survivalist — you know, when we choose to be all parts, and we elicit kindness, we elicit understanding to the capacity of understanding — we can say to another individual, "I do not understand thoroughly your experience, but I understand part of it and I understand my part in it. I understand what I have given here. Now in the clarity of my being I could have done better; I chose not to. But I do not understand the full impact of what you are going through because that is intimate and personal, and that is your path and you set that up on Bliss. Let me correct my part in it, not for you; for me."

So when we give understanding, we can be honest and say, "I cannot completely say and admit that I know what it is to walk in your shoes. I do bear wisdom of some things I have observed in you that I own, but you have to own those to see the colors that I see; otherwise it will make no sense to you." And they are opportunities. When we do that in life, when we elicit those unsolicited acts of kindness — because we can do something that on the surface appears unsolicited — we always have to check the ulterior motive because that is what we are going to be weighed against. That is what we are seeing in the end, and that is the place that we want to be the clearest. So every time that we have gone out of our way and that we have helped and that we have been kind without any thought of reward — nothing, just that it is its own reward — every time that we are patient, every time that we are strong in the feeling of weakness, those too are all seen and they are all weighed. And so we come from the experience, you know, bruised a little bit but feeling good, on the other hand, because our life was in some measure fulfilled in that we made life better for other people, because we made it better for ourselves.

You see, what you have to come to understand is that everything comes back to the ultimate creator, and the ultimate creator of every individual life is you. Why? Because you are the ones who are given the authority of free will and intention, and you get to use that however you see fit, without good or bad.

So what is the pain that we suffer? It is the pain that we give to others that hurts us. Our suffering is not about anyone else; it is about our suffering. And in that view, everything is weighed. And in so many lives, that unprovoked goodness does not outweigh the provoked intention to destroy, malign, or hurt for the sake of staying alive. So many lives are unjustly lived because they are lived for the sake of survival rather than the godhead itself. And so that which we do in each life weighs heavier in flaws than in perfection, so that is why every life you keep coming back. You keep going there, reviewing, coming back, and you start building it up until one day you tip the scale to where the remarkable good in you outweighs those flaws. That is what we are working for — polish. Now why? We could go anywhere else; correct? Well, yes? In the whole of the Void and indeed in the whole of the kingdom of heaven, you can go anywhere else.

But here is the point that you have got to understand. You can only do what you know. You can only go where you know and what you are attached to. And everyone is attached to the imperfection, in perfecting it. And for what reason; to be free? Why do we want freedom? Because we want to own this plane and we want to own the rapacious attitudes that seem to go along with culture. We want to own those to where we have none of them inside of us because we have a mission to do, to make known the unknown. In other words, we are explorers in the Void. We are voyagers to Infinite Unknown.

What kind of God would I be teaching you about if the only end to this life that you could see was a life lived like ordinary people in sort of a mundane situation that had no challenge to it, and had no adversity to it, and had no growth in it, to where every neighbor is trying to protect his or her own? What kind of God would give you such a life? I mean, is that the highest pinnacle of a life's achievement? No, and everyone has already lived that. The highest pinnacle is to address the adversity in life that we are vulnerable to and indeed to make short-order of it because we do not want to be attached to it. If we are attached to it in any sort of prejudice, we are going to be tied in at that moment of weighing ourselves in the light.

Now the remarkable gift — that some of you realize and not all of you yet realize — is the teaching yesterday. It is very profound because it suggests to you that if this were so — and it could be utterly possible that it is so, for what proof do you have that it isn't so? — that at this moment you know you are looking at you and, if not this moment, this moment is going to come, and how do you want to see it? Because this is a bus stop; this is a train station. And don't you have greater aspirations for life? What about all of those dreams that have flitted in and out that have gone unexperienced? How do we get those? By making room for them in our life. Well, how do we do that? By getting unstuck in our life and being so clear that we can entertain an idea, and it manifests without being clogged in the plumbing of the mind. How many of you understand that? So be it.

So when I say to you, think every thought as if it could be written across the sky for everyone to see — think every thought that in a hundred thousand years or a hundred years or five years that you would welcome that thought back, because it came from a state of honor — there are degrees of evolution; and everything you do, remember, consider doing them in the light of all eternity. What kind of revenge, petty revenge, is worth ten thousand reincarnated lifetimes? I daresay that the cost is just a little too heavy and that who is really worth that? No one is. No one is worth missing evolution for. That is the train I want you on.

Now in the light review, what happens is then when it is all said and done, then we are stripped of the emotions. They are being fed on by the light because they are polarized emotions. The lords of the light feed on polarized feelings — energy going this way and that way — because that is what light is, and we are stripped of it. And we are allowed to go off and rest and contemplate, and we are given exactly the most exquisite place that we could ever dream of to be in to do such a contemplation. And in that rest we have thousands of years — which may seem like an afternoon — thousands of years to ponder, to heal, to ripen, and to get ready to return.

168

COMMON THOUGHT IS WHAT CREATES OUR DAILY LIFE

Now does consciousness and energy on the Plane of Bliss work on the earth plane? Absolutely it does, because what happens at the lake of tranquility? What happens there? In contemplation, as we contemplate, as we view, as we remarkably and daringly become the whole self in any situation, we also become that in every desire. It is not simply a place to where we contemplate upon the misdeeds of our life. It is a place to where we contemplate upon the dreams of our life, and there we can have long dreams — long dreams. That oftentimes is the greatest healer of all, because the dreams can become so impassionate — impassionate on the Plane of Bliss is to mean analogical — that they become so analogical and so impactful that the whole of the being is there and transformed in the midst of the dream itself, and there they may dream dreams.

And you have done the same thing, especially when something tells you you can do that, that by virtue of dreaming it, what happens? Well, on the Plane of Bliss when the whole self is empowered and it analogically conceives a world, a life, an experience, it is not a matter of are you focusing there as a discipline. You really are just that. No matter what you do, you are in a state of focus that is very profound and so easy because that is the natural state on Bliss. You do not have a physical body pulling at you to be taken care of, unless you have been so physical that the idea of self cannot be understood unless it is understood inside of a body. But for the most part you are caught up in your spiritual body — beautiful, exquisite body, you know — and it doesn't pull on you. You do not have body problems. So naturally what happens in a state to where the self then is in contemplation or is in a dream? They are totally in a dream. There is no pull, none. So that is the state on Bliss.

How powerful is this? Here when you come to school and you learn — and then I endeavor for you, beseech you to carry that on into your life — I am endeavoring to get you to accept a state of focus and to be highly protective of the state of focus, because whatever sits there as common thought is reality. And by changing the ulterior motives in each of you intentionally helps dramatically alter the anatomy of common thought, you see, because if you are an unhappy person inside, your common thoughts just keep reflecting that. They just keep going out into your life.

Now I want you to listen to that because the seed of their flowering is the ulterior motive. If you are a revengeful person, you have hate in your heart, that is a seed, and it flowers common thought from it. Then an everyday exchange has an opportunity to be a flowering of a life. Here we have a flowering of poison, literally. That is the garden. That is the consciousness that is flowering in some of you. Well, that common thought is reality. And the idea is that if we can open up your chest, tear out all of the garbage that is in it, burnish those shelves and put one beautiful, brilliant thing there, that that becomes the ulterior motive, then the flowering of common thought from that will be assured that you will have a magical life and a sweet life, a life that is empowered, that is one with nature instead of warring against it, a life that allows the dream to come about quickly. You know, it is a light: the way you feel light in body, not heavy in body.

And on the Plane of Bliss our ulterior motive there is not buried — it is surface — and from that, there is a flowering in long dreams. Those who have the remarkable dreams of the future, that so analogical are they and such a long time are they in that state that when they incarnate, they seem to have a whole different agenda. They are not normal in the sense that other people are normal. What interests other people may interest them mildly for moments, but you begin to see that the thrust of this individual is much different, marginally different than people who do not come back with great dreams. And this becomes their ulterior motive, even as children, and that motive starts to build in their life. And they may build up rust and crust just from the harrowing experiences of society and culture, but for the most part so integrated is the dream from Bliss, the desire from Bliss, that it stays right underneath the surface. And all common thought that comes from it, though tainted by surface corrosion, is by and large much more powerful. These lives are going to be meaningful lives because the ulterior motive in them is meaningful — meaningful. See it as an innate goal that has been set into place.

When you don't dream those dreams and you are coming back with your mixed bag of things you have to take care of, then those are the ulterior motives that sit inside of you, and you come ⁓ere a harsh entity before, you are going to come again so that you have an opportunity in your ride it and turn it over. And you are going to d of individuals in your life as you did the last es they, who are endeavoring to learn too, for cur. So everything in one's life is an opportunity portunity to evolve, is an opportunity to change. : The soul feels here (chest). And why does it ssages? Because what we lay down in the carrier urn is the life plan for this existence. And that en we finish our contemplation, I am going to en the opportunity arises and we fall back into remember that the garbage can outweigh the We have a lot of garbage in there, and if we fall g, well, that is how I am; well, that is honorable, but now is not it honorable to say that this is my opportunity to change that in myself? Do I or don't I want to evolve? Do I want to grow or not? Do I want to partake of a life that I don't have to work so hard anymore in it, that I have laid down the good works in this life and that one day — because I am not finished here, I can't go anywhere else because my business is here, because I am too primitive to go anywhere else and too advanced to go somewhere else; I am caught right where I created it to be — that I can come back and have clarity and be so unattached but powerful? Yes, so somewhere we have to make up our mind to do the work.

Now when we go against that, you get this pain right here (chest). How many of you have felt it, again? You should listen to it. You should always listen to it because this is a log you laid down on Bliss. To go against it is then to have to repeat it. When do you get tired of doing that? Sometime you have to take a stand and make war and you conquer. Bring it on, and sharpen your sword and march. And I don't care; it is a humbling experience, but greatness comes from humbleness. Humble people are daringly bold. They are ostentatious.

When we live by this, when we feel fear in here — remember, the feelings are all the same — who is saying what this is? We are saying what it is. What are we afraid of? We always have to ask that question: Why am I afraid? Am I afraid of this confrontation? Am I afraid to be honest? What is the fear that I am feeling here? Or is that which I am feeling here being misinterpreted? Most of the time it is, because most people don't like to deal with their own conscience. That is why you have to have the whole self in the light review, because to view it from the self of personality is painful and it is difficult. That is the reason why the Observer is standing there, the Holy Spirit is there, that it can be switched with absolute love and support so that what can be seen will not be fearful. Our greatest fear is to make contact with our conscience, and we avoid it. That is what happens in here.

Now you have returned and are going to return with a bag of goodies. A lot of them just aren't pretty at all, but a lot of them are exquisite. And you are beautiful and you know that, and there are parts of you that love what you are. Maybe the wretchedness of you it far outweighs, but look for a little something. Hold onto it every day. I love this about myself. You know, that is the purposeful good. And you have to also put a smile on your face and say, "What is so marvelous about all of this, that these troubles that I have in my life, this personality that I have that is so hard to get along with, is that I know that about me. But what I celebrate is that I am so powerful I made me that way, and that is refreshing because I am really on the path to turning it around. I know I had the power to put it there. I know I have the power to erase it." You see? And maybe that is the only little thing that you can find that is sparkling about you, but that is enough.

There are others of you who are going to have just a whole lot of goodness. There is a whole, great, long margin of joy, a great margin. That joy is a natural effervescence of someone who has conquered. You know, there is more of that joy in their life than there is depression. These people have mastered. And that mastery is not about mastering other people; it is about ourselves. They have a natural state of joy that is a little disturbing because it almost smacks that they are really disinterested in your problems. But they are. They really are. And, you know, that just fries you. It fries you because, you know, you want people to feel sorry for you. And the people that don't, you know, you are not going to cater to them. You know, you want the woe-is-me group. Well, look around you. If you are a woe-is-me person, look around you; so are they.

But, you see, joy is a release and it is also wisdom, and that is what we get when we love ourselves enough to tackle our difficulties. To expect someone else to do it for us is meaningless. I, as your teacher, will not make you happy. I am here to tell you what you are — and you get to make choices from that — and to give you excellent knowledge that you can start to integrate, and to give you hope and to keep reminding you I am talking to Gods out here. I am talking to immortals that are so powerful that they can believe themselves into eternal death. That is how powerful you are. I am talking to Gods.

You see, that is what you keep forgetting. This is the pristine message. That is what you are going to know at the light. You know, you were worth coming and taking a second look at. Don't you see that? What if you weren't? What if this was it and then you went into the big sleep never to awaken again? This is what you keep forgetting, that you are a divine being. And that is so sweet because it means that you exist in the bosom of God, and that in there the only condemnation you ever have had is from yourself. And the only — only — reprieval that you will ever get is from yourself. And isn't that the way a sovereign should be? Absolutely.

YOU ARE GODS, THE CREATORS OF REALITY

When I talked to you yesterday about you already being dead, you just may be. But what I am here to remind you — and what you are going to hear again and I am going to be telling it to you when you view this life again — is you are God; remember that. You are divine; remember that. Everything is about choice and opportunity, which is your rightful place in the kingdom of heaven. And although the message yesterday seemed to cry out of doom and bewilderment, it was a message worthy for a divine ear. How many of you understand that?

Yes, you are worthy to hear that. That means you are a big person, a big being — a big being — and you are to remember that when you hear me again tell you that one blissful moment: You are God incarnated and you must choose the path to where that godhead is perceived as total power, total mind, total love, eternalness. You must create a life to where that remarkable character can be shining through you at all times; that I want you to remember that you have the power to have a life to where God is made manifest through you, and that the marvelous deeds of a supreme intelligence can be made manifest through you, and that all of the hurt and pain that you have created, you created.

It is never too late to say what do I want, to keep this game up or to be a marvelous being to where the power and love of the Holy Spirit flows through me? So how practical is that in life? Well, it enriches the job you are at. It shouldn't be a job; it should be an opportunity, a created, embellished opportunity to do better. It is an opportunity in your family to shine, to be unconditional love, to allow truth on every level; to your children, to love them unconditionally, to live a life to where you are a giant in their eyes instead of becoming small, when they are old enough to see your fallacy; that you live your life in such a way that is remarkable, that they being given in the care of you, you are exercising the great stewardship of showing another what it is to be better, to be greater, and to make certain that there is no hidden agenda that the child can see. This is an opportunity to be it to your lover, to your husbandman, to your wife.

When I told you yesterday why are you holding it together, that is more painful than being honest. It takes a great person to love you enough to say no, to love themselves enough to say no. Don't you want someone with substance, true character, that is dependable that you can count on? They are going to be at your back and by your side because they are worthy people; they are not hypocrites.

Why don't you let it fall apart? To many of you that sounded cruel. Why? Because you are taught to sacrifice, to hold it together? For what? A lie? What kind of fruit does that bear in a relationship? Let it go. I am talking about any level — wherever this problem is in your life — let it go. Shine. So what happens? Everyone packs up and moves; allow it. You call the shots here. You allow it. Why? Yes, it is emotionally hurtful, but what now is the new ulterior motive? It is honor; it is integrity. That sounds cruel; it sounds selfish. But isn't that what we are talking about here, is being in tune with self? And sometimes when you let it go, it is opening a cage and letting a bird fly. You never want to be a prisoner or a jailer, because when you are, you are that to yourself. Remember, we are coming back to the acts of the being who stands alone in a light review.

And you let it go. Let it fall apart. And you may fall apart, but there is an ulterior motive here for wellness. You don't have to say anything else. You have to excuse nothing. I don't feel anything but healing. That is enough. Anything else, that is subject to conjecture. How you are going to remold is going to be something that you have to allow to happen and allow yourself to grow according to the ulterior motive there. We have always got to make certain that is in place and it is clean.

So what happens? Many things are going to happen. The immature in your life are going to be dross and they are going to go away. Good. Good. It is about time. Let them go. The immature will always be yelping away, snapping and hissing at a distance, woe is me; woe is that. Now you get to see what you were holding together. Frightful, isn't it? A little frightening. You let it go because now everything becomes real clear to you — or what you let go of is feeling the same thing — and healing starts occurring in everyone's camp. Then what we have is a jump-start in a relationship, however, whatever, that relationship is. It could be you and a butterfly. Then you are off and running.

There are always alternatives, but the one that we care about the most is the one we bear ourselves. And that is the teaching because, I promise you, if you say I gave up my life and I lived it for this person, in the light you know what is going to be seen is resentment. That is not love, people. And what we want to do — and here was the lesson yesterday — we have an opportunity right now to be magnificent. Every opportunity is magnificent. We get to make a choice.

And we also have to do something else that is painful: We have to take our sword out and we have to cut the head off of our past. We have to raze it to the ground. Why? Because you want to do it in such a way that you never revisit it again — never, ever. Destroy it, everything about it. You destroy it because you never want to visit it again. I know it has served you. I know your victimization, your tyranny, your pain, your suffering, all that has served you. I know you use it against people to make them feel guilty, ashamed, feel sorry for you; it is all manipulation. It is manipulation. Are you that pitiful that you have to be so wretched to manipulate people? Are you really that pitiful? You see, I see you — and so does your God see you — as a wimp, a noxious wimp. Are you really so pitiful that you have to play games? No. Cut it to the bone. That is it. You were born two minutes ago. Two minutes ago you were reborn. That is what I am trying to tell you. This is a light review; you are going to be reborn again. Do you want to go back to your past? Want to go back to that previous life? Well, going back to your past is going back to a previous life. How many of you understand that?

Now here is an excellent example brought forward by a wonderful master. He said this (mystery of birth and death) is equal to the labyrinth.[12] And those of you who have had the sweet and wonderful opportunity to go and be a part of the labyrinth understand this, that very physical people all hang out together. And an advancing God in a spiritual life will go very far, can go very far into the labyrinth right into the Void, and it is done impeccably. Or you can say, "I know I can go on the adventure to the Void, but I am going to go back and retrace my steps and hang out back here with you. In other words, I would rather live in the aisleways than in the Void. Why? Well, that is my past, after all. It is important to me, so why am I even making an effort to go forward? Let me just stay here. It is no problem. It is my past." Or it is like going all the way and there is one more ladder that takes you into Bliss and you say, "No, I don't think I want to go there. I want to go back to my past. I have friends back there over the

12 In other words, it is equal to the discipline of The Tank™.

worms and I want to go back there and stay there for the rest of the day."[13] Isn't it like that? How many of you understand?

Being Consistent in the Disciplines of the Great Work

Now we are going to talk about last night. I left you with a teaching that you create the atmosphere and that all is life. You see, there is a school of thought that talks about the transmigration of souls to where starting with a lowly amoeba and a rock, their souls will start to migrate.[14] Well, that is true to a degree because everything is in evolution. And who are the engines of evolution? You are. And if the lowly amoeba got its haphazardly little start from something you were talking about with your God and off shoots an amoeba, well, then the amoeba actually represents that conversation.

Remember this right here? All energy waves are carriers of an idea, an intelligence, a thought. And, you know, this is what common thought looks like.

Fig. 8: Collapse of the Energy Wave into a Particle

---

13 The worms referred to are not living organisms. They are an aspect of the labyrinth structure and experience in the discipline of The Tank™.

14 The belief in the transmigration of souls is commonly referred to as metempsychosis: the belief in the passing of soul, Spirit, or personality upon death into another body, whether of the same or a different species. The Greek roots of this word are "meta," meaning change, and "psyche," meaning soul. Metempsychosis is another word for reincarnation. This belief was held broadly in all the religions of ancient Greece and the religions of the East. It is a belief that has been held by the majority of people who have ever lived.

This is a child's drawing but, you know, in that we learn the sweetest. Now this is what common thought looks like, and it is carrying thought out like this: It radiates from you like a central sun. Now in your bands you radiate common thought. And obviously this little entity is a pretty happy entity, so that the ulterior motive here is like a sunshine. And so because that sits at the basis of the mindful intelligence of this individual, then common thoughts are moving out into conscious energy potentials and they just start spiraling around us. You know, you are just dropping this stuff — here is an amoeba — and you don't even know that you are doing it.

You see, every thought that is radiating out there (the bands), it is doing this (see fig. 8) and then it is spiraling into it (the bands), and that is how we create reality. And when you come to school and you begin your mastership studies, you begin to see that this is what you have always done and that the reason you haven't seen remarkable things in your life is because they are all around you always. It is sort of like, you know, a fish wanting a drink of water. What do you say to a fish that says I am thirsty? Well, that is what you begin to understand. It starts to come together. And you really start to get a sense of this on the Plane of Bliss, and that because everything is already formed around you, you don't see that as miraculous, but in fact all of this has been making your reality continuously. And so if we say why is my life the way it is, then we have to search and find the seed, right here (the brain), that is causing that to happen.

Now if we know then that common thought is the power manifester, when we come to school we learn the diligence of discipline: focused concentration and long periods in the field (Fieldwork™), doing your List, going through the labyrinth. All disciplines we do here are about creating reality intentionally. We are intentionally doing something that is a natural state to you. But what is so marvelous about it is that it consists of ideas, thoughts — I give them to you; you start drawing them — that when you intentionally focus on them, they start radiating out of you. That wasn't just there on its own. It wasn't stimulated on its own because your modus operandi is a motive that is sitting there that the brain is hardwired to think every day. How many of you understand? And the teaching was every time you got your card on some marvelous thing that you had drawn, there was such a happiness inside of you because you saw it as such a miraculous sort of thing. I mean, there is such a joy in being able to do that about you, that you know what it is like when you find that first card — and you focus so hard and you have been impeccable and you find that card — and there it is, and your breath is taken away. I mean, you actually did this. But, you see, you actually do that every day. We have just artificially introduced an idea that you haven't thought about. How many of you understand? But the greatness of it is that idea manifested in the field. Now if that idea had taken hold as an ulterior motive, you would be radiating it every day.

So why did I teach you how to do the List? The List, for the sincere student, literally became a way to rewire the neuronet and, in doing so, to rearrange intent, except with most people what began to happen is that their intent or ulterior motive is ingrained so strongly when it comes to different things on the List, they don't believe in it. So when they come there, there is the ulterior motive that is not supporting the List, and that also comes off like this (see fig. 8). It is almost an intentional negation of something wonderful for you.

Now for the serious student in this school, it can look at its List and say, "Now all right. I have been able to manifest these things on my List, and as long as I do it consistently, I am radiating that thought out that it is going to happen. Why have certain things on my List not happened?" That is an indicator of what the ulterior motive is, and it is about self-discovery.

And what about why haven't you been able to do, you know, a remarkable healing? Because you don't believe that; that is the ulterior motive. And you can't trust that you can do it when you don't believe it. In other words, you have a house divided against itself. You have an opportunity for the miraculous but you have a decision that is already set inside of you that doesn't believe it, so you can't depend upon Blue Body™ work because it isn't the modus operandi in you. How many of you understand that?

So what do you do about that? Well, this is the work. You have to say to yourself, "If my card manifested in the field and these other things manifested, then I have a state of acceptance for them. If this doesn't, I don't have a state of acceptance," and why, and there is where you have to drag out the ulterior motive and look at it. And you say, "Did I get this from the Plane of Bliss?" Yes. Why? Maybe you have set it up not to be healed. Maybe you have set it up to be suffered. Maybe you need to suffer. Maybe that is how you set up the whole thing, because no-thing happens to you by accident; everything is intentional. All common thought is intentional. And sitting by the sea of tranquility, in that beautiful place, contemplation is radiating out of you like a great central sun.

So what was it? What is that thing that sits there that says you can have this but you can't have that? Is it changeable? Today it is changeable. Tell that to yourself reviewing this moment: "You change this. I am worthy of splendid health. You know why I am going to be worthy of it? Because I love myself and I love my life. I want to love my life throughout, and I just don't have room for anything other than life." So you have to look at it that way.

And then what do you do? You switch that out of your List and you put the ulterior motive in there. You change the motive. Instead of "I accept Blue Body™ healing," you put in there "I now accept life. I am worthy of health." And every time you say that and there is a balking in you, you say it a hundred more times until it surrenders — how many of you understand? — because it is easy to do it on the Plane of Bliss without the body. Here it is ingrained and it is a program in it, and you have to change the program. This is a part of being a master.

The other part is that if you don't, you are always radiating that you are not worthy of life, and it undermines everything. And that is the common thought that goes out, inasmuch as we have a sourpuss sitting up here that is hateful and vengeful. Well, as much as you sit there with terror and anger and malice, look at that. No matter what goes on during the day, you can wake up in the morning and the birds will be singing and you would just as soon that they be dead. Get them out of here. Your child wakes up happy and you don't want to see them. And everything has got this ugly little edge to it. That is common thought. What is it? Something sitting there. When are you going to get tired of that?

How many of you understand?

Now this is also about joy. God forbid you be happy. God forbid you be happy; don't want you to have one really happy day. I suffer. Look at this. You know, pigeons poop on their heads. Well, this could be a person who is not worthy of life, you know, and that radiates. It is in every little statement. It is in every little action. It is in every little feeling. It is just they are dripping with it. Why? Why don't you change that? Just change it; just change it; deal with it.

Then there are people who can't seem to make their fabulous wealth happen. Well, you know, self-worth is a marvelous thing because worth we see as energy exchange, self-worth. And there are people that if they don't feel worthy because they are burdened with guilt or shame or something on that order then, you see, when it comes to accepting fabulous wealth, wealth is equal to worth. And the lack of self-worth always undermines it. How can you keep saying I accept my fabulous wealth when the real core about worth negates that? How many of you understand that? You know, you have to change that. You have to say what am I not worthy of? Let us not talk of dollars and cents and rubies and gold. What do I not feel worthy about? Who convinced me, and what lie did I believe that I had no worth and no value? What did I accept that I keep negating opportunities with? You ask yourself that and don't be afraid to know the truth. Don't be afraid to feel what it is. Remember, the most thing you fear is your human conscience. Get into it and find out what did you do that causes you to have such lack in your life. And lack, it will have nothing to do with money; it will have everything to do with self-esteem. Have you programmed that into this incarnation some way, that your bag is so heavy on this side you don't feel worthy?

Well, we have to change that right now because any moment karma is neutralized. The moment ulterior motive is changed, there is no more karma. It is done. It is done. We are not God on a payment plan; it is done. We only have to find the seed right here (the brain).

Now happiness: You know, when we are ready to accept joy, we cannot accept joy based upon another person. Indeed, we cannot accept joy based on money, and we cannot accept joy based on age and appearance. We must have joy unconditionally, without people, places, things, times, and events, because to base it in anything else is to give our power away and our fruitful happiness. You have to learn to be happy with three beans. You have to learn to be happy without anyone in your life. Aren't you good enough to just be alone? Aren't you good enough company? If you are not and you are afraid to be alone, then maybe you should take a look at who you are living with, meaning you. Why don't you enjoy your company? You don't like your thoughts, eh? You don't like what you do? Well, that should be a clear indicator to you that no one will ever make you happy — not your children, not your appearance, not your disappearance, not how much money you have. Nothing is going to make you happy if you don't love yourself and come to terms with it, because that is who is going to stand in this light review, people.

And to do that is to love God. To do that is to have love for everyone else. To be happy without having to do something constantly and just sit and be mellow with your thought is an extraordinary something because it does this. When you are doing something and you are being entertained all of the time, your ulterior motive is coated with conversation. That is what you are radiating out there. To be happy with yourself is to be so clean that the sun comes out. That is when your great work is done. Now this isn't mass conversion; it is individual transformation. How many of you understand that?

These are the remarkable lessons that you are going to hear again. You are going to hear my voice tell you this when you are standing with your Holy Spirit. I want you to remember that. Remember, it is coming again and you are going to hear this again. And perhaps by the time you hear it again, you will have become it and the soul weighs like a feather. How exquisite.

Can you imagine on a human level how that makes me feel? Now you understand what my mission is? Now do you understand why I have such patience with you, why I love you so much? Do you understand why I talk and teach you the way that I do and I don't let you slide away with anything? Because it is going to come around again, and I know when you are standing there, I am going to be with you. And you are going to really realize that there really is something that just loves you. Your God just loves you, and this messenger really loves you and understands this is going to come again, every word, and every nod from you, and every movement, and everything you feel and don't feel. And by the time this comes around again and you are simply that and you are beautiful and you have cleaned your house, we are going to shine together.

How do you think I feel? Don't you know? You see, it isn't a matter about believing in me. Listen to what I am telling you: Believe in yourself. That is why I am back here, because every class we do is meaningful, and if it doesn't change you now, it is going to change you. If I don't get to you now, I am going to get to you. Do you understand? Don't be a buffoon and think this won't be remembered. Do not be a buffoon. Do not be so stupid as to think that this is going to be left out in your light review. It is in there.

So think about this for a moment, will you, because now you are getting to understand me. And you are getting to think much loftier. You are getting to have thought patterns much greater than that small, little, tiny, little life that you have had. You are starting to; you are opening up now. Think about this. What if everything you are seeing now you have become? Think about that. How does your conscience feel today? Is it heavy or is it getting lighter? Is it getting lighter? Well, you see, that then is evolution and that is getting those wings unstuck — you understand? — and you are starting to feel lighter and more effervescent. That radiates out of you.

Then what kind of rest period are you going to have after this review? I mean, I have given you such knowledge — that I haven't even scratched the surface — to get you to understand how to think and to tell you things that are going to be poignant to you, the moment that you look at this, that are going to turn you. It is like saying to you that I know that you have a choice in picking the body up or going on, and you can make another body, but sometime you are going to come to have to love this one. You have made it your master. You have given it the power to have dominion over you. But in doing that, you have done it a disservice because you are not there to rescue it when it is in trouble. And you don't know how to rescue it and you don't have the power to do it. You don't know how to keep it from aging. You don't know how to keep it well, how to give it peace, tranquility. You don't know how to do that. And by not being the master of it, you have given it a disservice.

And when you are standing there — this will come so quickly — and you say get back into your body, let us pray that you have loved your body enough by that point by being its master instead of its slave, and that you are no longer interested in appearances; you are interested in health. You are not interested in appearances, so stop blaming your body for getting someone or not getting someone, because it is going to die and be eaten up by a worm.

TRIUMPH OVER DEATH AND THE ALCHEMY OF TRANSMUTATION

When you love yourself enough to go back, then you are going to join a great group of masters because you are going to come back, and that heart is going to start beating, and you are bringing cognizant memory here and power. And then, you know, you can erase age; you can create glamour. You can become young, old, whatever. You have the power. The thing is, it is the gift that never dies so that you now have a body without loss of knowledge and memory, and that you can finish this up and slowly get lighter and lighter and lighter and lighter.

And what is a flaw, now you will correct because you are all beautiful. There is no such thing as ugliness in the kingdom of God. And be you judged by God, not by man, not by woman — be you judged by yourself, not others — then that is being absolutely pure and beautiful. And those of you who choose to do that are going to come back so extraordinarily enlightened, and you have seen the other side and you know this is the truth. You know it is. So everything else I have told you is the truth, and you know it is and you are victorious. You have championed death and live life in ultimate freedom. There are no gray areas. There is only ulterior motive.

And there are others of you that will say, "Ah, no. I know so much now that I want to make my body. I know how to do that now. I know how to make it, and I know how to make it to where it won't forget this moment." And you will do that because that is the range of knowledge you are going to have versus those pitiful Christians that go there to the light waiting for Jesus, you know, to save them or something; and then the Buddhists who just go to oblivion — orange oblivion — wing-tips and all.

You are going to have real knowledge to pose about life because life isn't bad. We made this life. All of these marvelous atoms that surround you, look at them, how they fall off of you. Well, you know, they fell off of you in every atmosphere that you have created, at every one of these kingdoms. Just by having a dream and analogically compressing it and moving back impregnates, pulls all of this energy with the idea itself. It is there and it just falls off of you. It is manifestation. Look around you; you are walking in your own stuff. Now that stuff, that primordial stuff, is intelligence and is you. The alchemists want to take the humblest to the greatest. Why do they want to do that? They want to take the humblest. Well, you know, there is nothing more humble than dirt. They want to take dirt and turn it back into this original right here (Point Zero). They have to go pretty far up to do that. Look at where they go (seventh plane).

The philosopher's stone is manifested right here (seventh plane). It actually is multiplied right there, sent back down, sent back up, involution, evolution, and there it is. You see, alchemy is about involution and evolution. It is about the transcendental life of particles into mass, out of mass. And why did they know that it is the great arcanum and the great panacea, meaning that it is the cure-all and the elixir of immortality? Because it was conceived on the seventh plane. It is right there with Point Zero, the beginning. How eternal do we get? And their thrust is to take the common to the uncommon, take it all the way back to the moment that we first did this (see fig. 6). Whatever is existing right there is the philosopher's stone right there.

Is it possible? Yes, because every particle is made up of particles within itself. And this is what they look like when they are unwound. So what is that then? We are consuming a substance that has been unwound as an idea we first had as God. Oh, cool; yes, that is very cool. We are consuming our consciousness and energy at this level (seventh plane). Oh, what does that do to the body? What does that do to all of the bodies? It is a powerful, radiating force that transforms. The body is no longer subject to time here (first plane). It is subject to eternity at Point Zero. How many of you understand that? It changes the molecular structure of the body and wholly opens the brain. What is it? Think of this: You are going to eat the substance of the first thought. You are eating your own original thought. You are eating your own idea. You are consuming the first bodies of God. Turn around and explain that. Now you understand an alchemist?

A true alchemist will always create the stone. Do you know why? Because what makes a true alchemist is the knowledge of the seven levels. They have to have a gnostic mind — a gnostic mind — to understand the beginning, Point Zero; the descent, involution; experience, evolution. And they understood that. Furthermore, they also understood that all substance, all things, were a natural fallout of that beginning so that there were levels to particles that contained literally the divine itself.

Now Yeshua ben Joseph said a most remarkable thing, as long as people understood it — so did Apollonius of Tyana — when he said the kingdom of heaven can be found in a grain of sand or a mustard seed. No one ever explained that adequately but, you see, what it meant was that in that small of a thing contained all the heavens. It contained it in atmospheric consciousness and energy. The ideas that exist there, the knowledge that exists there, are contained in a grain of sand.

The alchemists who understood consciousness and energy create the nature of reality, and not every one of them understood that — they did not understand energy carrying an idea with it — but those who did were the ones who were successful in developing the stone. Why? Because they understood then that dirt is an idea and it is a fallout from heaven. It is a fallout from Point Zero. It is a fallout from the seventh plane, the sixth plane, the fifth plane, the fourth plane; they understood that. And so they understood then what they needed to do was to take a grain of sand and to decay it.

Now remember when I talked to you about that the moment that you die, that the Spirit and soul leave the body, decay starts in immediately? How many of you remember that? Rigor mortis within minutes or hours; that is how fast decay happens. Move away from something that you love and then return within two weeks; there is a decay that has gone on in your absence. Are you listening to me? A decay. Why? Because you hold things together. When you leave, when the Spirit leaves the house, the house starts to decay. What is decay? It is simply the unraveling.

Now in the grain of sand, alchemists knew that they had to decay the grain of sand; in other words, they had to get it to decay. So the grain of sand molecularly started to fall apart, and each molecule containing those particles also started to separate. And in separation, each one of those particles were doing this inside of a molecule that itself is breaking up. How many of you see that? And along with it is coming the idea, isn't it?

So at first the intent has to leave the grain of sand. The intent has to leave it. And a master can make the intent leave the grain of sand. When the intent goes — look at it this way — the Spirit has left it, and what they were after was the Spirit escaping. We are after the Spirit escaping because the Spirit escaping is this, is the idea of it. How many of you understand? Now in its liquefaction, what used to be solid is in liquid flux. It is decaying, so it is coming apart. It is just like a caterpillar in a chrysalis, that the Spirit that holds the caterpillar together has left and there is a new Spirit; it is called a butterfly. Well, in the decay, the particle of sand goes together in a liquid form and all of this free energy is moving around in it. And all they have to do is to keep decaying this out of the different levels of energy.

In other words, they are taking this little grain of sand and they are going up with it with heat — with heat. Remember heat? What is heat? Why, it is nothing more than the friction of energy in atmosphere. Well, with heat they change its atmosphere. That is the way it works. And with continual change, then what happens is that this little particle of sand finally gets changed all the way up to where its nucleus is starting to come apart in its atomic structure. And as soon as we get the nucleus to come apart, then we take the eggs (subatomic particles) inside of the nucleus and we let those dissolve. We keep releasing. We keep getting the Spirit out of even the quarks that are inside of them and we dissolve them. And quarks are not going to dissolve until about here (fifth plane). When they come out, they have their whole energy, their whole short energy, that belongs to this plane here (fifth plane). And then from them, we are going to relax them until we get them up here (sixth plane) and we get it right to here (seventh plane).

When we get a grain of sand to relax all the way back to the beginning of its idea, we have opened up the idea of the seventh plane and the seventh body. We are right next to Point Zero, and that is sheer immortality. And then when you feed that and consume that into a physical body, it does exactly what it is supposed to do: The idea turns back on the giver and restores the brain of the original giver. That means the subconscious comes alive because in it, it has the exact moment that that idea came into being, and it is activated. And then we have a body whose vibratory rate is extraordinary and it is going through a metamorphosis. It is being dissolved slowly into the immortal. And it will always be beautiful. Turn to your neighbor and explain. You have learned? So be it. I love you. So be it.

Fig. 9: The Atomic Structure

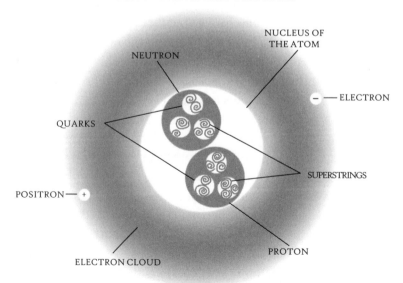

CHAPTER 6
CONCLUSION: DIMENSIONAL MIND VS. LINEAR MIND

"When one creates an ideal in consciousness, he should know without a shadow of a doubt that it is a reality in life without the need for justification from the senses. You have the power to create the miraculous. Expand your boundaries to include the extraordinary."
— *Ramtha*

Well, where are you?[1] Is it happening? Yes, it is. Now for the fanatics in the audience, you do not need to call the telephone company and say, "I am dead, so I don't have to pay my bill anyway." They just may haul you away, and that certainly wasn't in the program now, was it?

You know, great masterful people are extremely compassionate beings, as you can imagine. And they are heavy-laden with wisdom — heavy-laden with wisdom. Imagine for a moment how they then must think. You got a taste of it this weekend. What is on their mind? Well, what is on their mind is their ulterior motive; it is always their motive. And it can be as vast as the Void at midnight. It will never be small. It will be lofty and progressive. They have come by this way and, with their heavy-laden wisdom, there is often a temptation to help ignorant people. But they also have wisdom that teaches them that ignorant people also carry with them the baggage of victimization and that sometimes help can be the greatest hindrance, because in trying to help someone, who only sees life as a victim sees life, then any help they consider that which is termed making life difficult for them. It becomes harder.

Well, what kind of important insight do you need when you are working with people? You have got to be able to see their thoughts and their intent and to see all the potentials that come off of them, just like that: to be able to know their soul, to be able to read their thoughts, to be able to understand who needs it and who doesn't need it. Obviously everyone needs it but not everyone is mature enough to get it. Not everyone, as it were, is ready to advance in their life. That is the reason why so many people are so closed-minded and they are so lazy. They would rather have someone else think for them than they do it themselves.

Now not everyone will understand this message. Not everyone will understand it because they cannot fathom anything other than a linear mind. They cannot fathom the split picture happening simultaneously. They cannot possibly imagine that it has already happened and they are reviewing it, and then that the next set of occurrences and enlightenment will be that if it is so, then I can change it in any moment. They can't think that way. They only

1 Are we alive or dead and reviewing our life?

think linearly: up and down, born, dead, back and forth. They cannot think multiple.

Well, a dimensional mind is exactly what a master must have because a master knows they are consciousness and energy. Why would they choose a linear path? Why wouldn't they choose all paths simultaneously? Interesting concept, isn't it? Instead of becoming, they have already become. Do you understand? And to be able to see all potentials simultaneously, how do they do that? They made it their intent to do that. Just as you make it your intent to be a certain way, their intent is to know all things. And they get it. What is going to stop them?

Isn't creating reality equal to what you can dream? Isn't it equal to that which is termed the level of knowledge which one possesses? Why, it is the difference between a child dreaming and an adult dreaming. As we gather more information and more data, it broadens our horizons. So this weekend is endeavoring to do that. But you have to know lofty beings think lofty thoughts. They think them in just the same way: This moment, in the light of all eternity, I exist. How shall I shine? What sort of benefits do I want to come back to me? What path do I want to walk, because the path that I walk will be sprinkled with the sand of my consciousness. Is that going to be a prickly path? Is it going to be a dangerous path? Are the sands that you walk upon — the ideals that are coagulated underneath your feet, that saffron dust — are those explosive particles? Are they poisonous particles? Are they dangerous particles? Are they ideas of love, opportunity, and unlimitedness? How is your path coagulated?

You cannot walk on anyone else's path. Well, look at this, this little creature here. I adore this. It looks like New Year's, doesn't it?[2]

FIG. 10: THE ATOM

2 See fig. 10.

Look at this coming down here coagulating (see fig. 8). The very ground you walk on, you change. The very path, the very day-to-day existence of your life, is made up of your own consciousness. So when you are unraveling that bit of sand and taking it back to the seventh level, you can bet there is going to be some rocky road ahead because of the way you laid it down.

From this day forward, take a look at where you are standing; take a look at what surrounds you. What is the glue that holds that cabin together? What is the mind force in those things around you? Were they built upon a consciousness whose seat was anger? What was their ulterior motive, because that is coagulated in the stuff around you and the stuff you are standing on.[3] Think about it. It is how a master thinks. A master would not walk on any ground but their own. They won't walk on any ground but their own. Remember, the moment you leave your house, it starts to decay. Think about that. And if someone comes in and fixes it up, it is their energy they fix up. How many of you understand that? How could an enlightened being stand on the ground of a reality of anyone else except themselves?

So now you begin to understand those mysteries about those masters that walked the path of saffron dust. And the creatures, they are adored by them and they lay down at their feet. And the birds, they land upon them. And flowers bloom where they walk, that those masters walk the path of healing. And whoever follows right behind them is healed, just stepping on the same ground they stepped on. It is because the ground is them. We are not separated from our environment. Our environment is the coagulated force of common thought.

Where do you get the idea that a place is haunted? Isn't there

3 Edward Witten, a physicist at the Institute for Advanced Study at Princeton, is the leading proponent of superstring theory, which holds that quarks are constructed of strings. Superstrings exist in a ten-dimensional space-time. The extra six dimensions are enfolded to form the internal structures of quarks and electrons. The size of the string scale is 10^{-33} cm, a billion, billion times smaller than the size of a proton at 10^{-13} cm. Superstrings have been described as vibrating threads of energy or rips in the fabric of space-time. They are either open-ended like lengths of rope or looped like rubber bands. Each string — like a piano string — has many different modes of vibration or harmonics. One of these modes has the properties that describe the long sought-after graviton, the quantum of gravitational waves. In contrast to conventional quantum theory, which makes gravity impossible, string theory requires gravity. Thus string theory unifies the theories of general relativity and quantum theory, the models of

truth to that wives' tale or husbands' tale? Isn't there? It is true that earthbound spirits, people who are very carnal individuals, do not have knowledge except live day to day for their bodies. They cannot fathom themselves without the body because the body was every bit their consciousness. It was their path. And yet it is into rot now and decay. And they are earthbound and they stay within the areas to where they have energy. They stay in the atmosphere. They stay in the place they occupy because that is where they are grounded at. Now also the ground in which they were grounded at continuously replays an energy. So what is a vaporous vision? Indeed, what is it? What is it that sometimes, in the vapor rising off certain pieces of ground, that you can see a faint image? You know why? Because that ground was made up of that common thought.

There is much to be said then about the American Indian or the South American Indian who believed that Spirits live of their grandfathers in the mountains, or Spirits of their mothers upon the prairies, or that the great chiefs gather in some canyon or some mountaintop, or the Spirit of the great buffalo still exists. Why would they have that idea? Why? Because the spiritual energy has made that place what it was. That is why it is sacred. That is why they can go and powwow in that place and sit upon the very ground of intense common thought and receive the energy of their elders. It is a truth.

Why wouldn't it be a truth? How else is the stuff of matter made? By accident? No. There are no accidents in God's kingdom; there is only intention. What makes a holy place? A holy thought. The field is a holy place.[4] This arena, the Great Hall, is a holy

elementary particles and the four forces. From 1970 to 1994, five superstring theories and one supergravity theory were developed, each differing significantly from the others in the general properties of the strings. In 1995, Witten united all six of the theories into a single, more fundamental theory he called the M Theory. The M stands for matrix or membrane and has eleven dimensions. In M Theory, strings and loops are anchored to sheets and bubbles called d-membranes or d-branes. They also describe the theoretical subatomic black holes speculated by some scientists. Ramtha's eight-spatial diagram, showing the sevenfold involution of consciousness and energy from Point Zero (see fig. 3), can be described in terms of the M Theory. Point Zero would be similar to a subatomic black hole. The superstrings would correlate to the seven planes of existence, six of which are rolled up or enfolded, plus the dimension of time and the three dimensions of space: length, width, and depth.
4 The field used for Fieldwork™.

place because you have sat here and you have done great work here. If this had been a great arena of great tragedies, you would be sitting in sorrow and you would feel it. Why? Because the particles that are in slow decay here are oozing with the energy of that sorrow. How many of you have experienced that? So be it.

Now that is why sometimes in destroying your past, sometimes that is exactly what you need to do. You need to unfurl that which is termed the energy and let it rot. Let it go back and let it be purified. Purification by fire is a long ritual of burning — of burning — a place of sorrow, of burning a place of memory, of burning a haunt. What is burning doing? It creates the internal sulfur of the wood itself to ignite and unravel, and the common thought goes up in smoke. Turn to your neighbor and explain. How many of you understand? That is the reason why in doing Consciousness & Energy™ work, you do not wear jewelry while you are doing focusing — particularly metals having to do with the past — because the past is looped into the energy.

Metal is perhaps the greatest retainer of consciousness and energy there is. That is why gold is given in friendship and love. And when the feeling is no longer there, it should be taken off and melted down, because otherwise if you continue to wear it, you are continuously getting fed a thought. How many of you understand? You do? Beautiful.

Now does this mean that you go home and set brush fires? I don't want you to do that. I want you to understand that sometimes maybe that invisible depression you are feeling is where you are standing. It is the room you are at. It is something that is around you and that it is feeding back to you — how many of you understand? — and that needs to be taken care of. Remember, we cannot stand on any ground that has not been affected. All ground is affected. Masters create their own path. How many of you understand that? I ask you to do that, because to see wherever you step and wherever you go, simply to be the extending environment of your choice, is still an immature master; it is an immature student. Understand the effect is everywhere and that the fallout of common thought is coagulating all of the time.

Think about this: how many times you have had a room that has nearly been hermetically sealed, and you come back and there is dust. Where did it come from? It is your thoughts coagulating in the room or it is the room in decay. You don't have to have any source for it to come in; it will just come of itself. It is in the atmosphere. How many of you understand? So be it. Now we are talking of layers of magic here.

So what happens then when you create a change in the ulterior motive? Then you start broadcasting common thought, and it just starts manifesting around you. When masters don't want dirt on their garments because that is not where it belongs, it never gets there. When masters walk lightly on their path, it is because their common thought is light common thought. When masters seemingly have a seamless life, it is because they made it that way. And it seems that no matter what they do, they do it well and things always work out for them. That is because that is the way they have made it. That is because they fundamentally think that way and everything within their orbit is wound up in such thinking. Do you understand?

Now this should be very impactful for you. You should go home and take a look at what depresses you and take a look at where you are at. What is stored in the fabric around you, what kinds of thoughts? They should be changed. Furthermore, you should remember to remind yourself that when you do create your day dutifully, as you have been taught to do, that when you create your day, that this is how you are creating it and that day becomes the fallout of this common thought — an intentional common thought.

So you are not at the place at this very moment that you simply wake up and start thinking like a master. You are in the habit of thinking, "Oh, my God, it is morning; and the hour, it is late, and I wish to sleep longer." You see, you are not in the habit of opening your eyes and by the time you have opened them, you have already created half of your day just by the way that you think. You have to discipline yourself to create those common thoughts of creating your day exactly the way you want it. And it is like magic. Why? Because the fallout is happening through common thought coagulating as your path, as your day itself.

What couldn't you include in it? If your intention is to have a marvelous day, a magical day, a healing day, an energetic day, a miracle day, that is the common thought you have to radiate, and that day will give you exactly that. It works every time unless, of course, you have got sitting there some wretched ulterior motive that is going yeah, yeah, yeah, yeah, yeah. You have got to get rid of those things. Then the day has the fallout of the miraculous — how many of you understand that? — and God does not disappoint you.

So what about this life? It is the fallout from the Plane of Bliss. What about this light review? It is the fallout from your life. What about this review? It will be remembered. What do you get from it? All the advantages of extended wisdom, opportunity, choice, and change. Now what you do with that is entirely up to you because you are the Lord God of your being, a sovereign. But never let a day be wasted. It is precious life, one day closer to eternity.

And, remember, speak all things and think all things by the measuring stick of the light of all eternity. When you do, you will have learned the rule of the masters and your life will be richer, happier, more joyful, more peaceful, more comfortable, more beautiful, and more wonderfully predictable. When you are living that way, there is nothing to be afraid of.

Moreover, if this weekend has taught you about ulterior motive and your intention — and you understand that the greatest fear that you have in your chest is confronting your own conscience — perhaps it is time you did that and you got in there and saw what you have been afraid to see and start to change it. If you do, you will understand the Plane of Bliss. And this life — this life — can be the Plane of Bliss.

Remember, you have the opportunity to be a linear-thinking God or a multidimensional one. I would say go for it on every level, and you live this day multidimensional, and you live it in such a way that it can be viewed over and over and over as if this day is the day you are viewing it, and how do you want it lived. So be it.

I love you. I will see you in the light.

O my beloved God,
give I thanks greatly
for this review.
And of this life,
I do cherish
and honor.
O my beloved God,
I desire
clarity
and adventure.
Free my life
from my illusions,
that my adventure
may begin.
So be it.

RAMTHA'S GLOSSARY

Abstract thought. Abstract thoughts are concepts of the unknown. They are paradigms of thought that have not been experienced yet and thus have no emotional charge.

Aeroship. It refers to a spaceship, UFO, or airplane.

Age of God. The Age of God is a time when scientific developments will bloom greater than ever before. This age will come about through a deliberate change in time and the values of time. Disease, suffering, hatred, aging, death, and war will no longer be upon this plane, but continuous life. It is through knowledge, understanding, and profound love that these things will come forth in the life of each entity.

Ahk Men Ra. It is the name of one of the individual groups of Ramtha's school of Enlightenment created by Ramtha. He named and empowered each group with a specific mission and purpose that gives unity and identity to its members.

Akasha. It is a term of Sanskrit origin used in Hindu philosophy to describe the netherworld, the ether, or spiritual realm.

Altered ego. Altered ego is a qualified version of the psychological term of Latin origin, the *alter ego*. It refers to the human limited personality, and it expressly indicates the alteration and suppression of the true and divine self of the individual done by the individual.

Altered thinking. Refers to the thought processes of the altered ego.

Analogical. Being analogical means living in the Now. It is the creative moment and is outside of time, the past, and the emotions.

Analogical mind. Analogical mind means one mind. It is the result of the alignment of primary consciousness and secondary consciousness, the Observer, and the personality. The fourth, fifth, sixth, and seventh seals of the body are opened in this state of mind. The bands spin in opposite directions, like a wheel within a wheel, creating a powerful vortex that allows the thoughts held in the frontal lobe to coagulate and manifest.

Ancient wisdom. It refers to the wisdom of the ages, the knowledge of every great master who has ever lived and become enlightened. It is the truth behind the disciplines of the Great Work and the content of Ramtha's teachings.

Antichrist. The Antichrist is the altered Christ, the limited human personality that destroys our true divine self. It refers to anything or anyone who suppresses and robs humanity from its birthright and divinity.

Ascended master. An ascended master is a person who has mastered the physical plane, the limitations of space and time, and conquered death. These masters have attained the ability to increase the frequency of their physical bodies to a point where they can leave this plane and manifest themselves in any other plane of existence or dimension they choose. Ramtha, Yeshua ben Joseph, Buddha, Rathabim, Zarathustra, Takahshunuman, Apollonius of Tyana, among others, are all ascended masters. Ramtha was the first member of the human race to transcend this plane and ascend without ever experiencing death.

Ascension. Ascension is the natural result of becoming enlightened. It is the result of opening all of the energy centers in the human body and the complete blooming of the subconscious mind which results in the absolute freedom over all the planes of existence. Ramtha was the first human being born of man and woman to ascend from this plane without ever experiencing death. He elevated himself above his people after teaching them for 120 days all that he had learned about the Unknown God. After saluting them farewell, he raised the frequency of his body to a lofty place until he disappeared with a flash of blinding light. Yeshua ben Joseph is recorded to have experienced ascension from the physical plane after his death and resurrection in front of his disciples by the Sea of Galilee.

Assay. It means the test of the initiate. These events are usually ten days and allow the students to test their level of accomplishment.

Atlatian. Atlatian is the same as Atlantean. It refers to a person from the continent of Atlantis.

Atrium of the Constants. A plane of existence of higher frequency than the physical plane where the souls await their opportunity to be incarnated into a physical body.

Avatar. A master who has the power to manifest at will but who has yet to be fully realized as a master and conquer death.

Awakened being. It is a person who is enlightened and is no longer a victim of their genetics or environment. This phrase describes a master who consciously creates their own reality.

Bands, the. The bands are the two sets of seven frequencies that surround the human body and hold it together. Each of the seven-frequency layers of each band corresponds to the seven seals of seven levels of consciousness in the human body. The bands are the auric field that allow the processes of binary and analogical mind.

Binary mind. This term means two minds. It is the mind produced by accessing the knowledge of the human personality and the physical body without accessing our deep subconscious mind. Binary mind relies solely on the knowledge, perception, and thought processes of the neocortex and the first three seals. The fourth, fifth, sixth, and seventh seals remain closed in this state of mind.

Blue Body™. It is the body that belongs to the fourth plane of existence, the bridge consciousness, and the ultraviolet frequency band. The Blue Body™ is the lord over the lightbody and the physical plane.

Blue Body™ Dance. It is a discipline taught by Ramtha in which the student lifts its conscious awareness to the consciousness of the fourth plane. This discipline allows the Blue Body™ to be accessed and the forth seal to be opened.

Blue Body™ Healing. It is a discipline taught by Ramtha in which the student lifts its conscious awareness to the consciousness of the fourth plane and the Blue Body™ for the purpose of healing or changing the physical body.

Blue Plane. *See* **Fourth plane.**

Blue webs. The blue webs represent the basic structure at a subtle level of the physical body. It is the invisible skeletal structure of the physical realm vibrating at the level of ultraviolet frequency.

Body/mind. Body/mind consciousness is the consciousness that belongs to the physical plane and the human body.

Boktau. It means the great test. It is the name of a long retreat in Ramtha's School of Enlightenment that usually lasts at least thirty days. A mini-Boktau is a shorter version of this retreat, which usually lasts about a fortnight.

Book of Evolution. It is the record of all the experiences of the soul in its journey from the first plane of physicality back to the seventh plane and Point Zero.

Book of Involution. It is the record of all the experiences of the soul in its journey from Point Zero to the densest plane of existence, the physical plane.

Book of Life. Ramtha refers to the soul as the Book of Life, where the whole journey of involution and evolution of each individual is recorded in the form of wisdom.

Box, the. The box refers to the set of attitudes, habits, beliefs, and thought processes accepted by the human person that keeps it from exploring new paradigms of thought and experience. The box is the same as the neuronet and the human personality.

Breasts of Isis. Ramtha calls the amygdala and the hippocampus the Breasts of Isis.

C&E™ = R. Consciousness and energy create the nature of reality.

C&E™. Abbreviation of Consciousness & Energy™. This is the trademark of the fundamental discipline of manifestation and the raising of consciousness taught in Ramtha's School of Enlightenment. Through this discipline the student learns to create an analogical state of mind, open up its higher seals, and create reality from the Void. A beginning C&E™ workshop is the name of the introductory workshop for beginning students in which they learn the fundamental concepts and disciplines of Ramtha's teachings. The teachings of the beginning C&E™ workshop can be found in *Ramtha, A Beginner's Guide to Creating Reality,* REVISED AND EXPANDED ED. (Yelm: JZK Publishing, a division of JZK, Inc., 2000), and in *Ramtha: Creating Personal Reality*, Video ed. (Yelm: JZK Publishing, a division of JZK, Inc., 1998).

Carbule. Carbule refers to the carbon tubules, the microtubules, or skeleton of the cell.

Cartouche. It is a symbol that represents the essence of an idea or a person.

Chakra. Chakra is a Sanskrit word. A chakra is where two lines of energy cross. A chakra point is an intersection point of energy, something quite different from the seven seals or centers of consciousness in the human body.

Christ. Christ is not the name or title of a single individual. Christ is the name given to all those individuals who have mastered the physical plane and conquered death. The Christ in the human person refers to the God within, the divine aspect of the person.

Christ walk. The Christ walk is a discipline designed by Ramtha in which the student learns to walk very slowly and acutely aware. In this discipline the students learn to manifest with each step they take the mind of a Christ.

Christ-in-mass. This term refers to the feast of Christmas. It also refers to the Christ consciousness being present in human flesh.

Collective attitude. It is a set of attitudes and thought patterns common to a group of people.

Collective consciousness. This concept is similar to Karl Jung's collective unconscious. A collective consciousness is a recognizable state of mind that a group of people, country, or culture, share in common.

Collective subconscious. It is a collective state of consciousness common to humanity, although most people are unaware of it. It is also called social consciousness or body/mind consciousness. It is the consciousness of the physical plane and the first three seals.

Common thought. Common thoughts are the thoughts that have already been hardwired in the brain through experience and are common to the human personality.

Consciousness. Consciousness is the child who was born from the Void's contemplation of itself. It is the essence and fabric of all being. Everything that exists originated in consciousness and manifested outwardly through its handmaiden energy. A stream of consciousness refers to the continuum of the mind of God.

Consciousness and energy. Consciousness and energy are the dynamic force of creation and are inextricably combined. Everything that exists originated in consciousness and manifested through the modulation of its energy impact into mass.

Consciousness & Energy™. *See* **C&E™.**

Constants. Beings who live in the Atrium of the Constants, who are the overlords responsible for the cycles and the balance of the natural kingdom.

Cosmic glue. It is the term Ramtha uses to describe the force that holds the universe together. He describes love as the cosmic glue.

Critical mass. It refers to the manifestation and coagulation of consciousness into mass.

Crosham. It is the name of the broadsword Ramtha used in his lifetime. This sword was so large that it took the hands of ten men to hold its hilt.

Crossover. This term is used to describe the souls who wanted to understand the opposite sex in their next incarnation while retaining the perspective of their gender. Crossovers can be understood as men living in women's bodies and vice versa. Some of the people who are confused about their sexual orientation oftentimes are crossovers, although not always.

Dark night of the soul. It is a time of great emotional suffering that results from profound changes in the person's understanding of itself. It is when energy rushes through the emotional body and becomes purified and freed from the attachments we placed on it. It is a reverse charge into the brain that activates the energy field of the body and causes suffering.

Daughter of God. This concept expresses the divine inheritance of every individual, making special emphasis on the equality of women.

Dialogue days. The Dialogue days refers to the sessions people had with Ramtha in which the participants were encouraged to ask personal and direct questions to Ramtha. These sessions were held before Ramtha's School of Enlightenment was established in 1988.

Dimension. A dimension is the atmosphere or environment created between any two points of consciousness. There are seven major planes of existence and an infinite number of dimensions to each of them.

Dimensional mind. A dimensional mind is the mind of a master who no longer thinks in terms of linear time or one dimension of time and space. A dimensional mind is a mind that is able to see all potentials simultaneously.

Disciplines of the Great Work. Ramtha's School of Ancient Wisdom is dedicated to the Great Work. The disciplines of the Great Work practiced in Ramtha's School of Enlightenment are all designed in their entirety by Ramtha. These practices are powerful initiations where the student has the opportunity to apply and experience firsthand the teachings of Ramtha.

Dreams. Dreams find their source in human consciousness. They are the realities of other dimensions of thought and not just mere fantasies. Dreams are the medium by which the subconscious mind communicates with the physical body and repairs it during sleep. Most dreams fall under this category, although some dreams can also be prophetic in character. A conscious dream is a form of creating and manifesting reality at will, which is used in the disciplines of the Great Work.

Earthbound spirits. Earthbound spirits are the spirits of people who have died but who have not let go of their former life and physical existence. They exist in the infrared frequency band and are commonly known as ghosts.

Ego. The ego is the self, the true identity of the human person.

Electrum. This term refers to an electromagnetic field that has positive and negative poles called electricity.

Elohim. It is the name of one of the individual groups of Ramtha's school of Enlightenment created by Ramtha. He named and empowered each group with a specific mission and purpose that gives unity and identity to its members. This Hebrew word literally means the Gods, and it is sometimes used in reference to a specific group of the Gods that came to the planet earth.

Elohim Ka Men Ra. It is the name of one of the individual groups of Ramtha's School of Enlightenment created by Ramtha. He named and empowered each group with a specific mission and purpose that gives unity and identity to its members.

Emerald of your universe. The planet earth.

Emotional body. The emotional body is the collection of past emotions, attitudes, and electrochemical patterns that define the human personality of an individual. Ramtha describes it as the seduction of the unenlightened. It is the reason for cyclical reincarnation.

Emotions. An emotion is the physical, biochemical effect of an experience. Emotions belong to the past, for they are the expression of experiences that are already known and mapped in the neuropathways of the brain.

Enchantress. The enchantress is Ramtha's poetic name for the moon.

Energy. Energy is the counterpart of consciousness. All consciousness carries with it a dynamic energy impact, radiation, or natural expression of itself. Likewise, all forms of energy carry with it a consciousness that defines it.

Enlightenment. Enlightenment is the full realization of the human person, the attainment of immortality, and unlimited mind. It is the result of raising the kundalini energy sitting at the base of the spine to the seventh seal that opens the dormant parts of the brain. When the energy penetrates the lower cerebellum and the midbrain, and the subconscious mind is opened, the individual experiences a blinding flash of light called enlightenment.

Esoteric. This term refers to sacred or hidden knowledge.

Etheric. It is something that belongs to the netherworld, the ether, the spiritual order.

Evolution. Evolution is the journey back home from the slowest levels of frequency and mass to the highest levels of consciousness and Point Zero.

Exploding the volcano. This expression is used to describe the movement of the kundalini energy effected by the discipline of C&E™.

Fantastic realism. This concept describes the reality created by a lofty state of consciousness. It refers to the reality experienced by the masters.

Father, the. This term refers to the Source, God, Point Zero.

Field, the. *See* **Name-field.**

Fieldwork™. Fieldwork™ is one of the fundamental disciplines of Ramtha's School of Enlightenment. The students are taught to create a symbol of something they want to know and experience and draw it on a paper card. These cards are placed with the blank side facing out on the fence rails of a large field. The students blindfold themselves and focus on their symbol, allowing their body to walk freely right up to their card through the application of the law of consciousness and energy and analogical mind.

Fifth plane. The fifth plane of existence is the plane of superconsciousness and x-ray frequency. It is also known as the Golden Plane or paradise.

Fifth seal. The fifth seal is the center of our spiritual body that connects us to the fifth plane. This seal is associated with the thyroid gland and with speaking and living the truth without dualism.

First plane. It refers to the material or physical plane. It is the plane of the image consciousness and Hertzian frequency. It is the lowest and densest form of coagulated consciousness and energy.

First seal. The first seal is associated with the reproductive organs, sexuality, and survival.

First three seals. The first three seals are the seals of sexuality, survival, pain and suffering, victimization, and tyranny. These are the seals commonly at play in all of the complexities of the human drama.

Focus. The ability to focus on a thought is one of the main components of the disciplines of the Great Work. It is when a holographic picture representing a thought is held consciously and analogically in the frontal lobe of the brain.

Fourth plane. The fourth plane of existence is the realm of the bridge consciousness and ultraviolet frequency. This plane is described as the plane of Shiva, the destroyer of the old and creator of the new. In this plane, energy is not yet split into positive and negative charge. Any lasting changes or healing of the physical body must be changed first at the level of the fourth plane and the Blue Body™. This plane is also called the Blue Plane, or the plane of Shiva.

Fourth seal. The fourth seal is associated with unconditional love and the thymus gland. When this seal is activated, a hormone is released that maintains the body in perfect health and stops the aging process.

Free space. Free space is the experience of breaking free from the box and the molds of our limited personality. Free space is described as ecstasy. It is the experience of a broader, loftier perspective that allows the individuals to see with clarity and understand things that seemed chaotic and without solution in their lives before.

Frequency. Frequency is the vibratory speed that characterizes a wave of energy. Frequency is used to describe the vibratory rate of the particles and waves of a particular plane of existence.

Fruit of the vine. Wine.

Gnosis. Word of Greek origin, meaning knowledge. This word was used by the gnostic movements of the beginning of the Christian era to describe a system of knowledge or understanding of God, the creation, the human condition, and destiny, revealed by a transcendental source. This sacred knowledge had a redemptive or liberating effect on the individual.

Gnosticism. Gnosticism is an 18th century label for the gnostic movements of the beginning of the Christian era which present a vast array of teachings drawn from a variety of existing traditions. Their basic ideas are a dualistic view of the world. They believe that each human being has a spark of the divine that is trapped in matter, causing a conflict between light and darkness, knowledge and ignorance, good and evil. The revelation of sacred knowledge allows the soul of the individual to be liberated and escape from the flesh back to God, its source.

God. Ramtha's teachings are an exposition of the statement, "You are God." Humanity is described as the forgotten Gods. God is different from the Void. God is the point of awareness that sprang from the Void contemplating itself. It is consciousness and energy exploring and making known the unknown potentials of the Void. It is the omnipotent and omnipresent essence of all creation.

God within. It is the Observer, the true self, the primary consciousness, the Spirit, the God within the human person.

God/man. The full realization of a human being.

God/woman. The full realization of a human being.

Gods. The Gods are technologically advanced beings from other star systems that came to earth 455,000 years ago. These Gods manipulated the human race genetically, mixing and modifying our DNA with theirs. They are responsible for the evolution of the neocortex and used the human race as a subdued work force. Evidence of these events is recorded in the Sumerian tablets and artifacts. This term is also used to describe the true identity of humanity, the forgotten Gods.

Golden body. It is the body that belongs to the fifth plane, superconsciousness, and x-ray frequency.

Golden Plane. *See* **Fifth plane.**

Graymen. It is the group of very influential people who own the major banks and corporations that control the political and economical events of the world.

Great architect, the. The great architect refers to the brain and, more specifically, to the neocortex and the frontal lobe where holographic pictures or thoughts are created.

Great Work. The Great Work is the practical application of the teachings of the Schools of Ancient Wisdom. It refers to the disciplines by which the human person becomes enlightened and is transmuted into an immortal, divine being.

Hardwiring. Hardwiring is the process by which the neurological connections of the brain become established and mapped. The repetition of a thought pattern three times is all it takes to create a habit and record it in the neuronet.

Heaven. This term is used in three ways. It is used in reference to paradise. It is also used for a plane of existence in general. Heaven is used more specifically as the name of the quiet area of the neocortex, the frontal lobe.

Hell. Ramtha explains that the concept of hell originally meant a shallow grave. This form of burial was greatly undesirable since the body of the deceased would be exposed to the attack of savage animals. The only place where Ramtha found the existence of hell as a place of eternal punishment was in the consciousness of the men and women who believed in it.

Hertzian realm. *See* **First plane.**

Hierophant. A hierophant is a master teacher who is able to manifest what they teach and initiate their students into such knowledge.

Higher seals. *See* **Upper four seals.**

Hyperconsciousness. Hyperconsciousness is the consciousness of the sixth plane and gamma ray frequency.

Hypnotic ability. It is the ability to enter into an altered state of consciousness called analogical mind. In this state the activity of the neocortex is anesthetized and the midbrain and lower cerebellum are activated.

Iaut Aleph. It is the name of one of the individual groups of Ramtha's school of Enlightenment created by Ramtha. He named and empowered each group with a specific mission and purpose that gives unity and identity to its members.

Image, the. The image refers to social consciousness. It also refers to the mind produced by the neuronet or the personality.

Incarnation. It refers to a particular lifetime experience. The transpersonal, the Spirit, or true self of the individual is a child of the Void and immortal in nature. The soul is different from the Spirit. It is the recorder of the experiences of the immortal Spirit. Thus both the Spirit and the soul get to take on a physical embodiment in an incarnation for the purpose of interaction with the physical plane of existence. At death, both the Spirit and the soul leave the physical body and get an opportunity to take on a new incarnation, a new physical body to complete what it is they want to learn in this plane.

Infinite Unknown. It is the frequency band of the seventh plane of existence and ultraconsciousness.

Involution. Involution is the journey from Point Zero and the seventh plane to the slowest and densest levels of frequency and mass.

Ionia. Ionia is a region of the continent of Atlantis where Macedonia is located today.

Jehovah. Jehovah is a technologically advanced being who was highly insecure, warlike, and who hated his sister. He was responsible for Abraham's journey out of Babylon into the land of Canaan for the creation of the Hebrew people and for Moses' journey out of Egypt into the Promised Land.

JZ Knight. JZ Knight is the only person appointed by Ramtha to channel him. Ramtha refers to JZ as his beloved daughter. She was Ramaya, one of the children of the House of the Ram in Ramtha's lifetime.

Ka. Ka is an Egyptian term that refers to the lightbody of a person.

Karma. Karma is the natural consequence of a person's thoughts and actions. Karma comprises all the unresolved issues, attitudes, and emotions that a person has not yet owned into wisdom. Those issues not yet resolved by the soul are the real cause of the repetitious cycle of reincarnation.

Kingdom of God. This concept refers to a plane of existence or dimension of mind where the unlimited mind of God reigns.

Kingdom of heaven. *See* **Kingdom of God.**

Kirlian photography. This term refers to a photographic process developed by Russian technicians that is able to capture the auric field of a living object.

Knowingness. Knowingness is the ability to know something without the aid of sensory perception. Knowingness refers to the act of accessing the knowledge of the subconscious mind.

Kundalini. Kundalini energy is the life force of a person that descends from the higher seals to the base of the spine at puberty. It is a large packet of energy reserved for human evolution, commonly pictured as a coiled serpent that sits at the base of the spine. This energy is different from the energy coming out of the first three seals responsible for sexuality, pain and suffering, power, and victimization. It is commonly described as the sleeping serpent or the sleeping dragon. The journey of the kundalini energy to the crown of the head is called the journey of enlightenment. This journey takes place when this serpent wakes up and starts to split and dance around the spine, ionizing the spinal fluid and changing its molecular structure. This action causes the opening of the midbrain and the door to the subconscious mind.

Leave the body. It describes the initiation of an out-of-body experience.

Life force. The life force is the Father, the Spirit, the breath of life within the person that is the platform from which the person creates its illusions, imagination, and dreams.

Life review. It is the review of the previous incarnation that occurs when the person reaches the third plane after death. The person gets the opportunity to be the Observer, the actor, and the recipient of its own actions. The unresolved issues from that lifetime that emerge at the life review set the agenda for the next incarnation.

Lifeline. It is a potential timeline or probability of events that result from a particular state of mind or consciousness of a person.

Light review. *See* **Life review.**

Light, the. The light refers to the third plane of existence.

Lightbeing. It is a being from the third plane of existence.

Lightbody. It is the same as the radiant body. It is the body that belongs to the third plane of conscious awareness and the visible light frequency band.

Limited thought. This concept refers to a thought bound by the limitations of physical space and time. It refers to the thought processes of the human personality and the consciousness of the first three seals.

Linear physics. It is a name descriptive of classical or Newtonian physics.

List, the. The List is the discipline taught by Ramtha where the student gets to write a list of items they desire to know and experience and then learn to focus on it in an analogical state of consciousness. The List is the map used to design, change, and reprogram the neuronet of the person. It is the tool that helps to bring meaningful and lasting changes in the person and their reality.

Lord of the Wind. It is one of Ramtha's titles. The wind represents the freedom, power, and transcendence of the Spirit. Ramtha became the Lord of the Wind when he became enlightened.

Making known the unknown. This phrase expresses the original divine mandate given to the Source consciousness to manifest and bring to conscious awareness all of the infinite potentials of the Void. This statement represents the basic intent that inspires the dynamic process of evolution.

Mass to mass. This concept refers to the approach to physical reality from the perspective of physicality.

Master. A master is a person who is consciously aware of their divinity and applies this knowledge in their everyday life. Ramtha calls his students masters, for they are learning to think and act as masters.

Master General. The Master Generals are the staff members of Ramtha's School of Enlightenment who are responsible for the organization and execution of the retreats and events of the school.

Master Teacher. A master teacher is an ascended master who has the ability to initiate their students into the mysteries of sacred knowledge.

Material plane. *See* **First plane.**

Materialize. This term refers to the coagulation and manifestation of a thought into physical form.

Merkabah. The Merkabah is the name of a very large mother ship from the people beyond the North Star.

Mind. Mind is the product of streams of consciousness and energy acting on the brain creating thought forms, holographic segments, or neurosynaptic patterns called memory. The streams of consciousness and energy are what keep the brain alive. They are its power source. A person's ability to think is what gives them a mind.

Mind of God. The mind of God comprises the mind and wisdom of every lifeform that ever lived on any dimension, in any time, or that ever will live on any planet or any star.

Moment, the. This term describes the creative and eternal Now, the present.

Monkey-mind. Monkey-mind refers to the flickering mind of the personality.

Mother/Father principle. It is the source of all life, God the Father, the eternal Mother, Point Zero.

Motheren. Mother.

Mu. Mu is the continent of Lemuria that lies under the Pacific Ocean.

Nabor. Nabor was the city in the valley of Nazire where Ramtha was run through with a sword.

Name-field. The name-field is the name of the large field where the discipline of Fieldwork™ is practiced.

Neewollah. It is the feast of Halloween spelled backwards.

Neophyte. A neophyte is a beginning student of the Great Work.

No-time. This concept refers to the experience of the Now — the eternal, creative, analogical moment. Time is the consequence, manifestation, and experience of this creative moment.

Observer. It refers to the Observer responsible for collapsing the particle/wave of quantum mechanics. It represents the true self, the Spirit, primary consciousness, the God within the human person.

Om Akad. It is the name of one of the individual groups of Ramtha's School of Enlightenment created by Ramtha. He named and empowered each group with a specific mission and purpose that gives unity and identity to its members.

Onai. It was a southern-port city of the continent of Atlantis where Ramtha lived as a child with his mother, brother, and sister.

Our God. This concept refers to the God, the Spirit, the Observer, the divine element, the true self of the individual.

Outrageous. Ramtha uses this word in a positive way to express something or someone who is extraordinary and unusual, unrestrained in action, and excessively bold or fierce.

Outrageous thought. This type of thought refers to an unlimited, lofty, transcendental thought.

Past, the. The concept of the past, in its subjective context, refers to everything that is already known by the individual person through experience. The past in this sense comprises every emotional experience of the person in relation to people, places, things, times, and events. The past is the greatest deterrent of human evolution, for it cripples the ability of the individual to create new paradigms of thought and to make known the unknown.

People, places, things, times, and events. These are the main areas of human experience to which the personality is emotionally attached. These areas represent the past of the human person and constitute the content of the emotional body.

Personality, the. The personality is the secondary consciousness, the mirror consciousness, the traveler who forgot its divine origin and inheritance.

Philosopher's stone. It is an alchemical term that refers to the elixir of immortality.

Physical plane. *See* **First plane.**

Plane of Bliss. It refers to the plane of rest where souls get to plan their next incarnations after their life reviews. It is also known as heaven and paradise where there is no suffering, no pain, no need or lack, and where every wish is immediately manifested.

Plane of demonstration. The physical plane is also called the plane of demonstration. It is the plane where the person has the opportunity to demonstrate its creative potentiality in mass and witness consciousness in material form in order to expand its emotional understanding.

Plane of flesh. *see* **First plane.**

Point Zero. It refers to the original point of awareness created by the Void through its act of contemplating itself. Point Zero is the original child of the Void.

Prancing Pony Inn. This term refers to a pub or a dancing saloon. Ramtha borrowed this term from J.R.R. Tolkien, *The Lord of the Rings* (London: Grafton, 1991).

Prima materia. It is an alchemical term that refers to the ultimate essence of all things.

Prophecy. A prophecy is a potential future timeline based on the facts of the present moment. Prophesies should always accompany the statement "as it is seen now," for they are always subject to change as the collective consciousness changes. This understanding of prophecy is based on the law of consciousness and energy taught by Ramtha.

Psychic ability. Psychic ability is the ability to know without the aid of sensory perception. Psychic ability is developed when the midbrain is accessed and opened to receive information from the environment at a higher level of frequency than the Hertzian frequency band.

Ra. Ra is the name of an Egyptian God. Ra is the name Ramtha uses for the sun.

Radiant body. *See* **Lightbody.**

Ram. Ram is a shorter version of the name Ramtha. Ramtha means the Father.

Ramuste. Ramuste is the name of the collective house of soul emotion that Ramtha chose to be born into. The emotional understanding of this collective consciousness was the power to master.

Red energy. This term is used in reference to kundalini energy and psychic energy.

Red Lion. It is an alchemical term that refers to the elixir of immortality.

Red serpent. The kundalini energy rising from the base of the spine through the seals is visualized as a double red serpent undulating and crossing itself like the medical symbol of the caduceus. It is also used to describe psychic energy.

Reincarnation. Reincarnation is the repetitious cycle of incarnation.

Righteousness. It is the right use of something. It is the moral quality of impeccability.

Runner. A runner in Ramtha's lifetime was responsible for bringing specific messages or information. A master teacher has the ability to send runners to other people that manifest their words or intent in the form of an experience or an event.

Satan. Satan is not the name or title of a single being. Rather it is everything and anything that robs us from our divinity and from change. Satan, the accuser, is what keeps the human person locked in the emotions of the past.

School of Ancient Wisdom. This is the title given to the various schools throughout history where the sacred knowledge of the Great Work was taught. Ramtha has been largely responsible for all of these schools.

Season of blood. This term refers to the cycle of menstruation.

Second plane. It is the plane of existence of social consciousness and the infrared frequency band. It is associated with pain and suffering. This plane is the negative polarity of the third plane of visible light frequency.

Second seal. This seal is the energy center of social consciousness and the infrared frequency band. It is associated with pain and suffering and is located in the lower abdominal area.

Self, the. The self is the true identity of the human person. It is the transcendental aspect of the person. It refers to the Observer, the primary consciousness.

Sending-and-receiving. Sending-and-receiving is the name of the discipline taught by Ramtha in which the student learns to access information using the faculties of the midbrain to the exclusion of sensory perception. This discipline develops the student's psychic ability of telepathy and divination.

Seven seals. The seven seals are powerful energy centers that constitute seven levels of consciousness in the human body. The bands are the way in which the physical body is held together according to these seals. In every human being there is energy spiraling out of the first three seals or centers. The energy pulsating out of the first three seals manifests itself respectively as sexuality, pain, or power. When the upper seals are unlocked, a higher level of awareness is activated.

Seven Sisters. This is another name for the Pleiades constellation.

Seventh plane. The seventh plane is the plane of ultraconsciousness and the Infinite Unknown frequency band. This plane is where the journey of involution began. This plane was created by Point Zero when it imitated the act of contemplation of the Void and the mirror or secondary consciousness was created. A plane of existence or dimension of space and time exists between two points of consciousness. All the other planes were created by slowing down the time and frequency band of the seventh plane.

Seventh seal. This seal is associated with the crown of the head, the pituitary gland, and the attainment of enlightenment.

Shambhala. It is the name of an ancient forest that existed near the northeastern region of the River Indus during Ramtha's lifetime.

Shiva. The Lord God Shiva represents the Lord of the Blue Plane and the Blue Body™. Shiva is not used in reference to a singular deity from Hinduism. It is rather the representation of a state of consciousness that belongs to the fourth plane, the ultraviolet frequency band, and the opening of the fourth seal. Shiva is neither male nor female. It is an androgynous being, for the energy of the fourth plane has not yet been split into positive and negative polarity. This is an important distinction from the traditional Hindu representation of Shiva as a male deity who has a wife. The tiger skin at its feet, the trident staff, and the sun and the moon at the level of the head represent the mastery of this body over the first three seals of consciousness. The kundalini energy is pictured as fiery energy shooting from the base of the spine through the head. This is another distinction from some Hindu representations of Shiva with the serpent energy coming out at the level of the fifth seal or throat. Another symbolic image of Shiva is the long threads of dark hair and an abundance of pearl necklaces, which represent its richness of experience owned into wisdom. The quiver and bow and arrows are the agent by which Shiva shoots its powerful will and destroys imperfection and creates the new.

Sign of the star. The sign of the star is a more complex version of the sign of the triad, which is practiced by the advancing group of students.

Sign of the triad. Beginning students are taught to make the sign of the triad with their blinders on when they engage in any of the disciplines of the Great Work. The students begin this discipline by pointing to their forehead, or seventh seal, which is the apex of the triad. They continue to focus and complete the triad by moving their hand slowly towards their left knee, then their right knee, and finally back to the forehead. This triad represents the journey of involution and evolution.

Sixth plane. The sixth plane is the realm of hyperconsciousness and the gamma ray frequency band. In this plane the awareness of being one with the whole of life is experienced.

Sixth seal. This seal is associated with the pineal gland and the gamma ray frequency band. The reticular formation that filters and veils the knowingness of the subconscious mind is opened when this seal is activated. The opening of the brain refers to the opening of this seal and the activation of its consciousness and energy.

Social consciousness. It is the consciousness of the second plane and the infrared frequency band. It is also called the image of the human personality and the mind of the first three seals. Social consciousness refers to the collective consciousness of human society. It is the collection of thoughts, assumptions, judgments, prejudices, laws, morality, values, attitudes, ideals, and emotions of the fraternity of the human race.

Son of God. The son or daughter of God is the individual who is born to a loftier and broader state of consciousness than the one belonging to the first three seals. To act like the son or daughter of God is to live from the perspective of our divine consciousness rather than our human consciousness.

Son of man. This concept refers to the human and physical aspect of the person. A person acts like the son or daughter of man and woman when they choose to follow their humanity rather than their divinity.

Soul. Ramtha refers to the soul as the Book of Life, where the whole journey of involution and evolution of the individual is recorded in the form of wisdom.

Spill your seed. Sperm ejaculation.

Subconscious mind. The seat of the subconscious mind is the lower cerebellum or reptilian brain. This part of the brain has its own independent connections to the frontal lobe and the whole of the body and has the power to access the mind of God, the wisdom of the ages.

Superconsciousness. This is the consciousness of the fifth plane and the x-ray frequency band.

Tahumo. Tahumo is the discipline taught by Ramtha in which the student learns the ability to master the effects of the natural environment — cold and heat — on the human body.

Tank field. It is the name of the large field with the labyrinth that is used for the discipline of The Tank™.

Tank™, The. It is the name given to the labyrinth used as part of the disciplines of Ramtha's School of Enlightenment. The students are taught to find the entry to this labyrinth blindfolded and move through it focusing on the Void without touching the walls or using the eyes or the senses. The objective of this discipline is to find, blindfolded, the center of the labyrinth or a room designated and representative of the Void.

Terra. It is the name the Gods gave to planet earth 455,000 years ago when they first came to visit it.

Third plane. This is the plane of conscious awareness and the visible light frequency band. It is also known as the light plane and the mental plane. When the energy of the Blue Plane is lowered down to this frequency band, it splits into positive and negative polarity. It is at this point that the soul splits into two, giving origin to the phenomenon of soulmates.

Third seal. This seal is the energy center of conscious awareness and the visible light frequency band. It is associated with control, tyranny, victimization, and power. It is located in the region of the solar plexus.

Thought. Thought is different from consciousness. The brain processes a stream of consciousness modifying it into segments — holographic pictures — of neurological, electrical, and chemical prints called thoughts. Thoughts are the building blocks of mind.

Timeline. It is a potential probability of events that result from a particular state of consciousness.

Transpersonal. The transpersonal refers to the spiritual order, the transcendental aspects of the human person.

Truth. Truth is not mere data or information. Truth is the full realization of a concept or paradigm of thought into experience and personal wisdom.

Twilight™. This term is used to describe the discipline taught by Ramtha in which the students learn to put their bodies in a catatonic state similar to deep sleep, yet retaining their conscious awareness.

Twilight™ Visualization Process. It is the process used to practice the discipline of the List or other visualization formats.

Ultraconsciousness. It is the consciousness of the seventh plane and the Infinite Unknown frequency band. It is the consciousness of an ascended master.

Unaccustomed freedom. This type of freedom is experienced when the individual breaks through the box into free space.

Unawakened being. It is a person who is ignorant of their divinity. It refers to a being who lives under the illusion of duality and separation from the Source and is a victim of its environment.

Unconditional love. Unconditional love is the expression of the consciousness of the fourth seal. It is the beginning of enlightenment and the cessation of dualism, lack, and separation perceived by the personality. It is love in freedom without any emotional attachments. Unconditional love is a state of mind that is creative and giving in nature. It is the closest representation of God.

Unconsciousness. Unconsciousness is the loss of awareness.

Unknown God. The Unknown God was the single God of Ramtha's ancestors, the Lemurians. The Unknown God also represents the forgotten divinity and divine origin of the human person.

Upper four seals. The upper four seals are the fourth, fifth, sixth, and seventh seals.

Villager. A villager is a person who is ignorant of their true identity and divine origin. A villager is the opposite of a master.

Vishmalodu. It is the Lemurian name for the Unknown God.

Void, the. The Void is defined as one vast nothing materially, yet all things potentially.

Weed, the. Marijuana.

White Brotherhood. The White Brotherhood is an unseen brotherhood of ascended masters who love, observe, and aid in the evolution of humankind.

Winged Pharaoh. Winged Pharaoh was a title reserved for female Pharaohs who wore the sacred symbol of the winged disk. Female Pharaohs were the greatest of masters, loved by the people, who could heal with a touch and lead their people with wisdom and justice. This dynasty of Pharaohs existed before the known records of Egyptian history.

Yahweh. Yahweh is a different being from Jehovah. Yahweh disagreed with the enslavement Jehovah brought to the people of the earth. Yahweh and the God Id warred against Jehovah and endeavored to teach humanity about the

Unknown God within the human person.

Yellow brain. The yellow brain is Ramtha's name for the neocortex, the house of analytical and emotional thought. The reason why it is called the yellow brain is because the neocortices were colored yellow in the original two-dimensional, caricature-style drawing Ramtha used for his teaching on the function of the brain and its processes. He explained that the different aspects of the brain in this particular drawing are exaggerated and colorfully highlighted for the sake of study and understanding. This specific drawing became the standard tool used in all the subsequent teachings on the brain.

Yeshua ben Joseph. Ramtha refers to Jesus Christ by the name Yeshua ben Joseph, following the Jewish traditions of that time.

Your God. This phrase refers to the Spirit, the Observer, the God within the human person.

Zarathustra. Zarathustra is the uncorrupted version of the name Zoroaster, the founder of Zoroastrianism. Ramtha explains that Zarathustra became enlightened and an immortal master.

Bibliography

A Beginner's Guide to Creating Reality. Revised and Expanded ed. Yelm: JZK Publishing, a division of JZK, Inc., 2000.

Crossing the River Part I. Tape 346 ed. Yelm: Ramtha Dialogues, 1997.

Crossing the River Part II. Tape 347 ed. Yelm: Ramtha Dialogues, 1997.

Only One Thing. Tape 336 ed. Yelm: Ramtha Dialogues, 1996.

Plane of Bliss I — On Earth As It Is In Heaven: Our Journey Through Life, Death, and Beyond. Tape 348 ed. Yelm: Ramtha Dialogues, 1997.

Plane of Bliss II. Tape 355 ed. Yelm: Ramtha Dialogues, 1997.

Reese, William L. *Dictionary of Philosophy and Religion, Eastern and Western Thought.* Expanded ed. New York: Humanity Books, 1999.

Selected Stories III: Shambhala — Leaving No Footprints. Specialty Tape 033 ed. Yelm: Ramtha Dialogues, 1989.

The Bridge to Infinity. Tape 269 ed. Yelm: Ramtha Dialogues, 1989.

The Complete Works of William Shakespeare. Art-Type ed. New York: Books, Inc.

The Plateau for Learning. Tape 268 ed. Yelm: Ramtha Dialogues, 1989.

Update on Change. Tape 302 ed. Yelm: Ramtha Dialogues, 1991.

Wallis, E.A. *The Egyptian Book of the Dead; the Papyrus of Ani, Egyptian Text Transliteration and Translation.* New York: Dover Publications, Inc., 1967.

INDEX

A

abstract thought. *See* thought
abuse 87
adrenaline/epinephrine. *See*
 neurotransmitter
Ahk Men Ra 35
alchemist 76, 163, 185-187
alchemy 185
 philosopher's stone 163, 185-186
 prima materia 163
Aleph 151
altered ego 13, 74, 86, 90, 95
American Indians 193
analogical mind. *See* mind
anatomy
 heart 3, 40, 57, 75, 92, 104-105,
 118, 164-165, 184
 penis 40, 114-115, 119
 uterus 60, 92, 110, 115, 146
angel 65, 86, 150
anger. *See* emotions
anxiety/worry. *See* emotions
Apollonius of Tyana 186
archetype 72
arrogance. *See* attitude
art of imagination. *See* visualization
ascension 24, 26-27, 41, 90
atom 133-134, 143, 145, 161, 185, 187
 quark 155, 188
attitude 2, 9, 11-12, 14-15, 21-23,
 32, 42, 91, 100
 arrogance 32, 94
 blame 8, 10, 12, 18, 54, 56, 58,
 61-62, 80, 100, 184
 deceit 4, 13, 19, 22, 38, 61-62,
 111, 114, 125, 129, 175, 181
 fearlessness 36-37
 greed 42, 104

 hypocrisy 94, 111, 174
 jealousy 8, 12, 36, 43, 56, 80, 102
 lack 11-12, 14-16, 19-20, 30, 56,
 69, 80, 87, 94, 103, 181
 prejudice 80, 118-119, 148, 168
 selfishness 62, 112-113, 175
 survival 13, 15, 30, 58, 73, 79,
 88, 95, 111, 116, 118, 166
 tyranny 36, 59, 86-88, 104, 176
 victimization 8, 10, 12, 17, 30,
 54, 56-59, 68, 71, 79, 86-87,
 96, 100, 104, 111, 117, 144,
 159, 176, 190
 worthiness 29, 36-37, 159, 174,
 180-181

B

ba (Egyptian) 118
Bands, the 60, 88, 92, 110, 125,
 129, 178
belief. *See* faith
biochemistry 127, 139
biology 143
black hole 158
blame. *See* attitude
Blue Body™. *See* planes of existence
blue star 104
blue webs. *See* planes of existence
body/mind consciousness. *See* states
 of consciousness
Boktau 9
Book of Life. *See* soul
boredom 30, 62, 119
box, the. *See* human personality
brain 7, 10-11, 13, 19, 23, 26, 28,
 62, 69, 78, 83-84, 88, 91-92,
 115, 117, 122, 136-137, 148,
 165, 178, 181, 186, 188

brain's anatomy
  frontal lobe 21
  lower cerebellum 92
  neocortex 26
breath 3, 57, 99
broadsword. *See* sword
Buddhism 185

C

C&E™ 2, 21, 27, 31, 72, 98-99, 139
capitalism 87
cell 143
change 11, 13, 21, 29-31, 37, 44,
    47, 67, 74, 102-103, 105, 111,
    114, 118, 124, 126-127, 129,
    135, 141, 144-145, 147, 149,
    153, 171, 180-181, 183, 190,
    192, 194-196
chaos/adversity 93, 167
chemistry 148
children 23, 34-35, 37, 41, 45, 61,
    67, 91-92, 94, 115-116, 118,
    121, 127, 156, 170, 174, 180,
    182, 191
Christ 2, 17, 39, 76
Christianity 76, 185
civilization 78
closed-mindedness. *See* mind
common thought. *See* thought
compassion. *See* virtue
conceptual ideals 17, 39, 56, 62, 64,
    77-78, 84, 110, 132-133, 143,
    156-161, 165, 177-178, 185-
    188, 191
confusion 41, 43
conscience 172, 181, 183, 196
conscious awareness 23-27, 35, 47,
    59, 68, 98-100, 110, 124-125,
    149, 178, 184, 190
consciousness 23, 28, 36-38, 41-44,
    47-49, 59, 68, 84, 88-89, 91-
    92, 140, 149, 156, 162, 170,
    191-192

Consciousness & Energy™ 193
consciousness and energy 10, 25,
    47, 72, 84-85, 98, 110, 151,
    163, 169, 186, 191, 193
contemplation 18-19, 31, 41, 47, 49,
    63-64, 67, 80-81, 84, 87, 90-
    91, 120-121, 125, 133, 154,
    161, 168-169, 171, 180
  hall of contemplation 64-68, 70,
    75, 90, 121
control and power. *See* emotions
copulation. *See* sexuality
create your day. *See* mastership
creation 84, 88, 156-157, 166
  nature of reality 47, 58, 60, 68,
    70-71, 79, 83, 85, 98, 140, 151,
    157, 159, 163, 165, 170, 177-
    178, 185-186
  power to manifest 8-9, 32, 39, 47,
    56, 74, 77, 79-80, 84, 87-88, 92,
    111, 174, 178-180, 185, 194
  seven levels 4, 72, 112, 134, 174,
    185-186
Crosham. *See* sword
culture 9, 143, 167, 170

D

dancing. *See* music
dark night, the. *See* soul
death 2, 7, 15, 23-24, 27, 31, 40, 60,
    75-76, 78, 90, 110, 122, 125,
    130-134, 140, 144, 146, 148,
    173, 184, 187
  the dead 28, 122, 124, 131-132,
    134, 136, 141, 145-146, 148-
    151, 153, 163, 173, 180
deceit. *See* attitude
decision 20-21, 27, 32, 36, 44, 47,
    53, 56-57, 59, 69, 75, 80-81,
    83, 96, 100, 104, 126, 140,
    143, 173, 176, 178-179, 183,
    193-196
déjà vu 135

demons 13-15, 17, 56
dendrites. *See* neuron
depression. *See* emotions
destiny 53-55, 71, 80, 83-85
detachment 12, 17-18, 20-21, 25, 30, 98, 125, 160
devil 14, 42, 86
Dialogue days 157
dimension 22, 24, 26, 47, 93, 158
   multidimensional 6, 41, 64, 112, 131, 134, 156, 190-191, 196
   three-dimensional reality 47, 112
dimensional mind. *See* mind
disciplines 20, 31, 44, 98, 100, 106, 169, 178, 195
disease 15, 19, 29, 48, 78, 87, 118
   plagues 42
divinity 18-20, 38, 41, 55, 57, 59, 63, 72, 86, 105, 124, 158, 173, 186
dogma. *See* religion
doubt 79, 92
dreams 48, 52, 57, 62, 66-67, 72, 78-80, 106, 122, 153, 159, 163, 168-171, 185, 191
drugs 12, 23, 81

E

earth 26, 48, 90, 92, 151, 155-156, 158
earthbound spirits. *See* Spirit
ecstasy 115
Egypt 28
Egyptian Book of the Dead 28, 151
electromagnetism 62, 163
Elohim 35
emotional body 3, 57, 81, 88, 97, 125
emotions 2-3, 12, 27, 41-47, 49, 62-63, 66, 88-89, 95, 101, 114, 125-127, 143, 164-165, 168, 175, 181
   anger 12, 61, 180, 192
   anxiety/worry 47, 71, 86, 97
   control and power 111, 114-115, 117-118, 127, 176

depression 194
envy 8, 43, 56, 102, 127
failure 38, 58, 78, 102, 148
fear 2, 13, 15, 17, 19, 22, 27, 35, 40, 43, 47, 56, 58, 97, 125-127, 165, 172, 175, 180-182, 196
guilt 119, 124, 127, 165, 176, 181
hate 12, 37, 43-44, 56, 73, 78, 144, 170
pain and suffering 2-3, 10-11, 15, 30-31, 38, 41-42, 44-47, 57-58, 61-62, 66-67, 71, 74, 79-81, 86, 89, 101, 111-112, 115, 118, 124, 167, 172, 174, 176, 181
passion 121, 123-124, 134, 150, 159, 161, 164, 169
regret 66, 97, 99, 101-102, 112
resentment 12, 102, 175
sadness 32, 46
sorrow 193
unhappiness 170
energy 3, 14, 21, 41, 43-44, 55-57, 59-60, 62, 72, 81, 83, 85-86, 88-89, 94, 97-98, 101, 103-104, 110, 112, 117, 120-121, 133-134, 154-155, 157-158, 162, 165, 181, 185-187, 192-193
enlightenment 2, 12, 18, 102, 122, 134, 152, 184, 190, 192
envy. *See* emotions
equality 20
eternal life. *See* life
eternity 11, 39-40, 42-43, 66, 72, 84, 90, 94, 163, 174, 195
evil 15, 19, 56, 92
evolution 31, 35, 38, 40, 49, 53, 61, 83, 115, 129-130, 141, 153, 160, 163, 168, 171, 177, 183, 185-186
extraordinary realities 20, 25, 31, 38, 49, 57, 71-72, 75, 106, 121, 124, 134, 162-163, 174, 179, 182, 195-196

F

fabulous wealth. *See* wealth

failure. *See* emotions

faith
  belief 15, 19, 29, 32, 38, 140,
    144-145, 150, 159, 163, 173,
    179, 183
  surrender 25, 116, 164, 180

fall, the 80, 99, 158

family. *See* love

fanaticism 18, 113, 118

fanatics 190

fantasies. *See* thought

fear. *See* emotions

fearlessness. *See* attitude

Fieldwork™ 129, 178, 193

fifth plane. *See* planes of existence

fifth seal. *See* seven seals

first plane. *See* material plane

first seal. *See* seven seals

first three seals. *See* seven seals

focus thought. *See* thought

forgiveness 19-20, 74, 92, 97, 99, 101

fourth plane. *See* planes of existence

fourth seal. *See* seven seals

free space 14, 16, 19-20

free will. *See* will

freedom 2, 14, 19-21, 25, 32, 39,
    44, 47-48, 66, 73-75, 79, 93,
    96, 100, 102-103, 106, 118,
    122, 125, 146, 152, 167, 184

frequency 27, 41, 49, 60, 155, 187-188
  gamma ray 24
  hertz 161
  Infinite Unknown 167
  infrared 26, 28, 60
  ultraviolet blue 24, 28, 162
  visible light 26, 28, 135-136, 145-
    146, 152-153, 163-164, 168,
    170, 173, 175, 196
  x-ray 24, 162

frontal lobe. *See* brain's anatomy

future, the. *See* time

G

galaxy 158

gamma ray. *See* frequency

generosity. *See* virtue

genetics 60, 66, 74, 91, 124, 143-144,
    151, 160
  genes 92, 143-144

genius 67, 71, 75, 77, 143

ghost 48, 70, 86, 123

glamour 184

glands 117, 164

God 31, 34, 38-39, 42, 54, 58-59,
    61-63, 65-66, 69, 72, 79-80,
    83-84, 86-87, 91, 93-98, 100-
    103, 120, 123, 126, 131, 134-
    135, 147, 150, 155, 159, 162,
    165, 167, 176, 181, 184, 186,
    195-196

God within 39, 54, 86, 88, 104,
    112, 146, 149, 163, 173, 177

God/man, God/woman realized
    74, 76

Goddess 16-17

Gods 28, 36-38, 40, 73, 75, 77,
    79, 88, 102-103, 118, 173-174

kingdom of God 27, 106, 124,
    167, 174, 184, 186, 193

love of God 16, 104, 112, 174,
    182-183

gold 194

golden body. *See* planes of existence

government 37, 42, 115, 118

Great Work 11, 162, 171, 182, 193

greed. *See* attitude

guilt. *See* emotions

H

habit 80, 102, 115, 195

hall of contemplation. *See* contem-
    plation

happiness 53, 173, 178-182, 196

hate. *See* emotions

hauntings 192-193
health 12, 90, 175, 179-180, 184, 192, 195
heart. *See* anatomy
heaven 22, 52, 59, 65-66, 71, 76, 82, 85, 92, 96, 151, 186
hell 19, 42, 65
hertz. *See* frequency
history 37-38, 46, 75, 77-78, 94, 163
hologram 79, 83
Holy Spirit 77, 140, 146, 150, 165, 172, 174, 182
honesty. *See* virtue
honor. *See* virtue
hormones 36, 62, 88-89
horoscope 23
human limitations 20, 22, 35, 43, 47, 59, 72-73, 76, 78, 85-86, 89-90, 97, 100, 104-105, 149
human nature 38, 56, 71, 73-75, 77, 79-80, 93-94, 111, 119, 124, 131, 166
human personality 4, 9, 13, 15, 19, 38, 54, 71-72, 75, 78, 81, 91, 95, 112, 114, 117, 124-127, 129, 132, 141-142, 165, 172, 176
people, places, things, times, and events 9, 11-12, 14, 16, 18, 21, 31, 87-88, 99, 102-103, 114, 122, 182
the box 97
the image 44, 58, 71, 75, 83, 133, 182, 184
humankind 36, 48, 73, 94
humility. *See* virtue
hypnotism 44
hypocrisy. *See* attitude
hysteria 18, 127

ignorance 19, 22-23, 36, 44, 61-62, 67, 115, 125, 145, 190, 192
illusion 14, 21, 61, 130, 140, 153
image, the. *See* human personality

immortality 37, 39-40, 42-43, 47, 132-134, 150, 173, 185, 188
impeccability. *See* virtue
incarnation 7, 53, 59, 65, 74-75, 80, 85, 91, 96, 134-135, 139-140, 142, 144, 150, 158, 170, 174, 181
India 27
Infinite Unknown. *See* frequency
infrared. *See* frequency
infrared body. *See* planes of existence
initiation 133, 151, 160
injustice 165
innocence 61, 87, 116, 121, 158
insecurity 16, 127
intellectual mind. *See* mind
intelligence 43, 102, 139, 156, 158, 160-161, 174, 177-178, 185
involution 83, 158, 185-186, 192
Isness 21

J

Jacob's ladder 26, 29, 158
jealousy. *See* attitude
joy 37, 44, 47-48, 72, 89, 97, 111, 116, 172-173, 179, 181, 196
judgment 3, 27, 35, 38, 60-62, 65, 85-86, 89-90, 100, 113, 173, 184

K

ka (Egyptian) 118
karma 7, 9, 18, 144, 181
kindness. *See* virtue
kingdom of God. *See* God
knowingness 57, 66
knowledge 7-9, 13, 18, 21, 23, 26-28, 32, 39-40, 46, 53, 64, 82, 86, 91, 95-96, 110, 124-126, 132, 135-136, 140, 143, 149, 151, 154, 163, 173, 184-186, 191

knowledge (*continued*)
  making known the unknown 72,
    76-77, 84, 92, 122, 124, 134-
    135, 167
  sacred knowledge 40-41, 64, 96,
    183, 192
  the unknown 8, 26, 54-57, 66, 75-
    79, 84, 87, 101, 106, 136, 161,
    179

L

labyrinth of the mind. *See* mind
lack. *See* attitude
language 34-35, 45
law 8, 19, 32, 36, 39, 135, 154, 159,
    161
life 7-9, 14-17, 20-21, 27, 29, 31-
    32, 37, 53-57, 59-61, 67, 70,
    72, 75, 80, 85, 91, 106, 111,
    113, 121-125, 130, 144-145,
    148, 151, 154-155, 157, 162,
    166-170, 174, 177-178, 180-
    182, 185, 192, 194-195
  eternal life 2, 32, 48, 73, 90, 134,
    152, 184, 188
  life review 4, 24, 32, 60, 65, 68,
    85-86, 90, 99-100, 110-112,
    114, 116, 118, 120-125, 129-
    135, 140-142, 144-151, 153,
    159, 161, 165, 168, 172-173,
    175-176, 180, 182-183, 195
    weighed against the feather
    61, 113, 118, 151, 164, 166, 167,
    168, 182
  monastic life 9
  multiple lifetimes 7, 9-10, 18-19,
    22-23, 28, 31-32, 67, 71-72,
    91, 117, 124, 134, 167-168
  past lifetime 20, 22, 47, 59-60,
    67-69, 75, 85, 91, 110, 119,
    171, 176, 183
  present lifetime 2-3, 7-8, 10, 18-
    20, 22-24, 29-32, 40, 42, 48,
    52-59, 61, 63, 68-70, 75, 78,
    95, 97-98, 100, 132-133, 135,
    146, 195-196
life force 32, 97, 115, 132
life review. *See* life
lifeform 38, 49, 112
lightbody. *See* planes of existence
limited thought. *See* thought
linear time. *See* time
List, the (discipline) 163, 178-180
lofty thought. *See* thought
Lord of the Wind. *See* Ramtha
love 16, 18-20, 22, 30, 39, 43-45,
    47-49, 61-62, 76, 97, 106, 112,
    114, 130, 133, 175, 182, 187-
    188, 191
  family 27-28, 37-38, 46, 66, 80,
    88, 103, 125, 144-145, 174
  love of self 63, 80, 118, 123, 172-
    174, 180, 183-184
  lovers 40, 67, 71, 78, 120, 123,
    128, 174
  relationships 4, 15, 29, 66, 68, 70,
    88, 102-103, 114, 125-127,
    130, 148, 175, 194
  unconditional love 16-17, 21,
    147, 172, 174, 182
love of God. *See* God
lovers. *See* love
lower cerebellum. *See* brain's anatomy

M

magic 2, 32, 73, 92, 170, 194-195
magnetism 20, 30, 111
making known the unknown. *See*
  knowledge
male gender 40, 115
mandala 104-105
mantra 9
march, the. *See* Ramtha
Master Teacher 7, 20, 38, 41, 44-45,
    48, 83, 104, 131, 173, 182
mastership 9, 12, 14, 19, 25, 30, 32,
    56, 99, 122, 172, 178, 183-184,
    191

a master is 8, 13, 15, 18, 30, 38, 40, 57, 59, 77-78, 90, 101-102, 105-106, 111, 113, 131-134, 149, 151, 153-154, 159, 161-162, 176, 180, 184, 187, 190, 192, 194-195
    create your day 195
    runners 6-7, 28, 35, 41, 101
    walk of a master 55, 80
material plane. *See* planes of existence
materialism 71
melatonin. *See* neurotransmitter
memory 10, 18, 22, 26, 36, 42, 46-47, 49, 55, 58, 60, 84, 91-92, 141-142, 149, 160-161, 183-184, 193
men 20, 36, 39-41, 45-46, 56, 74, 80, 95, 114-116, 118-119, 142, 184
mercy. *See* virtue
metamorphosis 83, 188
mind 9, 26-28, 31, 35-36, 39, 44, 56, 60, 64-65, 69, 73, 77, 84, 115, 120, 135-136, 141, 155, 160, 162-163, 168, 171, 192
    analogical mind 115-116, 157-158, 162, 169-170, 185
    closed-mindedness 190
    dimensional mind 47, 49, 131, 191, 196
    intellectual mind 9, 12, 25, 35, 38, 77, 144
    labyrinth of the mind 68, 76-77
    mind of a master 2, 11, 41, 43, 131, 143, 153, 161, 190, 192, 194-195
    mind of God 76, 78, 85, 89, 134, 142, 152, 156
    monkey-mind 92
    subconscious mind 60, 188
    unlimited mind 31, 71, 85, 123, 144, 161, 174, 186, 191
miracles 19, 48, 57, 178-179, 195
molecules 186-187
monastic life. *See* life
money 2, 12, 75, 116, 121, 181

moon 22, 42, 47, 123
morality 35, 58
mortality 37, 45
multidimensional. *See* dimension
multiple lifetimes. *See* life
music 49
    dancing 40, 49
mutation 49
mystery 39, 44, 96, 134, 142
mystic 70, 84, 87
myth 44, 57

N

nature 8, 125, 156, 160
nature of reality. *See* creation
near-death experiences 147
necromancer 10
neocortex. *See* brain's anatomy
nervous breakdown 17
neuromemory. *See* neuron
neuron 11
    dendrites 11, 64
    neuromemory 23
neuronet 10, 12-13, 38, 55, 59, 62, 110-111, 117, 124, 178-179
neurotransmitter
    adrenaline/epinephrine 121
    melatonin 78
New Age 142
no-time. *See* time
nobility 38, 49, 95, 128, 130
Now, the. *See* time
Nut, Egyptian Goddess 151

O

objective truth. *See* truth
Observer 25, 61, 86, 90, 99, 110, 112, 117, 125-126, 134, 136, 145-146, 166, 172
Om Akad 35
One World Order 42
oppression 48
orgasm. *See* sexuality

Osiris, Egyptian God 118
out-of-body experience 24, 26, 28,
    122-123, 133, 151, 187
outrageous 172

P

pain and suffering. *See* emotions
paradise 48, 103, 120
parenthood 10, 20, 35, 37, 41, 55-56,
    60, 71, 87-88, 100, 142-143
passion. *See* emotions
past lifetime. *See* life
past, the. *See* time
peace 43, 48, 97, 105, 196
penis. *See* anatomy
people, places, things, times, and
    events. *See* human personality
philosopher's stone. *See* alchemy
philosophy 23, 28, 113, 124
physical body 7, 9, 12, 23-28, 35-36,
    38-40, 53, 57, 60, 62-63, 66,
    69, 72, 74, 76-80, 84, 88-92,
    105, 110, 122-124, 131, 133-
    134, 139-140, 143-144, 148-
    149, 152, 162-163, 169, 180,
    183-186, 188, 192
physics 83
plagues. *See* disease
Plane of Bliss. *See* planes of existence
plane of demonstration. *See* planes
    of existence
planes of existence 22, 24, 26, 60,
    64, 66, 72, 154, 157-158
    Blue Body™ 134, 179-180
    blue webs 28
    fifth plane 26, 60, 66, 99, 140,
        161-162, 186, 188
    fourth plane 26, 60, 90, 99, 140, 186
    golden body 134
    infrared body 134
    lightbody 60, 92, 134, 168
    material plane 7, 26-27, 37, 39, 42,
        53, 63, 67, 70-71, 76, 97, 119,
        132, 140, 160-163, 167, 169,

185-186
    Plane of Bliss 52, 55, 57, 59, 63-
        68, 70-72, 74-76, 78-79, 85,
        90-92, 95, 98-99, 110, 116-
        117, 120-121, 125, 132-133,
        140, 142-144, 147, 158, 160,
        165-166, 169-171, 178, 180,
        195-196
    plane of demonstration 38, 92, 143
    second plane 140
    seventh plane 27, 163, 185-186,
        188, 192
    sixth plane 140, 161-162, 186, 188
    third plane 3, 10, 24, 26, 46, 60, 90,
        99, 131-132, 134, 140
planet 28, 67, 154, 158
Point Zero 22, 29, 68, 72, 83, 98-99,
    127, 135, 139, 154, 161, 185-
    186, 188
politician 115, 118
potentials 23, 39, 49, 70-71, 99, 133,
    140, 145, 161, 178, 181, 190-
    191, 195
power to manifest. *See* creation
prayer 28, 151
preexistence 95
prejudice. *See* attitude
present lifetime. *See* life
preservation 43, 45, 47, 133, 163
priesthood 37, 118, 151
prima materia. *See* alchemy
primary consciousness 139, 141, 144,
    146, 149-150, 155-157, 159,
    162-163
procreation. *See* sexuality
prodigal son 3, 57, 97
psychiatry 126

Q

quantum physics 145
    quantum field of potential 65, 145,
        153, 191
    waves and particles 156, 177,
        185-187, 191, 193

quark. *See* atom

R

Ra, Egyptian God 22
Ramtha 26, 41, 48
  Lord of the Wind 32
  Ramtha's teachings 72, 98-99,
    106, 195
  the march 36-37, 41, 44-46, 48,
    75, 158-159, 171
rape. *See* sexuality
redemption 2, 39, 87, 185
regret. *See* emotions
reincarnation 7, 9, 12, 15, 18, 22,
    95, 125, 127, 132, 136, 141-
    142, 151, 164, 168, 172, 176,
    184
relationships. *See* love
religion 37, 42, 58
  dogma 25, 76, 83
  worship 36
remote-view 41, 46
resentment. *See* emotions
resurrection 76, 148-149, 151
revelation 28, 55, 59, 63, 73, 119, 134
righteousness. *See* virtue
runners. *See* mastership

S

sacred knowledge. *See* knowledge
sacrifice 21, 71, 175
sadness. *See* emotions
saint 18
School of Ancient Wisdom 7, 11, 13,
    19-20, 32, 37, 39-41, 44, 53-54,
    90, 123, 130, 132, 134-135, 140,
    144-145, 154, 158, 169, 178
science 28, 32, 36, 90, 98, 145
second plane. *See* planes of existence
secondary consciousness 139-141,
    149-150, 155-157, 159, 162
self, the 3, 8, 15, 22, 31, 52, 54-60,
    62-63, 66, 70-72, 74-75, 78-79,

82-87, 89-90, 92, 94-96, 98,
    100-101, 104, 113, 118, 123,
    126, 129, 140, 142, 146-147,
    169, 172, 175, 179
  the shadow 12-14, 17, 19
selfishness. *See* attitude
sensory perception 80-81, 160
seven levels. *See* creation
seven seals 116
  fifth seal 161-162
  first seal 116
  first three seals 74, 98-99, 111, 161
  fourth seal 99, 104, 161
  sixth seal 161
  upper four seals 98
seventh plane. *See* planes of existence
sexuality 80, 111, 116, 121, 126
  copulation 44, 74, 79, 116, 157
  orgasm 116, 133
  procreation 39, 73, 115
  rape 116, 122
shadow, the. *See* self, the
Shiva 26
sin 48
sixth plane. *See* planes of existence
sixth seal. *See* seven seals
slavery 22, 36, 40, 44-45, 71, 122,
    175, 184
social consciousness 8-9, 38, 55, 87, 95
society 2, 58, 170
sorrow. *See* emotions
soul 7, 10, 20, 29, 32, 43, 49, 60-61,
    69, 71, 84, 91-92, 94, 96, 110,
    112, 117-119, 122, 125, 135-
    136, 139, 141, 146, 151, 160,
    162, 164-165, 171, 177, 182,
    187, 190
  Book of Life 110
  the dark night 3, 57, 81, 88-89
  transmigration of the soul 135, 177
South America 193
sovereignty 79, 97, 195
space 140
spaceship 39
Spirit 7, 28-29, 35-36, 39, 60, 65, 69,

Spirit (*continued*)
  74, 80, 84, 90-91, 95, 98, 112,
    124, 132, 134-135, 140-141,
    143, 149, 162, 187-188, 193
  earthbound spirits 192
  spiritual journey 52, 54-55, 69, 80,
    85-86, 89-90, 95, 97-98, 100,
    103-105, 113, 124, 176, 192
  spiritual order 2, 7, 23, 28, 35, 53,
    55-56, 59-60, 67, 73-75, 80,
    83, 92, 99, 123, 133, 169
  states of consciousness 83, 170
    body/mind consciousness 89, 97,
    139-140, 143, 146, 149
  students of the Great Work 2-3, 40,
    45, 56, 104, 113, 128, 179
  subconscious mind. *See* mind
  subjective truth. *See* truth
  suicide 148
  sun 155, 160, 178, 180, 182
  superstition 18, 36
  surrender. *See* faith
  survival. *See* attitude
  sword 19, 36, 45-46, 171, 176
    broadsword 13, 18
    Crosham 41
  symbols 40, 104
  system of thought. *See* thought

T

  tachyon 155
  Tank™, The 176, 178
  teachings 7, 14, 17-18, 20, 27-28, 30,
    32, 89, 113, 141, 153, 179
  technology 77, 143
  temptation 127, 190
  third plane. *See* planes of existence
  thought 15, 19, 38, 47-49, 52, 61, 64,
    68, 73, 81, 85-86, 94, 112, 135,
    143, 157, 163-166, 168, 177-
    178, 186, 193-195
    abstract thought 62, 72, 79, 88,
    136, 154, 183
    common thought 61, 68, 81, 101,

    111, 123, 129, 161, 170, 177-
    180, 182, 185, 192-195
    fantasies 27, 116, 122
    focus thought 11, 18, 21, 28, 30,
    45, 60, 96, 101, 169, 178, 193
    limited thought 19, 83, 195
    lofty thought 38, 43, 47, 58, 81,
    85, 100, 111, 123, 126, 129, 141,
    145, 153, 161, 183, 190-191
    system of thought 177
  three-dimensional reality. *See*
    dimension
  time 7, 9-10, 18, 26, 34, 39, 41, 45,
    47-49, 52-53, 63, 66, 69, 72-
    73, 89, 128, 131, 133, 135,
    140, 154-155, 157, 170, 186,
    194, 196
    linear time 110, 131, 190-191, 196
    no-time 39, 42, 46, 63, 115
    the future 19, 37, 67, 71, 78, 91,
    101, 131, 170
    the Now 8, 12, 14, 19, 41, 46-47,
    49, 79, 97, 115, 131, 146, 162,
    168, 185
    the past 2, 8, 10, 14, 16-17, 19,
    21, 31, 41, 43, 45-49, 54-56,
    58, 64, 70-71, 74, 78, 80, 87,
    89, 96-97, 100-105, 127, 131,
    134, 154, 171, 176, 193
    timeline 10, 29, 34, 38, 41, 65-66,
    69-70, 77-79, 91-92, 96, 99, 171
  transcendence 123, 185
  transformation 53, 182
  transmigration of the soul. *See* soul
  transmutation 45, 47, 55, 60, 184, 186
  truth 15, 27, 34, 40, 45, 53, 58, 93,
    95, 98, 110, 119, 124, 128-130,
    143, 150, 160, 174, 181, 184,
    192-193
    objective truth 66, 80, 85
    subjective truth 28, 67, 80, 85, 129
  twenty-third universe. *See* universe
  Twilight™ 164
  tyranny. *See* attitude

U

ulterior motive 3, 95, 113-114, 116-
    123, 125-130, 134, 141, 144,
    147-148, 150, 166, 170-171,
    175, 178-182, 184, 190, 192,
    194-196
ultraviolet blue. *See* frequency
unconditional love. *See* love
unhappiness. *See* emotions
universe
    twenty-third universe 158
unknown, the. *See* knowledge
unlimited mind. *See* mind
upper four seals. *See* seven seals
uterus. *See* anatomy

V

Venus 158
victimization. *See* attitude
virtue 39, 93
    compassion 44, 166, 190
    generosity 94
    honesty 172, 174
    honor 31, 39-40, 80, 91, 95, 128,
        130, 168, 171, 175
    humility 20, 86, 172
    impeccability 3, 15, 39, 54, 58,
        113-114, 128, 147, 175-176
    kindness 94, 114, 166
    mercy 68
    righteousness 35, 57
virus 29
visible light. *See* frequency
visualization 30, 91, 104, 116, 131
    art of imagination 35, 57, 63-65,
        67, 72-73, 77, 79, 83-85, 92, 98-
        99, 101, 125, 132, 140, 169, 182
Void, the 9, 41, 49, 72, 76, 84, 90,
    98, 154, 156, 167, 176, 190

W

walk of a master. *See* mastership

war 36, 42, 72, 170
warrior 36-37, 41, 57, 159
waves and particles. *See* quantum
    physics
wealth 9, 12, 16, 19, 31, 39, 94-95,
    97, 195
    fabulous wealth 181
weighed against the feather. *See* life
white hole 158
will 19, 21, 36-38, 42, 45, 47, 54, 59,
    79, 110, 134
    free will 24, 39, 45, 47, 53-54,
        59, 100-101, 104
wine 12, 22, 39, 120
wisdom 2-3, 7-8, 22-23, 39, 41, 44,
    48-49, 59, 64-65, 81, 91-92,
    105, 166, 173, 190, 195
women 16-17, 20, 39, 43, 45, 56,
    74, 80, 95, 114-116, 118-119,
    122, 142, 159, 184
wormhole 28, 158
worship. *See* religion
worthiness. *See* attitude

X

x-ray. *See* frequency

Y

Yeshua ben Joseph 185-186

Other Ramtha Titles

The following is a list of additional books on Ramtha that can be purchased through Ramtha's School of Enlightenment and other fine bookstores. Also available is a whole library of recordings and videos of Ramtha's teachings. All products are available through mail order at:

RAMTHA'S SCHOOL OF ENLIGHTENMENT

P.O. Box 519
Yelm, Washington 98597 USA
www.ramtha.com
info@ramtha.com
For product information please call:
800.347.0439 or 360.458.4771
FAX: 360.458.2329
email: mailorder@ramtha.com
For information on events please call:
360.458.5201
email: audrey@ramtha.com

A BEGINNER'S GUIDE TO CREATING REALITY, Revised and Expanded Edition. *by JZK Publishing, a division of JZK, Inc. (238 pages).* This book is the general introduction to Ramtha and his teachings. It includes a detailed Glossary of terms and concepts used by Ramtha as well as an Index.

FINANCIAL FREEDOM *Edited by Judy Pope Zion (126 pages).* "If you think there is a demarcation between gold and God, you are not only a hypocrite, you are cutting your own throat." This book is also available in German and Spanish translations.

I AM RAMTHA *Edited by Richard Cohn, Cindy Black, and Greg Simmons (128 pages).* This book is a beautifully photographed book that accompanies thirteen of Ramtha's most universal teachings. Wonderful teachings on the subject of emotions, being at one with nature, unconditional love, and the prize that is called life.

LAST WALTZ OF THE TYRANTS *Edited by Judy Pope Koteen (154 pages)*. This book is a synthesis of Ramtha's teachings on the challenges we face by those who control the world economy and from the coming radical changes in nature. This book is also available in French, German, Italian, and Spanish translations.

RAMTHA (a/k/a THE WHITE BOOK) *Revised Edition by JZK Publishing, a division of JZK, Inc. (232 pages)*.

RAMTHA *Edited by Steven L. Weinberg, Ph.D. (218 pages)*. Also available in Spanish, French, Norwegian, Italian, and Japanese translations.

SPINNER OF TALES *Compiled by Deborah Kerins (228 pages)*. Ramtha has captivated audiences throughout the years with his storytelling. Now they have been put together in book form to be preserved and delight readers of all ages.

STATE OF MIND: MY STORY *JZ Knight (446 pages)*. The intimate account of JZ's life in her own words. Her story, which includes her humorous and poignant introduction to Ramtha, is a story of the triumph of the human Spirit.

THE ANCIENT SCHOOLS OF WISDOM *Compiled by Diane Munoz-Smith (172 pages)*. Ramtha tells how the ancient schools operated in times past and why their instruction was so precise to awaken the forgotten God within. This book is also available in German, Italian, and Spanish translations.

THE CHILDREN'S VIEW OF DESTINY AND PURPOSE *by JZK Publishing, a division of JZK, Inc. (50 pages)*. This children's book, illustrated by the children who attended this teaching, is a simple and yet profound understanding of life's destiny and life's purpose.

THE PLANE OF BLISS *by JZK Publishing, a division of JZK, Inc. (154 pages)*. This book describes the place where the soul travels after death — traditionally known as heaven or paradise — and the soul's life review. This book is also available in the Spanish translation.

TO LIFE *Compiled by Diane Munoz-Smith (152 pages)*. At the beginning of each audience, Ramtha elegantly and thought-provokingly salutes the God within with a toast. This book is a selection of the toasts from Ramtha's audiences from May 1988 to May 1996.

UFO'S AND THE NATURE OF REALITY *Edited by Judy Pope Koteen (222 pages)*. This book tells the story of alien intervention in our history, in our present time, and in our future. It exposes the limitations of subjective mind and encourages the reader to move into interdimensional mind. This book is also available in German, Italian, and Spanish translations.

Video Recordings
by JZK Publishing,
a division of JZK, Inc.

CREATING PERSONAL REALITY *(5-volume video set. 9 hours-NTSC/ PAL)*. This is an introductory instructional teaching given to all beginning students that want to be part of Ramtha's School of Enlightenment. Available in French, German, Italian, Japanese, and Spanish.

INTIMATE CONVERSATIONS *(27 minutes-NTSC/PAL)*. Two distinct beings — JZ Knight and Ramtha — one ancient, one modern, sharing provocative insights about God, about love, and about life. This video is also available in French, German, Italian, Japanese, and Spanish.

A LOOK WITHIN *(32 minutes-NTSC/PAL)*. This is the first video that highlights the disciplines done at the school. Included are interviews with students, scholars, and JZ Knight. This video is also available in French, German, Italian, Japanese, and Spanish.

TWO PATHS *(3-volume video set. 7 hours-NTSC/PAL)*. This is "a new teaching called the two paths: the emotional body of humanity and its agreement in mind control and, the second path — our natural path — which is God and follows this teaching of Christ." This video is also available in French, German, Italian, Japanese, and Spanish.

THE MAGICAL BRAIN *(1 hour 46 minutes-NTSC/PAL)*. In this video Ramtha shares his knowledge on the brain and its relationship to consciousness, energy, and the creation of reality, as well as detailed instructions on how to harness its enourmous power for manifestation.

THE BRAIN: WHERE SCIENCE AND SPIRIT MEET *(1 hour 35 minutes-NTSC/PAL)*. Dr. Joe Dispenza shared his presentation on the role and function of the brain in the creation of reality that he delivered at the World Parliament of Religions with the student body of Ramtha's School of Enlightenment.

THE ULTIMATE CHALLENGE FOR RELIGION — THE QUANTUM AGE *(1 hour 56 minutes-NTSC/PAL)*. Dr. Miceal Ledwith places Ramtha's teachings and the implications of Quantum Physics in contrast with the major religions of the world.

IN SEARCH OF THE SELF: THE ROLE OF CONSCIOUSNESS IN THE CONSTRUCTION OF REALITY. *A Conference on Contemporary Spirituality, February 8-9, 1997, Yelm, Washington (8-volume video set. 9 hours 38 minutes-NTSC/PAL)*. An international group of scholars from the fields of physics, psychology, sociology, and religious studies gathered at Ramtha's School of Enlightenment to discuss key issues concerning the nature of consciousness and its implications on science and spirituality. This two-day conference captures the conclusions of the scholars who spent up to a year studying and analyzing Ramtha, JZ Knight, and Ramtha's School of Enlightenment.